1,000,000 Books

are available to read at

Forgotten Books

www.ForgottenBooks.com

Read online
Download PDF
Purchase in print

ISBN 978-1-332-10359-1
PIBN 10285079

This book is a reproduction of an important historical work. Forgotten Books uses state-of-the-art technology to digitally reconstruct the work, preserving the original format whilst repairing imperfections present in the aged copy. In rare cases, an imperfection in the original, such as a blemish or missing page, may be replicated in our edition. We do, however, repair the vast majority of imperfections successfully; any imperfections that remain are intentionally left to preserve the state of such historical works.

Forgotten Books is a registered trademark of FB &c Ltd.
Copyright © 2018 FB &c Ltd.
FB &c Ltd, Dalton House, 60 Windsor Avenue, London, SW19 2RR.
Company number 08720141. Registered in England and Wales.

For support please visit www.forgottenbooks.com

1 MONTH OF FREE READING

at

www.ForgottenBooks.com

By purchasing this book you are eligible for one month membership to ForgottenBooks.com, giving you unlimited access to our entire collection of over 1,000,000 titles via our web site and mobile apps.

To claim your free month visit:

www.forgottenbooks.com/free285079

* Offer is valid for 45 days from date of purchase. Terms and conditions apply.

English
Français
Deutsche
Italiano
Español
Português

www.forgottenbooks.com

Mythology Photography **Fiction** Fishing Christianity **Art** Cooking Essays Buddhism Freemasonry Medicine **Biology** Music **Ancient Egypt** Evolution Carpentry Physics Dance Geology **Mathematics** Fitness Shakespeare **Folklore** Yoga Marketing **Confidence** Immortality Biographies Poetry **Psychology** Witchcraft Electronics Chemistry History **Law** Accounting **Philosophy** Anthropology Alchemy Drama Quantum Mechanics Atheism Sexual Health **Ancient History** **Entrepreneurship** Languages Sport Paleontology Needlework Islam **Metaphysics** Investment Archaeology Parenting Statistics Criminology **Motivational**

BAPTISM:

By J. DITZLER, D.D.

"PROVE ALL THINGS."—*Paul.*

NASHVILLE, TENN.:
SOUTHERN METHODIST PUBLISHING HOUSE.
1886.

COPYRIGHTED, 1881.

To My Beloved and Esteemed Former
Preceptor,

Rev. B. H. McCOWN, D.D.

of anchorage, ky.

This Work is Respectfully Dedicated

By the Author.

Rev. B. H. McCown, D.D.:

Dear Sir—For several years after attending college I had the honor of pursuing the languages under your direction. You were present, as you told me, during the discussion between Mr. Campbell and Rice at Lexington, Ky. Elder A. Campbell, as the debate shows, selected you as a most proper authority to whom, on his part, he preferred referring a philological point in dispute. You are presumed, therefore, on both sides of this controversy, to be an impartial and able witness. Not on this account only, but because of your former kindness toward and interest in the Author, I have dedicated this Book, the result of so much pains and toil, to you, as an humble token of regard, and subscribe myself,

Yours in Christ,
J. DITZLER.

Longview, Louisville, Ky., 1880.

CHAPTER I.

INTRODUCTION.

Dr. T. O. Summers justly complains to Bishop Andrew of the many trashy works on baptism. Rev. J. D. Hudson, of Alabama, does the same, regretting the commonplace repetitions of the various compilations on this subject. While Drs. M. Stuart, Rice, Rosser, Chapman, Seiss, Hibbard, E. Beecher, Edwards, Bishop Merrell, and Summers have done excellent service, it can not be stated that they have thrown any new light on the subject, and it really stands where it was left by Lightfoot in the seventeenth century. We will have occasion to point out important facts on this subject on many occasions. As a sample of the carelessness of writers and their indifference to the progress of investigation, we feel it to be our duty to select one sample page from the work of Dr. Summers himself. We should not do this but for his repeating it in editions that ought to have corrected the blunders, especially when the bishops had honored his book as *our standard* on baptism. In the "New and Revised Edition" of 1878, from a revised edition of June 6, 1874, after we had published correct reports of those authors, Dr. Summers in one single page (222) thus copies some authorities:

BAPTIDZO.

"Gazes: *brecho, pluno, louo, antlo.*" This is a mere scrap of Gazes's definition, yet the same may be found in a host of compilations. Turn now to our list of lexicons and see how defective is the above. He reports Scapula as saying it means "to dip." He does not say so. He reports him as saying that it means "to *dye*." This is preposterous. He says Stephanus gives "dip." He does not. He thus reports Schleusner: "To plunge, immerse; to cleanse, wash, purify with water, etc." Turn to my list and see how defective is this as a citation of the great German.

He quotes Suidas as defining it, "To sink, plunge, immerse, wet, wash, cleanse, purify." Suidas does not define the word, and this is simply repeating the blunders of former compilations. These are only a part of the errors of a part of one page! Is not a text-book accurate at least in all citations and texts most desirable?

Gale, Booth, Carson, Cox, E. Beecher, Conant, Dale, Moses Stuart profess to treat the subject *philologically*, as also A. Campbell, Prof. Ripley, and Ingham of London. Conant being so favorably surrounded excelled all men in collecting classic occurrences of *baptidzo*. Dale stands next in point of merit there, and before all others in his research in patristic literature on Mode, though of little value; for after the third century, not to say the close of the *first*, small is the help we get *philologically*, save of the few whose work as translators compelled them to be philological and not so dogmatic, not to say superstitious. While Dr. Dale did much in Latin and Greek literatures we think he failed as a philologist *in toto*, as will be abundantly shown when we come to the classics on *bapto* and *baptidzo*.

The utterly unscientific method always followed on this subject by both sides may well account for the unsettled state of the controversy. Long delay in the correct and complete solution of a disturbing question is not proof that the friends of truth and Christian fraternity may not hope for a complete solution.

To the bishops, the many ministers of both the great wings of Methodism, many Presbyterian and Congregational ministers, who for ten years past have urged us to publish the result of our labors and researches on this question, we return our grateful thanks. Our delay has been unavoidable from 1869, but afforded opportunity to incorporate refutations of the most recent blunders of many authors, and to add the facts developed by Max Müller confirming the views and methods always maintained by us on the science of language.

It has cost us much pains to adapt the work to both the learned and the unlearned. To do this we have kept the quotations that are in the languages in foot-notes as well as some more elaborate criticisms, so as not to impede the plain English scholar, and yet enable him to see the force of the most learned arguments if he choses to read the notes.

It will be seen that we give prominence to the ancient versions very far beyond other works on this subject, for most just reasons. Our opponents have attached the greatest importance to this field. It will be seen by comparison that as yet the field had not been touched, comparatively, by the one side—excessively misused by the other.

It will be seen how lexicons were almost totally misquoted, the original generally not given, and the great masters, as a rule, wholly ignored, or so indifferently cited as to leave the reader in total ignorance of what they said. Many samples will be presented. In Oriental languages we produce from their original works the great masters, Schindler, Buxtorf, Castell, Fürst, Leigh, etc.; in Greek classics, Passow, Rost, Palm, Pape, as the most accurate and learned and recent; Schneider, Gazes, Wahl, Schleusner, earlier; and among the older lexicons, classic and biblical, Stephanus, Suicer, Stokius, etc.

We flatter ourselves that we have exhibited the exact use of classic Greek. We have aimed to point out its abuses and cited authorities in abundance on such matters. In philology, in the science of languages, in the discovery of primary meanings, the classic Greek is of vast importance. The difference between *baptidzo* as a classic and religious word we have aimed to make so clear that only very willful stupidity can reject the evidences.

Since all my manuscripts were ready for the press (1872-1875) the Carrollton debate occurred between J. R. Graves, LL.D., and myself, and was published by the Baptist House in Memphis, Tenn., under the eye and in the same house where the doctor edits his paper, The Baptist. It is with regret that we have to expose the astounding conduct of our opponent in that debate. After I had written out my speeches, as agreed, and left them with the publisher, Dr. Mayfield, and left for Texas, Dr. Graves took out my speeches—on my return I saw him with them—and rewrote all of his. This was done after we both had our names, February 15, 1876, subscribed to the declaration that it was a correct report of the debate. As the phonographer failed utterly to get my speeches, speaking so rapidly, I had to write them out from my notes. All will see that much of minor importance and nearly all repartee would be lost—unavoidably so. After thus subscribing ourselves, and after he had professedly published his speeches on Mode in his paper, Dr. G. took my manuscripts and rewrote all of his, adding as many as six, eight, ten, and even twelve pages

INTRODUCTION.

of new matter at a time in single speeches, not a line of which was used during debate, and leaving out what he did say wherever exposed. Whatever he says of covenants is just the reverse of the facts *in toto*. As I returned from Texas through Memphis I examined parts of several of his speeches on Mode — the fourteenth and fifteenth, besides much already added from the eighth on. I sat down in their room and added a few pages to my twelfth and thirteenth speeches to meet some of his additions from the sixth to twelfth, and rewrote my fourteenth and fifteenth in reply to his, making them far longer than half-hour speeches can be made; added several pages to the sixteenth on Mode, and never was permitted to see his seventeenth, eighteenth, and nineteenth speeches on Mode, nor any thereafter, *not even the proof-sheets*. Not a page after my seventeenth speech in the book was proofed by me. In these he makes his daring assertions he dared not make when I was there. He purposely delayed his manuscripts under various pretenses till a public debate at Stanford, Ky., April 2d to 9th, called me away. I wrote for the proofs of our speeches, but neither his nor mine were ever sent to me. One of my speeches of half hour I rewrote, making it a reply to three or four he had slipped in without my knowledge of the enormous changes. The seventeenth, though I never got his seventeenth as *rewritten* by himself, I prepared in McKenzie, Tenn., where I stopped on my way, and where I wrote for a return of my last two speeches to recast them, in view of what he might do in his seventeenth, eighteenth, and nineteenth speeches; but they telegraphed they were nearly in print and would be next day. They were not for yet *two weeks*. Innumerable typographical errors blot the work, and in places where my own comments were made and carefully placed in brackets, the brackets are removed and I charged by Dr. G. with trying to impose the bracketed words on the people as my own! We will attend to many of his bold and reckless assertions in this work.

In that debate we did all we could to force or draw him out on Baptist succession, on history, or on the ancient versions, and on them all he was dumb as an oyster. Yet in the *published* debate he fills whole speeches with a reckless mass of crudities, defies me, and challenges refutation. Well he knew there would be in the book no answer, because I would never see it till the book should be in print! He was afflicted with a painful soreness of throat, spoke very slowly—on an average not over one word to my two. Hence his opening speech on Mode, on which he was one hour and ten minutes—extra time allowed to finish his points—makes but twelve pages and six lines. His next full half-hour speech fills four pages and a third solid. Compare these with those half-hour speeches that have eighteen, twenty, twenty-two, twenty-seven pages, much of it finer print, and all can see the truth. Again, let any one examine his first eight or even ten speeches on Mode and see how pointedly they are refuted; his fourteenth and fifteenth, that I caught him slipping in "on the sly" as I came from Texas; see their exposure, and he will see enough to prove that I never saw the remainder of his speeches.

CHAPTER II.

Baptism—Administrator—Design.

In preparing a book on the MODE of baptism, it is not deemed necessary to treat of the *administrator* of baptism, because: First. All Protestant churches are *practically* agreed on this subject, whatever may be the abstract theories of some parties. As a rule only the *ministers* of all these bodies baptize. Second. So far as theory or practice goes, the New Testament does not throw any light upon it of a positive character. We know not who baptized the converts of Pentecost (Acts ii, 41) nor the first Gentile converts (Acts x, 44-47). We never will know who did the baptizing among Christ's earlier disciples (John iii, 22-25; iv, 2) before he had selected his apostles. Compare Mark i, 14, 16-20; Luke iv and v entire, and vi, 13-16. There is no record where any one of the twelve apostles ever baptized any person; and Paul, the one chosen out of the due order—the fourteenth one—really boasts of having baptized only the few named in 1 Corinthians i, 14-17, in person. Third. The fathers allowed of baptism by laymen as well as by ministers, yet mainly the ministers baptized.

As to the *design* of baptism, we will treat of that in a separate work, the errors in the design being too grave and numerous to be fully exposed and the true import of baptism set forth in a convenient volume. But the *real*, the *scriptural* design we propose to give, as it will shed light on the mode as well as on the subjects of the rite.

The immersionists hold that "immersion was the baptism commanded by Christ and practiced under the apostles." Of the most prominent writers of this class we may name in Europe and the United States, Drs. Gale, Carson, Cox, Hinton, Fuller, Booth, Conant, Mell, Ripley, Ingham,* A. Campbell, L. B. Wilkes, J. R. Graves, Brents (G. W., of Tennessee). These in substance rely on the following assumptions to sustain this hypothesis, namely, that

1. Baptism is an *anglicized* Greek word, *baptisma* (βαπτίσμα), from the verb *baptidzo*, and it is derived from the root *bapto*, and has a specific meaning which is immerse, dip, plunge. They assert that,

2. This is sustained by the *unanimous* testimony of all ancient and modern Greek lexicons or dictionaries, which do always give immerse, dip, plunge as the meaning of *baptidzo*, and *never* sprinkle or pour.

3. The Greek literature of nearly two thousand years fully sustains this, and is *the only real* standard of appeal.

4. All translations, ancient and modern, support this position by rendering *bapto* and *baptidzo* by words that mean to immerse, never by words meaning to sprinkle or pour; that the ancient versions being made by the most competent of all witnesses, are decisive of this question.

5. *Baptidzo* and *bapto*, its root, are translations of the Hebrew words *tabal* and *tzebă*, that always mean to immerse, dip, or plunge.

6. That these facts are admitted also by all the eminent pedobaptist critics and scholars; but they set up *tradi-*

---

*Ingham, 1865, a very exhaustive work, compiled merely, has it thus: 1. Lexicons; 2. Examples, especially in classic usage; 3. Versions, especially ancient—e. g. Syriac, etc.; . . . 9. The word can not represent actions as distinct as pouring, sprinkling, and immersing or dipping. (Pages 27, 38, 575.)

tions and the *authority of the church* as the grand reason for affusion, claiming the right to change the ordinances of the church.

7. That the practice of the early centuries of the church was altogether by immersion, and that no other practice was allowed till about the thirteenth century, save in case of sickness, and such cases were illegal, not "ecclesiastical."

8. That the prepositions used in connection with these words, such as *en, eis,* connecting them with the element—baptize "*in;*" went into the water; and *ek, apo,* out of, *from,* indicating *emersion,* "helping out of the water"—strengthen these arguments.

9. That the allusions to baptism in the New Testament, such as Romans vi, 3, 4; Colossians ii, 11, 12; 1 Corinthians x, 1, 2; Hebrews x, 22, clearly demonstrate immersion as the only apostolic practice, designed to symbolize the *death, burial,* and *resurrection* of Christ.

The *places* where baptism is represented as occurring—*in* Jordan, "in Ænon near to Salim, *because* there was much water there"; Philip and the eunuch, etc., additionally strengthen this view.

To give force and certainty to these assumptions all immersionists hold to certain theories as absolutely settled, undeniable; viz:

1. That in a given period and summary of literature, not at all commensurate with the actual literature of a language, and *all* dating *centuries* later than the origin of the language, and later than much of its best literature, the prevailing meaning of a word at any such later period *is its primary* meaning!

2. That if a word ever means, or implies, to dip, plunge, immerse, it can never mean, or apply to, sprinkle

or pour; and if to sprinkle or pour, it can never mean dip, plunge, immerse.

3. That wash, purify, cleanse are meanings of *baptidzo* in the New Testament and Apocrypha *because* derived from immerse. Hence the New Testament often alludes to baptism as a washing, cleansing, etc. (Eph. v, 26; Titus iii. 5; Acts xxii, 16; Heb. x, 22, etc.), while all ancient versions render baptize by wash, cleanse, purify, etc., as well as more recent ones in the sixteenth century.*

4. That classic Greek is the same as the New Testament Greek, and that *baptidzo* is to be explained and its New Testament use determined by the classics!

5. The less critical also advance the following absurdities as canons of interpretation, viz: That to sprinkle an object is "to scatter it in drops." Hence *baptidzo* can not mean to sprinkle, to pour upon, unless the object is invariably "scattered in drops." A. Campbell, G. W. Brents, and J. R. Graves adhere to this.

6. A number of immersionists maintain that if *baptidzo* means to *immerse*, sprinkle, pour, then no one is baptized until all three of these acts are accomplished upon him! We may hope that this silly sophistry has ceased to be repeated, especially as A. Campbell renders *baptidzo* by some twenty or more different words, Conant by fourteen, etc.; while drown, *intoxicate, soak, make drunk* figure in all immersion works as among the meanings.

7. They hold that dip, immerse, plunge are all synonymous in meaning. J. R. Graves, Alexander Campbell, Wilkes, etc.

We shall subject all these assumptions to a careful examination and test of facts.

* Syriac, *amad, secho;* Arabic, *amada, gasala;* Latin, *lavo;* German, *waschen;* etc.

CHAPTER III.

ORIGIN AND DESIGN OF BAPTISM.

If the origin and design of baptism has ever been explained, its real propriety presented, we have never met with it. Nor have we ever seen an explanation of the relation between the washing [baptism] with *water* and the cleansings effected by blood in Exodus, Leviticus, and Numbers. Tracing Christian baptism through proselyte baptism as Vossius, Witsius, Lightfoot, etc. do, does not bring us any nearer the matter. The real origin and design of baptism remains unexplained. The careless and excessively loose treatment it has received may well account for its horrid distortions.

Every rite must have some reason in it in the element used, if elements are used, and in the then current force of the word as used by the writers or speakers. Hence we must look for the origin of this rite in the religious import of the word *wash* (*rachats* in Hebrew), *cleanse*, and in the *symbolism* of water.

Among all nations, in every European language, Egyptian, and those of Asia Minor, water represented innocence and purity—cleansing. Cleansing made the party innocent. The outward symbolized and was declarative of his innocence, whether actually cleansed from actual guilt or really innocent.

In Homer's day, a thousand years before Christ, it was an old custom for parties before going to prayer to wash themselves at the hoary sea, or besprinkle themselves with clean water before praying to Minerva (*Athene.*)* They sprinkled with living water candidates for the Eleusis. In Ovid, Homer, Diogenes, Virgil, Porphyry, Herodotus, etc. these washings are often alluded to in connection with devotional exercises. Originally symbolic of innocence, purity, absence of guilt, it came to be corrupted in use as a real agency in purification, as an expiation of crime. To this base use of it Tertullian alludes at length.

In the earliest times, as Homer relates the earlier heathen customs, nearer the purer days of their religion, these washings and cleansings were symbolic of the object of their prayers and devotions—purity by which they became innocent. Hence they besprinkled themselves with water as the *first step*. It was not then initiatory *into* any body.

In the Bible water symbolizes innocence and purity—the one being implied in the other: "I will wash my hands in innocency; so will I compass thine altar, O Lord" (Ps. xxvi, 6; lxxiii, 13).† Here it anticipates the object of devotion—purity and innocence before God—symbolizes that object. Pilot, recognizing this Jewish use of water, washed his hands in token of innocence as to Christ's blood.

As religious innocence, implying purity, can be had only through the merit of "the blood of sprinkling" (1 Peter i, 2; Heb. x, 22; ix, 13-19; xii, 24; Num. xix, 9-13) applied by the Spirit, the water comes to represent the Spirit by

* In the full citation in Clemens Alexandrinus where the passage is given in full.

† In this Psalm, lxxiii, 13, "I have cleansed my heart in vain, and washed my hands in innocency." We must not forget the constant fact that the water and Spirit are named or implied together throughout the Bible—one inward, the other outward.

which we are actually cleansed as to its mode or action, as well as its real design. Ps. li, 1-10; Is. i, 16; iv, 4; xliv, 3; Ezek. xvi, 9; xxxvi, 25-27; Eph. v, 25, 26; Titus iii, 5, 6; Heb. x, 22; with Matt. iii, 11, 12; Acts x, 41-44. "Can any man forbid water that these should not be baptized who *have received the Holy Spirit as well as we?*" The constant association of the water in all these, as well as innumerable other passages, shows that the water was *always* symbolic of the innocence effected by the Spirit's application of Christ's blood, *and of nothing but that.* It was not initiatory into any thing. *Baptism is symbol and nothing else.*

In Moses's day the connection of the water and the blood—as *blood* was the *groundwork* of all religious innocence before God, the *procuring* cause—is striking. When Moses had led the people out of Egypt, he consecrated the priests and people with blood (Ex. xxviii, 41; xxix, 16-22), and sprinkled vessels, people, the book, and tabernacle with blood (Heb. ix, 17-22), and ordained that the priests and people wash or be cleansed with water. Ex. xxix, 4; xxx, 18-22; Lev. viii, 4-6; xv, xvi; Num. viii, 7; xix, 13-22. When David repented he alluded to water, to washing as a preliminary process (Ps. li, 2-10) as well as to the sprinkling with blood (verse 7, "Purge me with hyssop"), where it is a *spiritual* washing prayed for, as all will admit. The Greek, Syriac, and Latin read, "Sprinkle me with hyssop." Hebrews x, 22, unites the blood as the *real* work, the water as the symbol of cleansing—"having our *hearts* sprinkled—our *bodies* washed, etc."—i. e. symbolically cleansed, as Aaron's was (Lev. viii, 6).

When Moses washed Aaron and his sons with water (Lev. viii, 6) it was not initiatory but preliminary. He was first washed, and after this all that occurs throughout the long chapter, for *eight days,* occurred before he was a priest (chapter ix, 1-12). If baptism was a door into the church, all this was strange. Stranger still, as they baptized themselves *every day* before performing their duty. Did they initiate themselves into the church every day?

When God called people to repent (Is. i, 16), washing as a preliminary process, symbolic of purity, is alluded to in the spiritual washing: "Wash you, make you *clean*" (Is. i, 16). In Exodus xxx, 18, a laver is made for Aaron and his sons to "wash with water" thereat—"out of it," in the Greek and Hebrew. But what was the import, the design, the symbolism of the cleansing with water when the party was sprinkled with blood, etc. for a purification? In Leviticus xiv, 7, 8, 51-53, a person is sprinkled seven times with blood, and is pronounced *clean when sprinkled.* After this he is "to wash with water" [*hudati*]. The washing with water could only be declarative of the typical cleansing effected by the sprinkled blood, as Hebrews x, 22, also. The house was sprinkled seven times with blood and water, the water answering to that of the person cleansed, washed, sanctified (Num. viii, 7; Eph. v, 26). "And thus shalt thou do unto them *to cleanse* them, sprinkle water of purifying upon them." "Sanctify and cleanse *by the washing of water* by the word." Some assert that this was with water mingled with ashes of a burnt heifer (Num. xix, 9-22). But that latter rite was not introduced till between nineteen and thirty-seven years after this. See Numbers, chapter xx, in this connection also. In the case of the water of separation, of Numbers xix, the defiled was to "purify himself with it." If he failed to do so he was unclean, defiled the tabernacle, and was therefore to be cut off. Why? "Because the water of separation was not sprinkled upon him, he shall be unclean."

ORIGIN AND DESIGN OF BAPTISM. 19

The Targum of Jonathan is very emphatic on Numbers xix, 13, where the words "shall not purify himself" (verse 13) read "shall not *sprinkle* himself"—"Since the *waters* [*mon*] of sprinkling were not sprinkled upon him, he is unclean; as yet his pollution is upon him *until he besprinkles himself.*" The Persic is very much the same. Paul (Heb. ix, 13) agrees perfectly with this view: "Sprinkling the unclean, sanctifieth unto the *purifying of the flesh.*" In this case again the water betokened the typical cleansing—was declarative of its work. But in Numbers xix, 18, a tent and vessels of the ministry are purified by only sprinkling; but the person, after being sprinkled "for a purification for sin," was to wash his garments and his person (*hudati*) with water, and be [thus declared] clean, and if unclean it was "*because* the water of separation was not sprinkled upon him" (13, 20). The water in all these cases betokens the innocence secured by the blood of sprinkling—symbolic innocence—made actually innocent by Christ's blood. In all this the clear understanding of the typical baptisms when first introduced will enable us to see the real design of baptism; as well as to understand who are proper subjects of the rite. It opens the way to rid the public mind of the awful abuses that confuse the mind and blind the judgment of men. Initiatory rite, door into the church, sign of death, burial, and resurrection, communicating grace, for remission of sins—all these horrid distortions of the beautiful symbol are scattered to the four winds by a clear historic insight into the rite.

Now these "divers baptisms," as Paul calls them (Heb. ix, 10), different kinds of baptisms; some with mere blood; some with mere water sprinkled on them; some with blood and running water administered to men, houses, tents, vessels; some with water mingled with the ashes, were all to effect, declare, typical purity. The *person* had to wash after *he* was purified to declare and symbolize the fact. The whole truth then was, Christ's blood—"blood of sprinkling" (Heb. x, 22; ix, 14; xii, 24; 1 Pet. 1, 2)—was the only real cleansing from sin. The blood of animals typically cleansed from guilt or sin, and the water symbolized to the person that he *was cleansed.*

We see in all this the *origin* and *design* of baptism. *All* these sprinklings Paul calls baptisms—"*washings*," in our version. But all parties agree that the (*rachats, louo, nipto*) *washing* also of persons was baptism. And it is *the* one we have most to do with. It was, like the rest, wholly symbolic. That was its entire religious meaning and design. Infants were subjects of baptism in its original institution. As they purified by sprinkling them, Joel ii, 15-17, sufficiently shows that infants, "*those that suck the breasts,*" were a part of the "congregation" (Greek, *ekklesia, church*) sanctified by being "sprinkled with water."

They are born innocent, free from guilt, however tainted by the transmission of that distemper, as Mr. A. Campbell calls it, that ruined our race. As the blood of Christ covers their condition, and they are innocent and in a saved condition—their condition, the status to which *conversion* brings aliens (Matt. xviii, 1-5; Eph. ii, 13-19)—they of all persons are most properly entitled to baptism. Water does not *primarily* symbolize the Spirit, but innocence, then religious purity which makes innocence, because to an alien or sinner the Spirit *applies* the merit of Christ's blood to the actual washing away of actual sins. *Therefore,* water or baptism of water, symbolizes the means, the Spirit's application, to effect this innocence or purity. In 2 Maccabees i, 18, 21, 31, 33, we read that when the Jews got the opportunity to reform and attend to their religious duties they began by a general outward purification. "We proposed to keep the purifying of the temple." Hence, "Nehemiah commanded the priests to sprinkle the wood and the things laid thereon with water." They prayed that the sacrifices might be sanctified" (verse 26). The water was (verse 31) poured on the great stones; *therewith* "Nehemiah *purified* the sacrifices." It is not to be forgotten that as the Israelites passed the sea they were all baptized, infants and adults (1 Cor. x, 1, 2); to which David seems to allude most forcibly.(Ps. lxviii, 9) when God "confirms" his church or "heritage" when he sent a "plentiful rain" on them.

It is not surprising therefore that John came baptizing that Christ, who was to *thoroughly purge* his floor, actually cleanse, purify, and save the people, might be made manifest to Israel. It had all these centuries of precedents in its favor, that when John called the people to baptism it involved and implied to them the need and desire to seek purity. Is it possible it could *ever* change its import? NEVER. Hence today it is in the *name* of the *Trinity* involved in the work of our purification, making us *innocent*.

CHAPTER IV.

Baptism with Water.

Washing with water was familiar to all people. Mode was not implied. Washing is most constantly the effect of affusion all around us. The rain washes houses, trees, plants, herbs, grass from the dust or whatever may soil that it can remove. People wash their hands where they dip one into the water to apply it to both, rubbing. One may pour it on the hands of another, as is often done, and as was the custom in the days of Elijah (2 Kings iii, 11). People wash their faces and bodies with water. Baths are had both where the body is partially put into the water and where water is showered from above, or, as in olden times, a servant pours water over the body. In all these ways persons and things are *washed with water*. Such a process the Greeks would express by *lousetai en hudati* ("*wash with water*"); *nipsetai en hudati;* or simply omitting the *en* ("with"), *hudati*, ("*with water*"). As the Jews had been used to these expressions in the Pentateuch, and for *wash* we have *baptize* in the later Greek writers, hence in the New Testament it is not surprising that there we have this form so constantly recurring.

"I indeed baptize you with water. He shall baptize you with the Holy Ghost."* So Matthew, Mark, John

---

* Matt. iii, 11; Mark i, 8; John i, 31, 32. The Greek in these places is ἐν ὑδατι, *en hudati*. In Mark i, 8, however, the best Greek MSS. have no *en*.

and Luke and Peter and Christ declare.* This is the historic and comprehensive way of narrating it—baptism was *with water.* Water was the *instrument used with which* people were baptized. This language declares the *general*, the *universal* practice of baptism WITH WATER. "*He* shall *baptize with* (*en*) the Holy Spirit.*" Acts x, 45: "On the Gentiles also was *poured out* the gift of the Holy Ghost." It *fell on* them (verse 44). Now, says Peter, telling this to "the apostles and brethren" (Acts xi, 1), "As I began to speak, the Holy Ghost fell on them, as on us at the beginning. Then remembered I the word of the Lord, how that he said, John indeed baptized with water, but ye shall be baptized with the Holy Ghost" (Acts xi, 15-17). Notice here, first, they are baptized with water; second, they are baptized with the Holy Spirit; third, the *mode* of the *all-essential* baptism is given. It was "*poured* on them." It "fell on them." So in the Bible it is represented as "shed forth," "poured upon." It is often called "*anointing*," "unction."† All believers received this sealing power of the Spirit.‡ By one Spirit are we *all* BAPTIZED into one body." Christ *baptizes* us with the Spirit. Cornelius's house was thus baptized; that is, "it was poured out on them." It "fell on them"—they were baptized with it.

In Acts i, 5, it was poured on them. Some say it filled the house, and they were *immersed in it.* To *immerse in* an element is to put the object *into it.* Here it is claimed

* Luke iii, 16; Acts i, 5; xi, 17. In these cases it is simply *ύδατι, hudati.* Peter tells us "the Lord said" the same (Acts xi, 15, 16).

† Ezek. xviii, 31; xxxvii, 5-14; Jer. xxxi, 33; Is. xxxii, 15; xliv, 3; Prov. i, 23; Joel ii, 28; Acts i, 1-5, 33; ii, 28; x, 44, 45; xi, 14-17; 1 Peter i, 12; 1 John ii, 20, 27, 28; v, 6, 7, 10; 2 Cor. i, 21; Acts iv, 27; Titus iii, 5, 6.

‡ Titus iii, 5-7; Eph. i, 12-14; 1 Cor. xii, 3-13; and the above texts.

the Spirit filled the house where they were assembled. In *that* case it would overwhelm them, but not *dip* them, surely, or immerse them. But it is untrue that it filled the house. It does not say so. The sound as of a rushing mighty wind filled the house. So states the text. It (the sound) filled it. But in all the other places there is no such fact. And in all cases the Spirit was poured on them. The Spirit thus acting *baptized them*, Christ being the baptizer. Isaiah xliv, 3; Zechariah xii, 10; Joel ii, 28, of the Old Testament; Peter, Acts xi, 15, 16; Luke, in Acts x, 44, 45; Paul, Titus iii, 5, 6, tell us the Spirit was poured out on the people—six witnesses. Matthew iii, 11; Mark i, 8; Luke iii, 16; John i, 33; Acts i, 5; Peter, Acts xi, 15, 16; John the Baptizer, in Matthew iii, 11, etc.; Christ, Acts xi, 16; Paul, 1 Corinthians xii, 13— eight New Testament writers and speakers call this pouring on of the Spirit on the people, *baptizing* them with the Spirit. Is. xliv, 3: "I will pour water upon him that is thirsty" symbolizes the words in the same verse, "I will pour my Spirit upon thy seed." It was the "I baptize you with water, with the Spirit," of the above texts.

But it is answered, Is the Spirit literally poured upon men? Is it not present every where, filling all space, ubiquitous, above, around us? How then can it be poured on us when it is present every where? To this we reply:

1. Yes; but if it holds good as an argument, the possibility of the Spirit being literally poured on us, shed upon us, etc., or against the propriety of such language, how much more is it against the idea or possibility of being *dipped* in the Spirit? How can people be immersed in the Spirit from this standpoint? To be dipped implies not merely putting in, partially or wholly, but being withdrawn. How could they be immersed into that in which

already they were enveloped? Suppose people were already entirely under the water of a lake or river, how could they be dipped into it, when already enveloped in the water? So this dodge leaves the objector in a worse predicament than ever.

2. Hence the Spirit's influence or operation on man's moral nature is repeatedly called in the New Testament baptizing with the Spirit. It is called baptism.

3. The Bible throughout designates this act or work of the Spirit, baptizing them with the Spirit, pouring the Spirit on them, as just seen.*

4. Then, why do the prophets and apostles represent the Spirit as "poured" on the people in the baptismal act? A good reason must underlie such language. First, there was a grand reason for the action of the Spirit being compared to the wind (John iii, 8); second, there was a reason for representing us as begotten by the Spirit—"born of the Spirit"—we receive character, impress from it; third, why is it often represented as "an unction," "an anointing"? Because the wind literally does act as named, known by its *effects*, so is every one born of the Spirit. Because those "anointed" have the symbolizing oil *literally* poured on them, therefore we are anointed by the Spirit. Because seals of state were literally placed upon documents to give impress, character, passport, acceptance, we are "sealed with the Spirit of promise" (Eph. i, 13; 2 Cor. i, 22). Because in outward baptism the water was literally poured on those baptized, they are said to be baptized with the

---

*To those who, like Stokius in his lexicon, assert that *baptidzo* is used to express the *abundance* of the Spirit, or its gifts, though he tells us it was by pouring, we reply that χέω, *cheo*, to pour, is often so used in the classics and the Bible, and with certain prepositions it represents floods even, abundance, bounteousness. But where does dip or immerse represent these ideas?

Spirit, it is said to be poured on them. The water was a symbol, as was the oil a symbol from other standpoints. Hence the objection brings out the clearest argument possible.

No intelligent person is willing to rest a good cause on mere allusions, much less upon one or two highly-wrought *metaphors* that allude to baptism, whether it be by that of the Spirit or of water. Baptizing, *eis, epi* (Mark i, 9; Matt. iii, 13), *en*, at Jordan, in Ænon, because there was much water there; and Acts viii, 38; Romans vi, 4, give us no historic basis, *no fact*, as to the action or mode. A. Campbell states it only as an "*inference*" as to the eunuch. He can't say he was immersed. Dr. Wilkes puts it at best only as a "*hypothesis.*"* We now propose to give a historic basis on this question, and facts that will clearly account also for the going to Jordan, Ænon, etc. Surely the ordinary reasons assigned are absurd. Dr. Barclay (immersionist) in City of the Great King, Elder Wilkes, and Baptists as well, tell us of four acres of pools of water in Jerusalem from forty-five to forty-seven feet deep in the centers, showing plenty of water in which to immerse, in which the three thousand of Pentecost (Acts ii, 41) could have been plunged. Well, then, why did people go in great numbers from thence to Jordan for baptism if quantity or sufficiency of water for the mode of baptism was the motive? Again, why leave the Jordan and go to Ænon if that was the question? Again, as it is only in connection with *John's* baptism we ever read of Jordan and Ænon as to baptism, if the people had to go to Jordan and Ænon for a sufficiency of water for the baptismal act, how came no one to go to either place in all the sixty-seven years of baptisms under the

* Louisville Debate, page 582.

apostles? John's lasted only some six months. If John's subjects did go thence for the purpose of getting sufficient water for the mode, it is the strongest possible proof against immersion in the apostolic age.

1. John baptized at first "beyond Jordan," "in Bethany"* (John i, 28; x, 42), where Christ afterward dwelt for a time, "into the place where John at first baptized" (John x, 40).

2. He next baptized *at* (*epi*) the Jordan (Matt. iii, 13). Luke reads "about Jordan" (Luke iii, 3). Mark has it *eis*, at, in, or into (Mark i, 9); *en*, "at," "in," "by," "about" (verse 5).

That Mark's *en* does not indicate mode, but merely the place, location, in which the baptism was performed, is evident from the fact that where the action of the baptism is named it is in Mark "*with* water (Mark i, 8), not *in* water. And the correct texts of Tischendorf, Tregelles, etc. have no *en* in Mark i, 8, in the Greek either. That it does not indicate mode but merely place is further evident from Matthew's words, "at Jordan," Luke's, "about Jordan." The Hebrews stood still "in the midst of Jordan" (Josh. iii, 17); "stand still in Jordan" (Josh. iii, 8); "into Jordan" (verse 11), all on dry land, just as the people "came up out of Jordan"—repeated some five times (Josh. iv, 16-21). "The Israelites pitched (*en*) by a fountain" (1 Sam. xxix, 1). "Get thee hence, and hide thyself (*en*) the brook Cherith" (1 Kings xvii, 3). In Ezekiel i, 3; iii, 15; x, 15, 20, 22, in the Hebrew *in* (*be*) and *at* (*al*) the river interchange over and again for the same thing. But in Joshua the *en* (in) Jordan and *into*

---

* In James's version it reads Bethabara, but in Baptist Union Bible, A. Campbell's, and Anderson's and Wilson's immersion versions it reads Bethany, as well as in all ancient MSS. and versions, and is the only correct reading.

Jordan are expressly limited and *defined* (Josh. iii, 8) by *epi*, *at* or by the Jordan (Josh. iii, 8). *Epi* is there used as the limitation of *en* or *eis*. So the *en* and *eis* of Mark i, 5, 9, are limited and defined by Matthew's *epi*. And some manuscripts of Joshua iii, 8, expressly use *eis* for *epi* in that verse: "As ye come *eis* (*to*) the water;" others, "As ye come *epi* (to) the water."*

3. Every Jew baptized himself from once to two, three, four times a day in Christ's day (Mark vii, 3, 4; Luke xi, 38), with facts detailed in the laver argument. Did they all go to Jordan to find water enough for their baptism? We see in the laver argument that all Jews baptized daily, and baptized their furniture and their beds every day. When we are told of big cisterns twenty-two feet deep, sixteen or seventeen feet wide, that families had against the three, four, or five months of drouth every season, and that they could immerse in them, we again refer you to Leviticus xi, 30-36; Numbers xix, 22; xxxi, 23; Leviticus xv entire, etc. as an utter refutation of that. And in the face of those facts would a man, his wife, their six, eight, ten children, and often six, eight, ten servants, male and female, daily immerse in the cistern and daily immerse their *beds* in it, then use the water for drinking, for cooking, and the like. Immersion theories require this.

* Origen's Hexapla, in loc. So likewise *epi* and *en* interchange, e. g. Judith xii, 7, *epi*, at the fountain; some MSS. *en*, at, etc.

CHAPTER V.

Baptism of Paul (Saul).

In Acts ix, 18, we read in the Greek Testament, "And standing up [he] was baptized." The facts show that while Saul was praying he kneeled on his face, a habit very common then. Christ in the garden "fell on his face, and prayed" (Matt. xxvi, 39), where Luke says he kneeled (xxii, 41). Cornelius fell at the apostle's feet to pray (Acts x, 25). The jailer "fell down before" the apostle and Silas (Acts xvi, 29). 1 Corinthians xiv, 25, shows it was the common habit. Saul had been praying in the deepest humility of spirit (Acts ix, 11). It was while in this attitude that his sins were washed away, in the act of prayer, and the Spirit received (Acts ix, 16-18). Then he arose, stood up, and was baptized. So the other report of it (Acts xxii, 16): Arise, "standing up, be baptized, having washed away thy sins in calling on the name of the Lord." All ancient English versions—six in number—before James's read, "*in* calling on the name of the Lord."* Peter said to Cornelius (Acts x, 26), "Stand up" (anasthæthi), and he helped him to stand up.

Matt. iii, 13: "Jesus cometh [*epi*, ἐπί] to Jordan unto John, to be baptized." It was [*epi*] AT the Jordan, not

---

* Καὶ ἀναστὰς ἐβαπτίσθη, *kai anastas ebaptisthœ*. The Greek implies that *while* or *in the act of standing* he was baptized. There is no "and" (*kai*) in the Greek. Such a form of words shows he stood for the purpose of being baptized.

in or *into* it. Mark i, 9, has for this *eis, at, into, by, in*. Of *eis* Liddell & Scott's Greek Lexicon says its "*radical signification is direction toward, motion to, on,* or *into.*" So say Kühner, Buttman, Passow, Rost, Palm, Pape—all modern critics. It is toward, mere motion *toward, to, on,* or *into.* Hence the primary meaning is not *into;* that is a derived meaning resulting from the motion toward, etc. Joshua iii, 8, *epi, at, to* interchanges with *eis, at, to.* As *eis* means *to, at* primarily, and *epi* never implies *into*, but limits the object to mere location *on, at, by, to,* it settles this question. Though we could cite vast numbers of texts where *eis* means to, at, by—e. g. 1 Kings xviii, 19, "*at* Carmel"—yet let us take a few that *limit it to Jordan,* as this is a question about Jordan in Mark i, 9. 1 Kings ii, 6: "Meet me [*eis*] at Jordan." 2 Kings ii, 6: "For the Lord hath sent me [*eis*] to Jordan." 2 Kings v, 4: "The sons of the prophets came (*eis*) *to* the Jordan and cut wood." Add a few more.

Is. xxxvi, 2: "The king sent Rabshakeh from Lachish [*eis*] *to* Jerusalem"—not into it, for the city was not yet captured, and he remained outside by the potter's field, and they came out and met him there (verse 3). 2 Kings ii, 21: "Went forth [*eis*] unto the spring of waters." Josh. iii, 16: *Eis*, "toward the sea." Luke v, 4: "Launch out [*eis*] into the sea." Note it was a ship or boat already in the sea. In Mark i, 9, *eis Iōrdanaen* in the Peshito is *bh' Yurdhnon,* at Jordan—not [*le*] into. Acts viii, 38, it is *le,* into, to, etc. Rom. vi, 4: "Into death" is [*le*], into. Wesley's version, in his notes, renders Mark i, 9, "at Jordan," just as he does Matthew iii, 13, "at Jordan." H. T. Anderson, immersionist, reads, "to Jordan" (Matt. iii, 13).

In the above we have repeatedly *the very words* of Mark

i, 9, which immersionists render "*into the Jordan;*" yet in not one of these cases does it allow of this meaning. As all the places where *eis* occurs with Jordan compel us to reject this rendering and accept *at* as the force of the word, and Matthew's *epi*, "at," settles it, we do not propose to surrender such *facts* to mere bravado.

Again, the rendering of H. T. Anderson, immersionist most rigid; of the Bible of the Baptist Union; and of T. J. Conant, all of whom render Mark i, 10, and Matthew iii, 6, "he came up immediately *from* [*apo*] the water," confirms this. *Apo* can not apply to emergence. Hence Christ was not in nor under the water. The want of accurate knowledge of the Greek in James's day—1607 to 1610—led them to suppose that *apo* meant at times out of, and the old lexicographers of the previous century so rendered it. No scholar will pretend now that it ever means "*out of.*" Winer, Kühner, Jelf, Robinson, Passow, Pape, Liddell & Scott, etc. have utterly dissipated that delusion. Hence Dr. T. J. Conant, the prince of Baptist scholars in Europe or America, though so intolerant of affusion for baptism, says, "It has been erroneously supposed that the same thing is stated in Matthew iii, 16, and Mark i, 10. But the prep[osition] 'from' (*apo*) is there used [so does Luke iv, 1, rendered 'from' even in James's version]; and the proper rendering is 'up from the water.'"* Winer, the great German critic on idioms, shows that *apo* can not be applied to a case where a subject was literally *in* or *under* the water, but only to cases where he was near to, by, at, "*not in,*" says he.† Because

* *Baptizein*, page 98 *note*.

† "'Ανέβη ἀπὸ, up *from* the water" (Idioms, 298). If *baptidzo* means, as they say it does, *to dip*—as dip in all such uses implies *withdrawal*—how could he come up out of the water in *their* sense, if *dip* had already withdrawn him?

ek occurs in several of the best ancient manuscripts, Dr. Wilkes insists it is the correct reading of Mark i, 10, as in Tischendorf. 1. By the same and by far more authority he must reject Mark xvi, 15, 16. 2. Scholz, Winer, Bengel, Lange, Theile, Olshausen, Mill, Griesbach, Conant, Anderson, Baptist Union Bible, all retain *apo* there.* 3. Even if it were *ek* in Mark i, 10, it often means "from," while *apo* never means "out of." And all copies read *apo*, from, in Matthew iii, 16, and Luke iv, 1. Hence Christ never was literally in Jordan—i. e. the water—but only *epi*, at Jordan, when baptized.

But taking the incorrect renderings of James, Luke and John report the same matter thus: Luke iv, 1: "And Jesus being full of the Holy Ghost, *returned from* Jordan." That which by Matthew and Mark is reported "from the water" is here "returned from Jordan," showing that mere *departure* from the Jordan is meant by all the writers. John thus records it (iv, 3): "He *left* Judea and *departed* again into Galilee." Thus it is perfectly evident that the writers merely meant to tell of his prompt return, of his speedy temptation, and of his departure into Galilee; nothing indicating *emergence,* but *departure.*

PHILIP AND THE EUNUCH.

Acts viii, 38: The supposed confession of the eunuch is so evident a forgery that A. Campbell, Anderson, Wilson (formerly of their church), McGarvey, all threw it out of the text most justly. It is not in any ancient copy (MS.) of the Bible. Hence all correct Greek texts now reject it without hesitation.

---

* Conant, Anderson, Bible Union, Baptist, professedly corrected the Greek text, contrary to Wilkes's statement.

Next to Romans vi, 4, immersionists have made more capital out of the baptism of the eunuch than out of all else in James's version, especially as the ignorant masses go beyond all records and jumble up the "much water" of Ænon with this case, then add both places to Christ's baptism, quoting it as if he went straightway into the water!!

1. Does the fact that "they went down both into the water, both Philip and the eunuch," imply immersion? Or that "they came up out of the water?" These are the words relied on. Do "into" and "out of" imply immersion? Yes or no? If you say No, you give up the argument. If you say Yes, it destroys the immersion theory; for if "into" and "out of" here imply immersion or dipping, *baptidzo* does not; for *after* they went (*eis*)* "into the water," it reads, "and he baptized him;" i. e. it was *after* he had been "baptized" that "they came up out of the water."

2. If "into the water" and "out of the water" imply immersion, both Philip and the eunuch were immersed. "Both Philip and the eunuch" "went down into the water," both came up out of it. If it is answered, Philip had to go down into the water to immerse him, we reply, first, that destroys the "out of" and "into" argument; second, it assumes the very point to be proved, that he did immerse him. It begs the question altogether.

3. But it is asked why did they go down into the water if not for immersion? If sprinkling was the mode why did not Philip run down into the water and secure a cup or pitcher full of water? First, decency and good will would suggest that both go while one had to go; second,

* I follow James's rendering here, of course. Εἰς means, primarily, toward; then to, unto; then at, and into.

the laws of Moses show why. Wherever possible the law required running, i. e. living water, to be used for baptism, ritualistic washing. As yet Christianity had not gone to the Gentiles, and Moses's law was strictly kept (see Acts xv, 1-20; xxi entire; and Gal. iii) long after this. In the facts of the laver argument all these matters are fully presented, which see. It is also argued that the nobleman had vessels for his use in the chariot, and water could have been brought in the vessel from the place of water. But if he had such, by their use by one unclean, all such vessels were unclean, and water for any use could not be used from such, as Leviticus xi, 30-36; Numbers xix, 22; xxxi, 23, sufficiently tell us.

4. Bloomfield, Baumgarten, and other most eminent scholars believe Philip poured the water on him in the baptism.

5. Finally, we insist if *baptidzo* means to dip, and we know dip means that we put in and *withdraw* the object dipped; hence if he was *dipped*, he was withdrawn from the water by Philip, which leaves it impossible that he should go out of the water literally, being already *withdrawn* from it.

We deem it time and space lost to discuss, as puerile writers do, about whether there was sufficiency of water between Gaza and Jerusalem in which to immerse the eunuch, or to try to prove, as immersionists do, that the jailer was led off in search of water. The plain facts all indicate affusion as the mode, as to the three thousand, the five thousand, Lydia, Cornelius, Paul, and the jailer. The fact that in *no* instance did the parties in the whole history of Christian baptism, during sixty-seven years, go in search of water, so far as the record goes or hints—and we propose not to leave the record—is all so much evidence against immersion. We are *too bountifully* supplied with proofs of affusion *to weaken* our crushing facts by forcing into service matters that of themselves afford no help to either side. The language in Acts x, 46, 47, "Can any man *forbid* water," is strongly in favor of the idea of it being brought for the baptismal use as against immersion.

We, however, can not see how the theory of immersion can apply to the three thousand and five thousand on Pentecost and the next day, especially in view of this. All were Jews. Purification or cleansing, if *actual*, defiled the water, and only *one* could be cleansed, washed, or baptized in or with the same water. If *ceremonial*, then as soon as one was ceremonially washed, or baptized symbolically, the water became ceremonially unclean. "WHATSOEVER THE UNCLEAN TOUCHETH SHALL BE UNCLEAN." Certainly non-believing Jews, to say the least, would regard all those who received Christ as unclean. Would they have allowed the Jews converted to Christ to thus ceremonially pollute all their public waters? We can not suppose so for a moment. See this further under the head of *the laver*, Chapter VI. If confession of each was taken as Baptists and Disciples now do, it is difficult to see how so many could be examined, prepared, and immersed after the apostles closed their preaching (Acts ii, 41).

But we think the writers on both sides of this question have committed grave errors also in aiming to settle so great a controversy, almost if not altogether, by the constructions they put upon (so far as the English version goes, and largely as to the original):

1. The merest *incidental* "allusions" to baptism. Such are Mark i, 9 (εἰσ, *eis*), "in," "*at* Jordan;" Mark i, 5, *en*, "in the Jordan," at, in, or by Ænon near Salim, in

or at Bethany, into the water (Acts viii, 38); or, on the other side, the three thousand on Pentecost (Acts ii, 41); the five thousand (Acts v, 14); Lydia, the jailer (Acts xvi, 16, 33); Cornelius (Acts x, 43-47); Paul (Acts ix, 18, 19). These latter are just as decisive as the former, if not much more so; yet they are not a historic basis; are only incidental allusions, and all briefly given.

2. Metaphorical as well as incidental allusions, where almost every word is highly metaphorical; such texts must always be more or less uncertain as to their exact meaning when interpreted, at so remote a period, by a people not versed in the metaphors of those times. Take such examples as Romans vi, 3, 5; Colossians ii, 12; John iii, 5. Scholars have always, since the fourth century, been perplexed as to the real meaning and intent of these texts. We say the fourth century, for till then Romans vi, 4, was *never* referred to water baptism, but to spiritual, while mostly John iii, 5, was held to be spiritual water, just as Origen, Calvin, Beza, Zwingle, etc. held.

3. Those texts that are only *allusions to* the baptismal use of water and are not actual baptism, and expressed in highly metaphorical style, based upon the ancient use of water. Such are Ephesians v, 26; Titus iii, 5; Isaiah iv, 4; Isaiah i, 16; Psalm li, 2-9; Ezekiel xvi, 9; Hebrews x, 22, and are far more pertinent, since they are general allusions to baptism and especially indicate its proper symbolism, viz. cleansing.

What we demand is a *historic basis*, a *record of facts* in historic order, *then* the allusions and metaphors are to be explained *by well-ascertained facts*, not the *fact assumed*, then sought to be proved by mixed, uncertain, and metaphorical allusions; many of which are in themselves wholly uncertain.

METAPHORICAL INCIDENTAL ALLUSIONS TO WATER AND SPIRIT BAPTISM.

But as mere *incidental* allusions to baptism are exclusively relied on as to Bible arguments by our opponents, let us examine a few of the *acknowledged allusions to* WATER baptism, on which all parties are agreed that the allusion is to ritualistic baptism.

Eph. v, 25, 26: "As Christ also loved the church, and gave himself for it, that he might sanctify and cleanse it with the washing (cleansing) of water by the word."

1. All immersionists refer this to baptism. A. Campbell, Wilkes, Dr. Brents, and all their writers always cite it thus and quote Wesley, Clarke, Doddridge, etc. to back their statements.

2. It confirms affusion. What is done to effect the (*loutron*) washing here? Two words are used—(1) sanctify, (2) cleanse. (1) Sanctify. How did they ritualistically sanctify the church or people? Hebrews ix, 13, 19, with Numbers xix, 13, 18, tell us it is done by sprinkling the water. Josephus tells us Moses "sprinkled Aaron and his sons" for this purpose. See full quotations under the argument on the laver. (2) Cleanse. How did they cleanse them? Numbers viii, 7: "And thus shalt thou do unto them, *to cleanse* them: Sprinkle water of purifying upon them." Ezekiel xxxvi, 25, refers to this cleansing, and, like Paul, names only the sprinkling of water as affecting it: "Then will I sprinkle clean water upon you, and you shall be *clean*"—cleansed. Here we have Paul, Moses, and Ezekiel giving us *the mode* of this cleansing and sanctifying; it is by sprinkling clean or pure water upon the persons.

Hebews x, 22, they all say refers to "Christian baptism." Dr. Graves gives it special prominence (Debate, p. 186) as "Christian baptism." But the above facts, as well as the laver, show the washing was by affusion of clean or pure water on the parties. Where it says body—over and again the Bible says body where only the face, the head, etc., or a part is designated (John xiii, 9, compared with verse 10, "*he* that is washed;" verse 8, "if I wash *thee* not;" Matt. xxvi, 7, "poured it on *his head;*" verse 12, "on *my body;*" verse 10, "upon me;" Num. viii, 7, "shave all their flesh," body; Titus iii, 5, 6)—they all say alludes to or is baptism, the washing. Clearly enough it is an allusion to the baptismal use of water, just as Isaiah i, 16; Ezekiel xvi, 9; Psalm li, 1, 2, 7; Isaiah iv, 4, are—"wash me;" "I have washed thee with water," etc.; but "the washing of regeneration" is that "which he shed (*poured out*) upon us abundantly"—a metaphorical use of words based on the *actual* pouring of water on the baptized subjects, symbolizing the Spirit (Isaiah xliv, 3). Hence,

1. *In all cases in the Bible where the mode of* baptizing (Spirit) is given it is pouring.

2. In all cases where the mode in the *allusions* to baptism is given it is affusion.

3. Wherever such words as cleanse, sanctify are used, referring to water, where all admit it points to baptism, as Ephesians v, 26, it is affusion.

4. Immersion as an ordinance of God's church is a stranger and foreigner to the whole Bible.

CHAPTER VI.

Jordan.

The following facts will appear on examining the evidence appended thereto:

1. John did not baptize at or in the Jordan at the beginning of his ministry, but went "*away* again *beyond* Jordan," to Bethany.

2. Jordan is in one of the hottest valleys in the world, owing to its great depression at the lower part, where John baptized.

3. The water flows from regions of perpetual snow, in Hermon and Anti-Lebanon, and hence the water is very cold. Most of the way it is shaded by abrupt cliffs and mountains "thousands of feet high." The waters run down a steep of three thousand feet, hence so cool from such snow-regions on the mountains.

4. Smith's summary of the facts is: "From its fountain heads to the point where it is lost to nature (empties in the Dead Sea) *it rushes down one* CONTINUOUS INCLINED PLANE, *only broken by* a series of *rapids* or *precipitous falls.*" This is immersion authority. Where are those eddies, stagnant places, and conveniences we hear of?

5. John left such an unhealthy valley just as soon as the great press of the multitudes would allow—as soon as the numbers were so reduced that the springs or "fountains" at Ænon near Salim would accommodate their wants.

6. It was a physical impossibility for John to stand in the cold water so long as the immersion theory requires. Circulation of blood would have ceased, animal heat would have been promptly overcome, and death ensued in a short time.

7. It is a physical impossibility that John could have immersed so many, if even the smallest number that any reasonable estimate demands be granted, in so swift a stream as was and is the Jordan. When a steamboat runs eight miles to the hour, not to say ten, none but practiced persons can risk throwing a bucket into the water and drawing it out full of water. But here the stream is as swift or swifter than that, and persons much heavier and larger than a bucket certainly; and while a man could take another and dip him by being very careful, it is not possible that one man could immerse great numbers in such a rapid stream, for the physical labor, the certainty of many being swept away from his hold and drowning, forbid. In a few minutes the limbs would become so numb in such a cold stream as to make the action of the lower limbs impossible.

Let us now see the proofs. The length of the Jordan directly to the Dead Sea is sixty miles. By its windings it is two hundred miles. Its fall is over three thousand feet. Dr. Robinson, Lieut. Lynch, and Gage all show its fall to be over three thousand feet. As Dr. Wm. Smith is such a favorite with immersionists, we prefer quoting from him. In his Dictionary of the Bible, following Lynch, he says, "The depression .. of the Dead Sea below the Mediterranean is 1,316.7, and 653.3 feet below Tiberias." He then gives the height of the head of the Jordan above the level of the Mediterranean 1,700 feet. The mouth is 1,317 feet below it, making the fall of the Jordan in all "a height of more than three thousand feet." Divide this by two hundred miles, and we have the average fall to the mile fifteen feet. The actual distance is sixty miles, which divided into three thousand gives sixty feet to the mile. Some writers put the distance one hundred and twenty miles, twenty-five feet average. The upper Jordan has more fall than the lower, where John baptized. Robinson shows its fall where John baptized to be a little over *ten feet* to the mile. The fall of the Mississippi is a little over *five inches* to the mile, yet runs from three to five miles an hour, much as it winds.

Kitto says, "It becomes turbid; . . . the water is . . . *always cold.*"

Of the upper Jordan a writer in Harper, June number, 1870, says, "The river soon became a *roaring torrent,* in which no boat could live." Lynch tells us they often had to have their iron boats hauled around places, because so dangerous, owing to the current. One iron boat perished any how. The above writer of Harper says they were assailed by a mob, but "the current bore the canoe along too rapidly for them to keep up with it, but they cut across the *bend,*" and thus overtook it for a moment.

Rabbi Joseph Swarz, for sixteen years a resident in the Holy Land (p. 43), says, "The Jordan . . . is so rapid a stream that even the best swimmer can not bathe in it without endangering his life. In the neighborhood of Jericho (there is where John baptized) the bathers are compelled *to tie themselves together with ropes, to prevent their being swept away by the rapidity of the current.**

Rev. D. A. Randall, a Baptist, who traveled in Palestine thus writes: "According to the usual custom of visitors, we commenced arrangements for a bath, when our

* A Descriptive Geography, etc. of Palestine.

sheik interposed, declaring the current too swift, and that it would be dangerous to enter the stream; that a man had been drowned in this very place only a few days before. But we had not come so far to be thwarted in our plans by trifles. Being a good swimmer, I measured the strength of the current with my eye, and willing to risk it, plunged in, and my companions one after another followed. We found the current quite strong, so that we *could not venture to a great depth*, but *far enough* to accomplish our purpose of a *plunge bath*."* W. M. Thompson, missionary in Syria and Palestine twenty-five years, says of the current, "The current is astonishingly rapid. . . . It required the most expert swimmer to cross it, and one less skilled must inevitably be carried away, as we had melancholy proof. Two Christians and a Turk, who ventured too far, were drowned without the possibility of rescue, and the wonder is that more did not share the same fate."† This is at the place where "our blessed Savior was baptized." Some people "ducked the women;" men carried their little children for the same purpose, "trembling like so many lambs;" while "some had water poured on their heads in imitation of the baptism of the Savior" (*ibid.*).

Lieut. Lynch, who traversed the entire Jordan, and whose statements none questions—indeed, he seems to be an immersionist—gives us an account of his descent in iron boats, one of which was destroyed by the violent current dashing it to pieces against obstacles: "The shores (seemed) to flit by us. With its *tumultuous rush* the river hurried us onward, and we knew not what the next moment would bring forth—whether it would *dash us upon*

---

* The Handwriting of God, or . . . the Holy Land, Part II, pp. 233-4.

† The Land and the Book, or the Holy Land, by W. M. Thompson, D. D., vol. 2, pp. 445-6.

a rock, or plunge us down a cataract" (p. 255). This was the lower Jordan, where John baptized. They arrived at El Meshra, where John baptized. The banks are ten feet high, save at the ford, and the water is suddenly deep. Here he moralizes how "the Deity, veiled in flesh, descended the bank, . . . and the *impetuous* river, in grateful homage, must have stayed its course, and gently laved the body of its Lord" (p. 256). When pilgrims came to bathe, he anchored below them, "to be in readiness to render assistance should any of the crowd be swept down by the current, and in danger of drowning, . . . accidents, it is said, occurring every year" (pp. 261, 265).

They went on and soon passed "a camel in the river, washed down by the current in attempting to cross the ford last night" (p. 266). In five minutes they "passed another camel in the river, the poor beast leaning exhausted against the bank, and his owner seated despondingly above him. *We could not help him!*" (p. 266). Abridged Work, p. 170.

Immersion is absurd in the light of these facts. The facts show that,

1. John baptized not in Jordan at first, not till the news of his work excited general attention, and the great "multitudes" coming necessitated a place of much water. Every ablution, every drink, all cooking had to be with *clean* water. Had John been at a pond or tank of water with even enough to supply all with drinking, cooking, and cleansing waters, as well as for animals, that would not have been sufficient. The moment unclean people or animals, or dead bodies of any kind, should have touched the water it would be unsuited for drinking, for washing. Hence no place would have suited for John's ministry when such multitudes came but a place, first, of

plenty water; second, *running* water; for *a fountain"* or "confluence of waters" can not become unclean. This explains John's going to Jordan. When the great "multitudes" ceased to come, Ænon furnished by its springs enough running water for all purposes whatever. Hence,

2. We read (John x, 40-42), "And [Christ] went away again *beyond* (peran) the Jordan, (eis) *into the place where* John *at the first baptized,* and *there* remained. . . . And many believed on him *there."* Christ went *into* the place; *abode* in the place *where* John baptized; people believed on him there. As he baptized *at* Ænon, so at, or *in, as the locality,* the Jordan, and first *"beyond* Jordan."

Aside from all else, the following remarks are appropriate:

1. In *no case* is a word said in the New Testament about Jordan or Ænon and "much water" as the place where any one was baptized in all the sixty-seven or sixty-eight years of apostolic history, though "multitudes" were converted (Acts v, 14; xvii, 4; and xviii, 7; ix, 42; iv, 4).

2. In no case of baptism under the apostolic converts do we read of into or out of the water. Only in Acts viii, 38, where the deacon Philip baptized one man, is that language used, they being on a journey. See the case.

3. Hence, if the much water and the Jordan have to be appealed to to support immersion; if in John's six months' ministry people had to go so great a distance to be immersed, inasmuch as in sixty-seven or sixty-eight years of baptism under the commission that never occurs, it is strong proof that the Christian dispensation was without immersion.

1 Cor. x, 2: "Our fathers were all under the cloud, and

all passed through the sea, and were all baptized unto Moses in the cloud and in the sea," or as Luther and some versions have it, and as is equally correct with the English, "with the cloud and with the sea."

It is urged by immersionists that here we have a metaphorical baptism; that the sea congealed on each side in high walls; the cloud stood over making a pavilion, and as the Hebrews descended they were all shut in, enveloped by the cloud and sea, covered over, and, as it were, immersed! They never say "dipped" on this occasion. If the words "dip" and "immerse" are the same exactly, mean the same thing in the same place, why not read "dipped" in this case?

1. It is not a metaphorical but a *literal* baptism. As outward, literal baptism is never performed without contact with some *liquid*, and water was the only liquid here, it was *water* baptism.

2. They were not immersed in water, hence it was not immersion.

3. But it is urged they were "enveloped,"* etc. That the cloud was over them *while in the sea*. Paul does not say so. And Moses expressly says the reverse (Ex. xiv, 19-22). The cloud rose up, passed over them, stood between the two armies all that night, keeping back the Egyptians. So all this assumption of a cloud over them while in the sea is untrue. Wesley and others believe that "God sent a plentiful rain by which he confirmed his heritage" at that time (Ps. lxviii, 9; lxxvii, 17; lxxviii, 23), and thus baptized them. Josephus, a contemporary

* Since the publication of the debate I see Dr. Graves (page 392) asks, "How could the descent of Israel into the Red Sea, and *their being* BURIED *out of sight in the cloud?*" etc. What daring imposture this! He was careful not to say that in debate; but, like nearly all the rest, slip it in unseen.

of Paul and learned in the law and traditions of the Jews, says of this occasion expressly, "Showers of rain also came down from the sky."* It is next to absolute certainty that Paul knew of, and alludes to that as a fact, and denominates it baptism.

This much we know absolutely:

1. There was no immersion, no plunging into water, no dipping as to the Hebrews.

2. They were all baptized with water.

3. All the hosts of Pharaoh *were* immersed, not one of them was baptized. The Hebrew, Greek, and Latin read (Ex. xv, 1, 4, 5, 10), they were "immersed" (*tabha* in Hebrew; *katedusan* in Greek; *submersi sunt*, in Latin, submersed). The English reads "sank," which Conant, A. Campbell, Wilkes, Graves, all tell us is the English of immerse.

Rom. vi, 3, 4; Col. ii, 11: "*Buried by baptism into death.*" This is now regarded as the Gibralter of the immersion theory. We never hear it correctly quoted in popular addresses by them. Invariably we hear them say that Paul calls baptism a burial. It is a burial. We know a thing or person is not buried till completely covered up. Let us notice, therefore, in the outset, the groundless assumptions made on this text. It is falsely assumed that,

1. It is *water* baptism.

2. That "buried by baptism into death" is a *literal* burial of the *physical body*, when the very words of the text expose glaringly its absurdity.

3. That burial among the Romans was such an interment, covering over in the earth, as we in modern times practice in burial in Europe and America, which Robin-

* Antiquities, B. 11, chap. xvi, p. 93.

son, their own historian, tells them is not the case (page 550).*

4. That the "planted" of verse 5 implies covering up, as if it were as we plant corn, potatoes, when neither of these fruits of the soil was discovered till in America. The "planted in the likeness of his death" is in the Greek "born together," "grafted together." Was Christ's death accomplished *under water?* Is there any likeness between Christ's death on the cross and a dip under water?

Even the word bury in the Scripture does not necessarily imply interment. Jer. xxii, 19: "He shall be buried with the burial of an ass, drawn and cast forth beyond the gates of Jerusalem." Jer. xxxvi, 30: "His (Jehoiakim's) dead body shall be cast out in the day to the heat,

---

* Robinson says (page 55), "The first English Baptists, when they read the phrase "buried in baptism." instantly thought of an *English* burial, and therefore baptized by laying the body in the form of burying in their own country. But they might have observed that Paul wrote to Romans, and that Romans did not bury, but burned the dead, and buried nothing of the dead but their ashes in urns; so that no fair reasoning on the form of baptizing can be drawn from the mode of burying the dead in England." Yet now, driven from lexicons, all ancient versions, and utterly defeated on every favorite field, this metaphorical text is their last and only support from their own standpoint.

1. Baptism was symbolic of innocence, purity, for fifteen hundred years; never representing burial.

2. In John's day baptism never represented burial. No one pretends that it did.

3. Christ's commission (Matt. xxviii, 19, 20) *leaves it where it was as to mode or design*—symbolic of the Spirit's work, never hinting a change in its design.

4 The Acts never hint a change. Nowhere in apostolic use does any pretend that it symbolized death, burial, or resurrection.

5. Hence it is infinitely absurd to select a highly metaphorical text, giving it a meaning that has no foundation in any previous history, nor in a single *literal* text in the Bible, as an argument.

and in the night to the frost." This was called burying with the burial of an ass—left on top of the ground a prey to weather and animals. The verb here rendered "bury" (*thapto*) is rendered *"embalmed"* in Genesis 1, 26; xlix, 30, 31; l, 2, 7, and its noun *"embalmers"* or "physicians" who embalmed. The word is employed in Greek where the dead are laid on piles of wood to be burned, on scaffolds to be consumed by the elements. It does not necessarily imply interment.

5. But Wesley,* A. Clarke, etc. say it refers "to the ancient practice of baptizing by immersion." But as an offset we reply, M. Stuart, Hodge, and Beza, in their commentaries, as well as others, reject this view, and maintain it is not water baptism, not immersion, there alluded to, but spiritual baptism.

6. Worse still for immersion. *No Christian father of the first three hundred years cites that as water baptism.* Origen, the father of commentators, born only eighty-three years after John's death and the most learned scholar of the church for sixteen hundred years, maintains it elaborately as spiritual baptism. Not till superstition and idolatry had prostituted water baptism into a hideous and frightful monstrosity was this held to be water baptism.

7. Even Dr. Wilkes, usually a very careful man in his statements compared with others of that side, says, "Now, here is a baptism. It is declared to be a *burial*. It is also declared that we are 'raised up' again" (Lou. Debate, p. 602, after quoting Rom. vi, 3, 4). Notice the

*In Louisville debate I copied an edition of Wesley's Notes that had not the words "by immersion" in Romans vi, 4. But I find no other copy that leaves it off; besides, it is evident from his note on Colossians ii, 12, as well as the words on Romans vi, 4, found in him, that this one edition is changed, and "by immersion" were his words.

blunders here made: First, it is not called or declared to be a burial. The burial is not the baptism, but the spiritual *effect* of the baptism; second, it is not "declared that we are 'raised up' again." No such words occur in that text. He cites them with quotation-marks as if there. Christ was "raised up from *the dead*," not from *water*, and our part is, "we should walk in newness of life (verse 4). WE WALK IN NEWNESS OF LIFE IN OUR BURIED CONDITION. Hence it is not under water, but to be "delivered, baptized, buried by baptism into death "—" our lives hid with Christ in God."

8. Dr. Graves (Debate, p. 116) says, "The phrase 'planted in the likeness of death' is, if possible, still stronger [i. e. than buried by baptism into death]. What is *the* likeness of death? A *burial* is the likeness of death, and *the only* likeness of death." (Italics his.)

1. Here the doctor misquoted the passage, leaving out "*his*" before death, and makes it read "planted in the likeness of death" generally instead of likeness of "*his* death," which was by *crucifixion*, hanging on a cross. Where is there a likeness between a dip under the water and dying on a cross?

2. He makes this word "planted together" imply *modal* action, as people now plant corn, potatoes, and such other things as they "cover up!" Does he not know that "plant" in the English Bible never so applies? That trees, vineyards, etc. are "planted," but in no case "covered up?"

The word in Romans vi, 5, which he thinks is stronger than "buried by baptism into death" is *sumphutoi*, from *sumphuo*, *born*, *engraft*, planted, grow together. Anderson, immersionist, renders it in this place "united together in the likeness of his death." *In no case is it*

4

modal. If it were it is utterly destructive of immersion, as Christ's death was not under water, but hanging on a cross.

10. It can not be too strongly emphasized that any doctrine or view of Scripture that is supported by men's views of the most highly-wrought metaphors and by these alone, and only two such—they the same in substance—in all the Bible, without any literal verse any where, with no plain, historic record to give explanation or direction—we repeat, such a way of interpreting the Bible is so absurd, so pernicious, so destructive of all processes of discovering truth, that it is never allowed in law, never allowed in science, and never tolerated in the study of divinity, save by the most distempered partisanship and intolerable bigotry.

The "buried by baptism into death" is the *effect* of the "baptized into Jesus Christ" of verse 3. The "buried into death" is not the baptism, but the *effect* of the baptism. "*Therefore* we are buried by *the* baptism," so the Greek reads, "into death," i. e. to sin. The "buried" is the same as "crucified" (verse 6), as "grafted together in the likeness of his death" (verse 5); the same as "circumcised with the circumcision made without hands, . . . buried with him by baptism into death"—not into water (Col. ii, 11, 12). The parties are raised, as Anderson, Wesley, and others have it, "by your faith in the energy of God"—not by the arm of the minister, as in immersion.

12. Again, this buried condition is given by Paul as evidence that all who are in it "*are* dead to sin," "crucified with Christ," "grafted together in the likeness of his death," "freed from sin," etc. But no one believes that water baptism is proof that we "*are* dead to sin," etc.

The apostles never appeal to water baptism as proof of "death to sin." Hence it can not be water baptism.*

Wesley, Clarke, and the writers of modern times who agree with them mainly held proselyte baptism to be the baptism referred to; but immersionists unanimously hold that it came in later, and so reject the groundwork of Wesley's and Clarke's views. All those taking the immersion view translate "are" by "were buried." But,

1. All standards on Greek grammar are against this, as I abundantly show in the Louisville debate.

2. All ancient versions are against it.

3. By this change we have Paul saying, to be consistent, "we *were* dead to sin," but are not so now, but "continue in sin;" "our old man *was* crucified," but is not so now; "he that was dead *was* freed from sin;" "for you *were* dead, and your life *was* hid with Christ in God" (Col. ii, 12; iii, 3).†

It should be remarked that,

1. No *standard* lexicon ever renders *baptidzo* by "bury."

2. The very few inferior ones that give it put it as a remote, metaphorical meaning.

3. Immersionists sometimes dare render the *obruo*—"overwhelm" of the lexicons—by bury, so reckless are they.

* For many other arguments and an elaborate defense of the *present tense* of Romans vi, 4, in English, see Louisville Debate, Wilkes-Ditzler, pp. 644-648. In that, Winer, p. 217; Jelf, vol. 2, pp. 66, 67; Kühner, Gram. 346-7, and all authorities support our present version in the tense "*are* buried."

† Since I obtained Origen's Works (nine volumes folio) I was pleased to find that he cited all the texts I had cited in the Louisville debate:—"I die daily;" "*Always* bearing about in our body the dying of our Lord," etc. (2 Cor. iv, 10); "We who live are *always* delivered *eis* (into) death"—as the same as Romans vi, 4; Colossians ii, 12: "Always delivered;" "*are* buried by baptism into death;" "to sin;" "our lives *are* hid with Christ," etc.

John iii, 5, is quoted to support immersion, as if emergence out of the element was implied. It is here assumed,

1. That this is water baptism. It was not held to be water baptism by any writer we have ever met of the first three centuries; yet we have thought it did allude to water baptism, but NEVER to Christian baptism.

2. The Jews were accustomed to say, "born of circumcision" (Lightfoot's Horæ Heb. et Tal.). Did they emerge out of circumcision?

3. There is nothing modal in the Greek word here used. It implies no more than to be impressed, influenced to the extent of change. "I have begotten you" is the same word. It is often rendered "begotten" by A. Campbell, Anderson, and all immersionist translators. Hence,

4. It reads "born of water *and of the Spirit.*" Does "born of the Spirit" in the same sentence imply "emergence" out of the Spirit? Surely not, but to receive the Spirit poured out upon them.

As immersionists cling so desperately now to John's baptism, we must notice the use they make of *en* in connection with the water. It is common to all, from Carson or Gale to Dr. Graves and Wilkes, to insist that *en necessarily* involves the idea not of *instrumentality,*—"*with* water," but "*in* water." Hence we have produced a vast array of texts never produced before on this subject.

In the Greek from the Hebrew, *b'* or *v'* "*with,*" we have the expression scores of times in the laws of Moses, in every instance of which save two (unless I missed in count, and I was careful) the expression wash *with* water, rendered "bathe in water" sometimes in James's version, is simply *hudati*—*with* water. The *en* (ἐν) which the immersionists render "*in*" does not occur save in two instances. In other places the *en* occurs, clearly indicating, like the Hebrew preposition *be, instrumentality — with.* Ezek. xvi, 9: "I have washed thee (*en*) *with* water." If one shall say the "*en*" in that case points to immersion, we reply, first, the verse refutes that. "Then washed I thee with (*en*) water; yea, I *thoroughly washed away* thy blood from thee, and I *anointed* thee (*en*) *with oil*." This language clearly imports that the water is applied to the person. It is figurative of course; but, second, the *with* (*en*) oil settles the force of *en* to be *with*. The oil is *poured on* the party anointed. Yet *en* expresses it—*with* oil.* Half of the New Testament references *in the common text* use *en*, one half do not. In the places where *en* is used, the versions, like the Vulgate and Luther, have it *with* water. So Isaiah iv, 4: God will "purge away the filth of the daughters of Jerusalem, *en* with (or by) the spirit of burning."

In the books of Moses, in the Greek, *en* occurs forty-one times from Exodus xxix, 2, 4, etc. to Numbers xxxv, 25, *en elaiō*—"*with* oil;" not once is it simply *elaiō* where the oil is poured on the parties.

In Leviticus xiv, 51, "And [shall *pererranei*] sprinkle *with them*" [*en autois* in the LXX, used by the apostles— the hyssop, blood, etc.] upon "the house seven times" (verse 52). "And he shall cleanse the house (*en*) *en to haimati* [ἐν τῳ αἵματι] WITH the blood of the bird, and (*en*) WITH the running [living] water [ἐν τῳ ὕδατι], and (*en*) WITH the living bird, and (*en*) WITH the cedar-wood, and (*en*) WITH the hyssop, and (*en*) WITH the scarlet." Here consecutively *seven times en* occurs in the Greek Scriptures, used by the apostles and early Christians indicating instrumentality *every* time—is *repeated* before *every* noun, meaning WITH each time, as none will question. The house was

---

* The same force of *en* (ἐν) is seen in Exodus xiii, 9; Revelation xiv, 15; vi, 5; Isaiah iv, 4; 1 John v, 6; and many other places.

sprinkled *with* blood, *with* water, and *en* is used for the "*with*" EVERY time. In Exodus xii, 9, " sodden (*en hudati*) *with* water." 1 Kings xviii, 4: "And fed them [the one hundred prophets in caves by fifties] *en, with* bread and water" (verse 13), *en*, "with bread and water."

Ezek. xvi, 4: " In the day thou wast born, neither wast thou washed (*en hudati*) WITH water."

Often to see "*with* the eyes" is expressed by *en ophthalmois*. So Ezek. xl, 4; 2 Kings xxii, 20; Zech. ix, 8; Sirach xxxv, 7; li, 35. " *With* power," is expressed by *en dunamei* repeatedly (Acts iv, 7, etc.); with the voice, *en phonae*, often (2 Sam. xv, 25; 2 Kings viii, 56 (55 Gr.); xviii, 27).

In 1 Chronicles xv, 25, "with (ἐν) *en*, shouting, and (*en*) *with* sound of the cornet, and (*en*) *with* trumpets, and (*en*) *with* cymbals, and (*en*) with psalteries," etc. In the Greek the *en*, with, occurs *six* times in that one verse as here for *with*. So 2 Chronicles xv, 14, it occurs three times for *with*—"with a loud voice (*en*), *with* (*en*) trumpets," etc.

Cases could be multiplied indefinitely,* but these are more than are needed.

But our advantage is greater still. While the inferior Greek texts somewhat divide the case in the New Testament between the cases where *en* occurs with *hudati*, water, and simply *hudati* as dative of instrument, with water, the great modern scholars Tregelles, Tischendorf, Alford, etc., give us a far more correct Greek text with the *en* thrown out of Mark i, 8, also giving us Luke iii, 11, 16; Mark i, 8; Acts 1, 5; xi, 15, 16, against Matt. iii, 11; John i, 33, etc.—two who have *en*, and that *en* the facts just

---

*See e. g. Genesis xlix, 11; 2 Samuel xiii, 22; 2 Peter ii, 16; 1 Thessalonians iv, 10.

given show means *with*. Above all we have already seen that the mode was given—baptized with the Spirit sent down from above, poured upon them.

DECENCY—HEALTH—CONVENIENCE.

These questions are gravely discussed by Elder P. H. Mell, " Professor of Greek and Latin in Mercer University, Georgia," in a reply to Dr. Summers's Treatise on Baptism, pages 163-169. There are some facts to which we call their attention who favor immersion:

1. Immersionists wear suits of clothes made of India rubber and other water-proof materials to protect themselves when immersing candidates. Such suits are advertised for sale.

2. Suits of clothes are specially made for parties to be immersed, advertised as such, on questions of decency—designed to *guard against* indecencies in the act of immersion.

3. Baptisteries in such comparatively mild climates as Northern Kentucky, Ohio, Illinois, etc., have *furnaces* made under them to *warm the water* to guard against ill health, suffering, and discomfort.

4. In some cases in the same latitude the baptistery adjoins rooms that have special conveniences for warming and affording the immersed parties the means of changing clothes at once and without risk to health as well as improper exposure to gaze.

5. In one leading immersion church, corner of Fourth and Walnut ("Campbellite"), Louisville, Ky., screens exist to guard ladies from the sight of the audience while descending into the water, which are run back out of the way as soon as the lady is well fixed in the water to undergo

immersion. The screens are run back between her and the audience as soon as she is dipped, so that she can not be seen as she ascends out of the baptistery.

6. Is not this admission of the weight of all the charges brought? Is it not an *advertisement* of the fact that intelligent *immersionists* regard it as unhealthy, dangerous, indecent in appearance and also *impracticable* in a large part of the globe?

7. If warm rooms, furnace-furnished baptisteries, waterproof clothes for administrators, special suits for candidates be necessary in such latitudes as Louisville and Paris, Ky., Cincinnati, Chicago, and other cities, what of the regions in Northern Canada, Greenland, and various regions where it would take enough oil to support half a colony for months to make fire enough to melt ice enough to immerse one person, and he or she most certainly freeze to death before such candidate could be dressed and warmed? Is the gospel to be excluded forever from such latitudes? Without coal or wood, perpetual ice around them, in other less northerly regions so cold and chilly as that death is almost certain unless good furnaces were active under the baptistery and warmed houses adjoining, I can not see how any one can make immersion, as the one only mode, compatible with the teaching and spirit of the New Testament. In a large part of the world it is *utterly impossible*—in larger regions *impracticable*.

8. A person immersed in filthy water, in mere filthy ponds, *is not baptized at all.* "Having our bodies washed with PURE water" (Heb. x, 22) does not mean *filthy* water.

CHAPTER VII.

Baptism Out of the Laver.

The most perfect historic record of baptism that we have is that of the ancient Jews. It is that of the laver. Here we have a record—a history. It runs through fifteen hundred years. The *data* are most abundant. If we fail to get light from such a record, with such a vast literature, inspired and uninspired, encircling it, we may well despair of understanding the matter altogether.

In this, the origin of symbolic baptism as a divine rite, commanded by Jehovah and performed by his people, we may clearly see the design and correct the many abuses of baptism. We can clearly see that it was symbolic, but not of death, of burial, of resurrection; not a door into the church; not an initiatory rite; not for remission of sins; not really *sacramental.*

In Exodus xxx, 18-21, we read of the laver that stood between the altar of burnt offerings and the door of the tabernacle. "Aaron and his sons shall wash (*rachats*) their hands and their feet [*ek*, Heb. *min*] *out of it.*"* "And when they go into the tabernacle of the congregation, they shall wash with water, that they die not." " Thou shalt bring Aaron and his sons to the door of the tabernacle of the congregation, and *wash them with water* (Ex. xl, 12).

---

* Exodus xxx, 18-21: *Rachats;* Greek, καὶ, νίψεται ἐξ αὐτοῦ; xl, 30, νίπτωνται ἐξ αὐτοῦ; verse 31, ἐνίπτεται ἐξ αὐτοῦ. This is carelessly rendered in James's version " *thereat* " for " out of it."

Of the laver (verse 3): "And put water therein to wash (*ek*) *out of it.*" "Moses, and Aaron and his sons, washed their hands and their feet out of it (*ek*)."

In the first laver was water for washing both the Levites and the sacrificial meats. In the later laver, separate ones were made for washing the meats. The first time these baptisms were carried out is in Leviticus viii, 4-6, where Moses brought Aaron and his sons to the door of the tabernacle, according to the above commands, and washed them with water.

1. We are all agreed that these laver washings were baptisms.* We have no dispute here. It is a unanimous agreement of both sides. In Hebrews ix, 10, Paul tells of the tabernacle services that "stood in meats and drinks, and divers baptisms"—"divers washings" in our version. All immersionists refer these to the washings of the laver and other like washings. Fuller, Gale, Hinton, Carson, A. Campbell, Judd, Ingham, Graves, Wilkes, all assert they were immersions, baptisms. Judith xii, 7: "Washed herself [baptized herself] at the fountain of water." † Sirach (Ecclesiasticus, apocryphal) xxvi, 31 (some copies verses 31, 30): "He that baptizes himself from [touching] a dead body, if he touch it again, what is he profited by his washing?" Mark vii, 4; Luke xi, 38, apply *baptidzo* to the daily washings of the Jews. So do many other Greek and Hebrew writers. Hence there is no controversy here.

A. Campbell's language will represent them fully on the main issue. "And the laver filled with water. . . . In this laver . . . the priests always washed themselves

---

* In Hebrew expressed by *rachats;* νίπτω, λούω, etc. in Greek.

† ἐβαπτίζετο . . . ἐπὶ τῆσ πηνῆσ τοῦ ὑδατοσ. Conant tells us the Syriac reads "*immersed,*" etc. This is utterly untrue. It is *amad,* wash. See on Syriac Versions, *amad,* Chapter XXIV.

before they approached the sanctuary." "This vessel was called in Greek *loutaer*, and the water in it *loutron*. . . . Paul more than once alludes to this usage in the tabernacle in his epistles, and once substitutes Christian *immersion* in its place."* Again, "The divers washings [*baptismois*] of cups, etc. and things mentioned † among the traditions of the elders, and the *institutions* of *the laver* were for *ceremonial cleansing*. Hence all by immersion." ‡ Let it be noted here how explicitly he states the design of baptism as *originally* instituted—"CEREMONIAL CLEANSING."

The learned Baptist, Dr. Gale, elaborates the same thing (Reflections on Wall, vol. 2, p. 101, of Wall's History of Infant Baptism), urging that *rachats* "I think always, including dipping,"—tells of this laver, cites 2 Chronicles iv, 6, on it, and insists that they dipped in it—immersed.

2. The next point is to determine the mode of these baptisms that ran through fifteen hundred years of daily and hourly occurrence. Immersionists say they immersed themselves in the laver. We deny this, and for the following insurmountable reasons:

First. By the original command, already cited from Exodus, they were to wash, not *in*, but (*ek*) "out of it."

---

* Chris. Baptist, vol. 5, 401.

† Chris. Baptism, 167; Dr. Brents's Gospel Plan, 338-9, same in substance. A. Campbell cites the washings of persons in Leviticus xv and xvi entire, thus: In Leviticus xv, 5, 8, 10, 11, 13, 16, 18, 21, 22, 27. Here are ten divers bathings etc. Also Leviticus xvi, 26, 27; xvii, 15, 16. Also in Numbers xix, 7, 8, 19. He has it "sixteen different bathings." "These are therefore called by Paul divers baptisms, or baptisms on divers occasions"!! Chris. Baptism, 174, 177. Did mortal ever read such interpretations?

‡ It hardly deserves comment when a man tells us the Greek *diaphorois* refers to *different* occasions. It means always different in kind —diverse.

The words (*min, ek*) in Hebrew and Greek are repeated over and again by the sacred writer.

Second. In every place in the Pentateuch where they were to wash in connection with the laver, it was either said "wash out of it," or simply "wash with water."*

Third. If any thing in all the Bible is clearly and repeatedly stated it is that if any thing or person needed ceremonial cleansing from defilement, needed baptism, in every case where such person or thing touched a person or object it was defiled. If he touched water in any vessel it could not be used. If the unclean touched water, unless a fountain or confluence of running waters, the water became unclean, and could not be used for drinking, cooking, washing meats, or any thing (Lev. xi, 29-36). If water in a vessel was touched by an unclean object the vessel, if of earthen matter, was to be broken; if of wood, it must be rinsed out with water; if of metallic substance to endure fire, it must be burned out and sprinkled with water, and not used for seven days.†

---

* Νίψεται ὕδατι. In all the five books of Moses I found *en, ἐν,* only named once with wash with water. We have seen its force already in such connections.

† "These also *shall be* unclean unto you among the creeping things that creep upon the earth; the weasel, and the mouse, and the tortoise after his kind. And the ferret, and the chameleon, and the lizard, and the snail, and the mole. These *are* unclean to you among all that creep: whosoever doth touch them, when they be dead, shall be unclean until the even. And upon whatsoever *any* of them, when they are dead, doth fall, it shall be unclean; whether *it be* any vessel of wood, or raiment, or skin, or sack, whatsoever vessel *it be,* wherein *any* work is done, it must be put into water, and it shall be unclean until the even; so it shall be cleansed. And every earthen vessel, whereinto *any* of them falleth, whatsoever *is* in it shall be unclean: and ye shall break it. Of all meat which may be eaten, *that* on which *such* water cometh shall be unclean; and all the drink that may be drunk in every *such* vessel shall be unclean. And every *thing* whereupon *any part* of their carcass falleth shall be unclean; *whether it be* oven, or ranges for pots, they shall

"Whatsoever the unclean person toucheth shall be unclean." "He that toucheth the water of separation shall be unclean until even." "Whatsoever is in" any vessel wherein any unclean thing falleth "shall be unclean."

Hence we have the plain Bible record for it that if any person needing ceremonial cleansing had dipped even his fingers or hand in the laver, or into any vessel of water, the water would be unclean, have to be thrown away, and the vessel broken if of earthen matter, burnt out if able to endure the fire.

The ancient rabbins are full of additions to all this, so careful were they of outward ceremonies. In washing the hands, "If, therefore, the waters that went above the juncture (of the hand) *return* upon the hands, they are unclean."* If the return of the water that had touched other parts than the hand, by returning upon the hand defiled it again, how much more would immersion of the whole unclean person in the laver? And one after another would certainly not mitigate the matter.

Fourth. The laver in Solomon's temple for these washings was cast at the fords of Jordan, placed in the temple (1 Kings vii, 23; 2 Chron. iv, 2-8), and was of great size, viz. ten cubits in diameter, five cubits deep— i. e. eight feet nine inches, and held water enough, according to Josephus, to make three hundred and seventy-five forty-gallon barrels of water. According to Dr. Gale it held nearly a thousand of our barrels of water. It was placed upon twelve molten oxen, which made it twenty-

be broken down; *for* they *are* unclean, and shall be unclean unto you. Nevertheless a fountain or pit, *wherein there is* plenty of water, shall be clean; but that which toucheth their carcass shall be unclean." Lev. xi, 29-36. Num. xxxi, 23, 24; xix, 21, 22; Lev. xv and xvi; vi, 28; vii, 18-21. All these uncleannesses required baptism. Lev. xi, 26.

*Lightfoot, Horæ Heb. et Tal., II, 417; Alsop, 38; and many like cases given.

one feet from the level of the floor to the top of the laver.* The water was brought in aqueducts under ground some four miles from a distant fountain, and made to rise up through the hollow pedestal into the basin, and then there were, first two, later twelve cocks at the basis out of which the water ran, at which the priests baptized. The laver was thus made twenty-one feet high to keep any unclean person from touching the water by which it would be defiled.

If a person got into the vessel, then, he had, 1. To violate the express precept to "wash out of it; 2. He would violate all the facts in Leviticus and Numbers cited about not using defiled water; 3. He would violate the repeated precepts of the rabbins, who taught it "was better to die of thirst than disobey" the laws of rabbins. Lightfoot gives us many such facts; 4. He would have to leap *twenty-one feet* high to get to the top; 5. When in the vessel he would have to swim or drown, as it "contained" the amount of water named in 2 Chronicles iv; 6. He would have to leap down twenty-one feet on the solid stone pavement; 7. The vessel would then have to be emptied of all its water, burnt out, and cleansed for seven days before it could be used. All this is involved by the immersion theory; 8. All this must be done in the presence of multitudes of men and women—of course the clothes retained on the person.

"The basis of it [the laver] was so contrived as to receive the water which ran out of the laver at certain spouts. At these spouts the priests washed their hands and their feet before they entered upon their ministry; for if they had put their hands and feet into the laver the

---

* In the Louisville debate I thought it by shortest measure fourteen feet. Walton shows it was twenty-one feet.

BAPTISM OUT OF THE LAVER. 63

water would have been defiled by the first that washed therein. And the sea of brass made by Solomon was so high that they could not put their feet into it. The Talmudists tell us there were twelve spouts or cocks, in the form of a woman's breast, to let the water out of the laver,"* etc. The mode of washing the meat out of the laver is given—"that on which such water cometh" (Lev. xi, 34).

Fifth. Josephus, who lived in the apostolic age, was a high-priest of vast learning and candor, and baptized daily himself at the laver. He interchanges *wash* and *sprinkle* in speaking of the laver. "The sea to be for the washing of the hands and the feet of the priests." "Whence the priests might wash their hands *and sprinkle their feet.*" "When he [Moses] had sprinkled Aaron's vestments, himself and his sons."† He washed Aaron and his sons.

Sixth. The Bible habitually speaks of a person being washed, just as we and all people do who wash only a given part of the body. John xiii, 5-10, records where Christ washed the disciples' feet, yet said, "If I wash *thee* not," "He that is washed." In Matthew xxvi, 6-12, anointing the head with oil was done "to my body." Numbers viii, 7, applies the phrase "whole body;" in Greek ($\pi\tilde{\alpha}\nu\ \tau\grave{o}\ \sigma\tilde{\omega}\mu a$), to the face. So Job ix, 30. Hence (John ii, 6) the jars of water were for the purification of the Jews—washing. But did they immerse in those little water-pots and violate all their laws on purification at the same time?

Seventh. The Targum of Jonathan, being a paraphrase and not literal, like those of Onkelos and Ben Uzzial,

---

* Brown's Antiquities, II, 189-141; Kitto's Cyclo., Art. Laver; Encyclo. Rel. Knowledge, old edition, with pictures of it, and water running out for washing; Walton's immense picture of it, vol. 1, Polyglott.

† Antiquities, vol. 8, chap. 8, secs. 5, 6; vol. 3, chap. 6, sec. 2.

shows the same truth on this question. On Exodus xxx, 19, where they were to "wash out of it," he has it, "They shall take for a washing of purification *out of it*,* and Aaron and his sons shall sanctify (*kadosh*) with the waters their hands and feet." Again, "And put therein living waters for sanctifying, so that they should not fail nor become dead all days"—forever. "And Moses and Aaron and his sons received (*nasab*) out of it [water] for washing, and sanctified their hands and their *feet out of it*" (*minyeah*).

Eighth. That is not all. In Christ's day, in addition to all these requirements—baptizing every time they touched a dead body, an unclean animal, or one who had touched the unclean or entered the house where the dead were—Mark vii, 3, 4; Luke xi, 38, and all Talmudic writers show that "all the Jews" as well as "the Pharisees" baptized every time they came from the market-place—public square of the city. A. Campbell, Anderson, and the Baptists translate Mark vii, 4, immerse. It is wash in our version. We ask immersionists how these Jews, in a country so destitute of water as Palestine is from three to five months in every year, more or less, obtained water sufficient for such constant immersions? They tell us, then, of cisterns twenty-two feet deep, sixteen feet wide, in some cases hewn out of solid rocks, in which water is kept for the dry seasons. Very well. But did they immerse their entire bodies in these cisterns? Here is a family of ten—husband and wife and eight sons and daughters. They baptized their various pieces of table furniture (verses 4, 8) as well as their "*beds.*" Mr. Wilkes (Louisville Debate) and Dr. Graves, A. Campbell, Gale, and Carson, and Ing-

---

* Sirach xxx, 1, 30: βαπτιζομενοσ ἀπὸ νεκςῶν κ. τ. λ. with the "wash" of Numbers xix; Leviticus xi, 29-36; xv; xvi entire; etc.

ham quote Maimonides, where they baptize their beds, in his day "part by part." These families often have five, ten, twenty, thirty servants, all of whom have to baptize every day from once to three or four times. Now who believes they all immersed themselves daily—men, women, male and female servants, ten to twenty—in the cistern of water out of which they daily drank, took water for cooking, etc.? Then they baptized their furniture and beds. Who believes they immersed these beds, couches, etc. daily in the cistern, and still repeated it daily for three months, yet daily used the water for drinking, cooking, etc.? But you *have* to believe it to hold on to the immersion theory. But you know it is not true. Aside from the repeated laws already quoted decency tells us it is not true. Jews so doubly nice they would not allow themselves in Christ's day to *touch* a gentile or one unclean if possible to avoid it, and would not go in where Christ was being tried lest they by contact be defiled — *they* drink water thus used!! Yet the immersion theory says *they did!!* No, sir; they *all* baptized by affusion. Now, then, the laver baptism extended through fifteen hundred years. Every Jew baptized every day, often several times. They generally numbered five and six millions. Let us put it at the *lowest* figure. Fifteen hundred years, three hundred and sixty-five days in a year, make five hundred and forty-seven thousand five hundred days. Then multiply those days upon the number of Jews; put them at *four* millions on the average for fifteen hundred years—from Moses till the commission was given—we have ONE TRILLION SIX HUNDRED AND FORTY-FIVE BILLIONS FIVE HUNDRED MILLIONS (1,645,500,000,000) of instances of baptism, ALL BY AFFUSION, when John began to baptize Jews as a Jew that Christ might be made manifest to Israel. We can now all see the force of "*baptize with water.*" Now, then, at first we saw that John, when only the few as yet came—no noise, no multitude yet named—the baptisms at Bethany were so noiselessly carried on that it is only named by *one* writer, and then *incidentally;* so not a word is said of multitudes at Ænon—the noise and flush of the crowds are all over. At Jordan we have *the multitudes* (Mark i, 5; Matt. iii, 5)—"they at Jerusalem," as well as "all Judea," etc. Now *why* did he go to those three places, at two of which were *running* waters, we know, and *plenty* of it at the *first* one? when so few as yet came—no allusion is made to water at all—at Bethany or in Bethany simply.

1. Such crowds, with all their animals, *had* to have, *must* have water. Round-lake Camp-meeting is not there because of convenient places to *immerse*. Camp-meetings, armies *encamped for a few weeks*, have to have much water. Here are thousands of people for *many* weeks, *some months*. Then much water was needed. But,

2. That *much water had to be* RUNNING water *by the law* of God. We cited many passages, especially Leviticus xi, 38, showing that fountains—so the Syriac and Arabic render Ænon—or "gathering together, flowing together" of waters *could not be defiled*, because running off constantly, and fresh clean water coming into their place. If it had been even a convenient lake one hundred feet square and fifty deep in the middle, the moment one washed in it, or an unclean animal, person, or thing fell into it or stepped into it, or water running from your hands or face after ablution had fallen into it, it could not be used. But such crowds had to have water, use it for all customary purposes. Hence the running waters of the Jordan were sought.

The moment the flush of the crowds is over John leaves the hot, low region of lower Jordan—the lowest spot above water on our globe, deep between ranges of hills, in about the latitude of Memphis, Tennessee, and so *intensely* hot that no city or village ever was built upon its banks in that region—and we next find him at Ænon near Salim, for there was much water there, not *deep;* the word, *polla* never meant deep, but "many waters" or fountains is far more correct, as the Syriac and Arabic have it. There was enough water in the springs of those mountain regions for the numbers coming now for all customary purposes. Hence we have here *Bible* reasons for all we see. They baptized *in* Ænon *with* water. They had known no other mode than affusion for fifteen hundred years. Custom demands its acceptance here as the recognized mode. The *primary* meaning of *baptidzo* settles it as the mode. Instead of the facts forcing us from the primary import here they all point to it as the only mode. And if we want *current* or *general* usage, that has been the usage *fifteen hundred years.* Nay, the Jews of those days tell us how much water was necessary to their ablutions in general. "They allot *a one-fourth part of a log* for the washing of one person's hands, it may be of *two;* half a log for *three* or *four;* a *whole* log for *five* to *ten,* nay to *one hundred,* with this provision, saith Rabbi Jose, that the last that washed hath no less than a *fourth part of a log* for himself" (Lightfoot, Horæ, ii, 254). A log is five sixths ($\frac{5}{6}$) of a pint. One person then washed with nearly *one fifth* of a pint. Its mode is told us by Pocock also—*aqua effusa evase,* with water *poured out of a vessel,* cup, or bowl. Leigh gives the same citation.

So well was it known that the baptisms of Mark vii, 4, were all by sprinkling, that the learned Greeks who duplicated manuscripts, translate *baptisōntai* in that place *rantisōntai*, "sprinkle themselves." The two oldest copies of the New Testament known thus translate it. Seven others do so. The reason was, that was a mere traditional obligation, and the baptism was not by divine authority. As it was not even by pouring in any case—always single in mode, and regarded by Christians as *only* a mode, they translate it sprinkle themselves. These are *historic* facts, WITHOUT METAPHORS.

Hence, Theophylact, the Greek father, commenting on Luke xi, 38, says, "Deriding their foolish customs, I mean, *purifying* themselves (*katharidzesthai*) before eating." The apostolic constitution, 66, alluding to the Jews, says, "Unless they baptize themselves daily they do not eat. Still further, unless they *purify* (*katharosin*) *with water their couches* and seats they will not use them at all." John ii, 6, tells us of the "water-pots, after the manner of the purifying of the Jews," which held two or three firkins apiece—i. e. six gallons. Could people immerse themselves in these jars of six gallons? "Benaiah struck his foot against a *dead* tortoise, and went down to Siloam, where, *breaking all the little particles of hail*, he *baptized* himself."* He touched a dead body; that required baptism. His baptism was performed by means of melted hail—a handful of water. Hence, Lightfoot, than whom we have no higher authority on such subjects, says, alluding to the cases of Mark vii, 4, "That the plunging of the whole body is not understood here may be sufficiently proved hence; that such plunging is not used but when pollution is contracted from the more principal causes,†
... for an unclean thing, ... *from water of purifying,*

---

* Lightfoot, Horæ Heb. et Tal., vol. 3, 292, *we tebal.*
† And this only "*later,*" as Pocock and Castell say and show.

etc." (Rabbi Solomon).* "*Baptismous* washing applied to *all* these; . . . in respect to some things, of washing only (that is, pouring water); and in respect of others, of *sprinkling* only. †

THE LAVER-WASH AND MAIMONIDES.

Elder Wilkes, ‡ Dr. Graves, § and all other immersionists have relied on Maimonides, above all authorities to settle the issue between us and them on the import of *wash* among the Jews. They cite this Rabbi to prove that in all cases wash [*rachats*] involved a complete immersion of the whole body in water. It is thus cited: "Wherever in the law washing [*rachats*] of the flesh or clothes is mentioned, it means *nothing else* than dipping of the whole body in a laver; for if a man dips himself *all over* [notice that *wash* himself all over is the word in Maimonides] except the tip of his little finger, he is still *in his uncleanness.*" Not unbaptized. Below they quote again: "A bed that is *wholly* defiled, if he *dip it part by part* is pure." I have the original of this by the Rabbi.

1. Dr. Graves, as always he seems to do, blunders as follows in introducing M., thus: "But I want to know how I am committed to the theory that the purifications of the Old Testament were so many baptisms? I will tell him how I will commit myself to it. In every case of purification when *taval* is used, I will say that was by the

* Lightfoot, Horæ Heb. et Tal., vol. 2, 417, 418; Sol. in Relm., chap. 1.
† *Ibid.*
‡ Louisville Debate, 563.
§ Graves, Carrolton Debate, pp. 113, 493; Ingham's Hand-book on Baptism, 373.

immersion of the whole body, *but in no other cases*"* (p. 112, 113). The next point in this is that such a thing never occurs in the whole Bible. *Taval* is not once used for purification, or to accomplish its washing in a single place in the Bible. But,

2. I will give a close and literal translation of this Rabbi: "Wherever in the law washing [*rachats*] occurs, either of the body [*basha, flesh*] or of the garments, from [*min*] defilement, nothing else is to be understood than the washing [*tabelah*] of the whole body at a fountain [or in conceptacle of water]. And that which is said [here extra defilement is described and omitted here], 'and he shall not wash [*shataph*] his hands with water,' is to be understood as if he said he must wash [*shitabul, tebal*] his whole body with water. And after the same order shall other impurities be judged of; so that if one should *wash* himself all over [*kulo*], except the extremity of his little finger, he is yet in his uncleanness."

3. This was washing for extraordinary defilement, not ordinary purification.

4. It is here shown even by that version of it that one may baptize himself without washing or dipping himself "all over."

5. No question is here raised by the Rabbi about ordinary baptism by perfusion or dipping, but whether *for certain kinds* of pollution "washing all over" was not necessary.

6. It does not declare, taking *their* version, that dipping is necessary to baptism, but declares if any part in the case given be unwashed he is still unclean, simply.

*Had Dr. G. cited Rabbi M. in the actual debate, the exposure would have followed in the next speech. I did not find out he had slipped it and his authors in the published debate till my eighth speech, where I answer it.

7. It admits that complete immersion is not required even in complete defilement, but all parts must be touched by the water in such cases. "A bed that is *wholly* defiled, if a man dip it *part by part,* it is pure." Here their own citation shows that bury, cover, immerse, dip is no essential point. First one part of the bed then another is put into the water for cleansing. This is not immersion in the sense Baptists, etc. mean—only a small part in at a time. Do Baptists dip a subject "part by part?"

8. Let us analyze the further assumptions of immersionists here.

First. The word used for this wash is *rachats,* which never means immerse or dip, but primarily is "to pour out, drip." See the chapter on Wash.

Second. *Kabas* is used to define this word, which no lexicon ever renders by dip or immerse.

Third. *Shataph* figures as the main word for their "dip," "immerse," which Gesenius defines by a "pouring rain," Furst by a "rain-gust," and is used (1 Kings xxii, 38) for washing the chariot at the pool. Did he dip it?

Fourth. *Tabhal* is used several times, which primarily means "to sprinkle," and all the greatest authorities tell us is used where the "object is merely touched by the liquid in part or in whole."* See *tabhal.*

9. But after all this, Maimonides lived late in the twelfth century after Christ, was an Arab converted to Judaism in that century. He is just eleven hundred years too late to know of what he speaks only as he saw it in those dark ages. Against him we oppose Onkelos and

* It may be noted, Dr. Graves, forgetting himself, introduces Dr. Alting (Debate, p. 493) as "so distinguished a scholar" on Rabbi Maimonides's point, renders it "the WASHING of the whole body is either added or understood." Opera Tem. IV; Com. on Epis. Heb. 220. That is well, and refutes his assertions about Alting and Maimonides.

Jonathan Ben Uzzial, who lived before Christ (see them quoted in the Laver), and Josephus, who lived in the days of Paul, and Pocock, who above all men examined Maimonides, had all that Rabbi had and infinitely more besides, Castell, Lightfoot, Wetstein, Buxtorf, Leigh, Schindler, Stokius, Kimchi, and a host of others, besides the facts of the Bible in the laver baptisms. Of Maimonides, Dr. Gale, the most learned of all Baptists in Rabbinic learning, says, "As for Maimonides . . . [he was] perfectly besotted in the idle dreams in which their boasted knowledge chiefly consists, and consequently even he can not be much depended on; besides he lived not above six hundred years ago, . . . therefore could know what was practiced in our Savior's time no better than many can now." Reflections on Wall, Wall, vol. 2, 102, ed. 1862, in two volumes.

We dare not lose sight of the symbolic import of baptism if we wish to be scriptural in its use. As it had always been symbolic of the religious innocence or qualification effected in the sinner or priest by the "washing of regeneration," the spiritual cleansing, so Ephesians v, 25, 26; Titus iii, 5; Hebrews x, 22, show that in the latest apostolic records baptism represented the spiritual cleansing, was symbolic of "sanctify," "cleanse," "wash." But it is "with *pure* water." No one dipped in a muddy or filthy pond or creek of water where stagnation and accumulated filth stain the water is baptized. His body is not "washed with pure water." As this is spiritual water alluded to, just as the heart sprinkled in the same verse is spiritual, yet all such metaphorical allusions have the *literal* as their basis. Hence none but *pure* water can constitute symbolic baptism. It is because of the superstitious uses baptism has been devoted to, and the unscriptural supposition that mode is the baptism, that has led to dipping in filthy, stenchy, foul holes of half mud, half filth, etc. that utterly disgraces the rite and obscures its beauty.

If any one doubts the pure symbolic import of baptism let him examine in full its origin.

1. Exodus xxix, 4-6; xxx, 18-22; Leviticus viii, 4-6; Numbers viii, 7.

2. The allusions to it in the Prophets: Psalm li, 1-10; Isaiah i, 16; iv, 4; xliv, 3; Ezekiel xvi, 9; xxxvi, 25, 26.

3. John's baptism (John iii, 23-26), where it was a "purifying," and translated in the old Æthiopic and other ancient versions "baptism" (Matt. iii, 11) "with water *unto* (*eis*) repentance."

4. The allusions recited above. Acts xxii, 16, compared with ix, 18, 19, "Be baptized and wash away thy sins in calling on the name of the Lord"—the six versions made before James's all thus read. Eph. v, 26; Titus iii, 5; Heb. x, 22.

5. After John was imprisoned Christ called his apostles. Mark i, 1-4, 16-20; Luke iv entire; then v, 2-12, and vi, 12-14; Matt. ix, 9, etc. From that day till after his death Christ does not have any one baptized, does not name Christian baptism to any one till just before he ascended (Matt. xxviii, 18, 19); and hence as John's baptism was only symbolic of the Spirit's cleansing, it follows it is only so still, as the commission made no limitation nor gave it any new force save the naming of the Father, Son, and Spirit.

6. The apocryphal use is cleanse, and nothing more. Judith xii, 7; Eccles. xxxiv, 25: Washeth—baptizes—from a dead body, "What is he profited by his *cleansing* if he

touch it again?" So Tobit ii, 5: *Louo,* wash, after touching a dead body.

7. As before shown, the real import and design of any rite is always involved in the ground-form, or elements used, and if a mere action involving not external elements, then in the proper import of the word used, as circumcision.

Hence in the lamb and its blood is found the true symbolism of the Passover, pointing to Christ our Passover.

In the day God rested from labor is the ground of import to our Sabbath.

In the meaning of circumcision in the Hebrew, *cut off, separate,* is the symbolism of circumcision—the heart separated from sin (Col. ii, 12; Rom. ii, 28, 29), and the men, as Abraham, the Jews, etc., separated to themselves.

Hence among all nations on earth in all ages water represents cleansing and innocence in its symbolism. It never symbolizes *death,* but represents just the reverse—*life* constantly. It never represents burial nor resurrection. All that baptism was ever designed to represent is seen in its recognized import.

We have seen that for fifteen hundred years baptism, from its institution as a rite till Christ came, was by affusion in all cases. That in all cases it was symbolic also. We will see in the future that the Jews constantly used words that meant both pour and sprinkle—the same word or words. The plentiful pouring out of the Spirit prophesied of so often may have led the apostles to the preference they give to *pour* over sprinkle. Hence we may justly suppose pouring became their favorite mode over sprinkling. It is preposterous to suppose that the Jews who believed in Christ and who, even late in the apostolic age, like Paul, kept "the purifying of the Jews"

(Acts xxiv, 18; John ii, 6), as he was "purified in the temple," were immersed for baptism when affusion had been the universal practice for fifteen hundred years. Unless some fact shows *a change* we are to suppose the old practice was continued. Jesus gave the commission (Matt. xxviii, 18, 19, 20) under which we today act—disciple all nations, all the gentiles, "baptizing them," etc. He does not say "with water," for it had been used fifteen hundred years—was well understood. He makes no change in its *design, mode, purport*. The only modification given was, "In the name of the Father, and of the Son, and of the Holy Spirit." Hence the long-established mode was continued.

CHAPTER VIII.

Baptism—Revival of Learning—Classics— Lexicons.

From the dawning of the Reformation, 1520-1522, till the present time there has been a sad and almost ruinous war of words on the question of how much water is required to administer the ordinance of baptism. As the immersionist side was espoused in the main by very ignorant and fanatical and even turbulent men at first, and the church was settled by the state, scholars took little or no interest in the controversy. Being satisfied that affusion was scriptural they devoted their attention to other and (to them) more interesting matters. Not until the middle of the seventeenth century did any eminent scholar defend the extreme views of the anti-pedobaptists. The pedobaptists devoted all their attention, so far as baptism interested them, to a defense of infant baptism, especially from the historic standpoint.

In England since the days of Dr. Gale, and more recently Dr. Carson; and in the United States, especially within the last forty years, it has become the most absorbing topic in the catalogue of religious dogmas. In Germany it has never excited any attention among the learned worthy of notice.

The parties favoring affusion labored under a great disadvantage by allowing both sides to adhere to a course of argumentation destitute of, and antagonistic to, all sound and recognized rules and laws of philology. Word-building, root-derivation, and all the laws by which scholars arrive at a correct knowledge of the force and meaning of words were ignored, and a wholly unscientific method persued. The immersionists and many pedobaptists treated the subject as if *their* interpretation of Romans vi, 3, 4; Colossians ii, 11, 12, settled the meaning of the word, and so philology was ignored. Had Franklin, Morse, Galileo, Kepler, Newton, and Bacon investigated the phenomena of nature from such unscientific standpoints the world would still be in profound ignorance of electricity, philosophy, and astronomy.

The great body of pedobaptists who favor immersion, such as Selden, Wall, and many others, though admitting the scripturalness of affusion, assumed that Jewish proselyte baptism was practiced before and in the apostles' days. Baptist writers contend that it was a century or more, not to say three or four centuries, later than the apostolic age. The Jews of the Middle Ages baptized and still baptize gentile proselytes generally by immerson. Hence Selden, Wall, and other pedobaptists who favor immersion do so almost exclusively in the belief that the Jewish proselyte *immersion* of the fourth century A.D. was apostolic in its date and also *perpetuated by the apostles*. It is not fair to take the evidence of these men in favor of immersion, as all Baptists do, and yet utterly repudiate the only ground and evidence that these distinguished scholars relied on as furnishing the proofs of immersion.

Another fact has misled many and puzzled not a few. The allusions to the Spirit of God moving upon the waters; hovering over the waters; the voice of the Lord upon the flood, etc. induced the settled conviction among many fathers, such as Tertullian, Origen, and others, that the Spirit of God imparted a divine efficacy and virtue to the water, by which those who received baptism had the grace of God imbibed from the water. It had a "medical virtue" that sanctified the nature of man. The Jews superstitiously fell into the same error on the approach of the Dark Ages, and hence they would either merse the whole body under the water, or mersed the person waist or neck deep; both were practiced to imbibe the saving grace, while the baptismal water was poured upon the head. The many ancient pictures representing Christ and others as baptized standing in Jordan are illustrations. These superstitions led to the more general practice of immersion in the Dark Ages. The Latin and Greek fathers practiced trine-immersions—"three dips for one baptism"—for many centuries. A single dip for baptism was wholly unknown for the first three centuries of the church after Christ. Hence immersion was the prevailing, almost universal mode in Europe when learning was revived in the fifteenth and sixteenth centuries. It is only within the last forty years that the Indo-European languages, Greek, Latin, etc., have been studied from scientific standpoints, and those great laws and affinities of language discovered that underlie a correct knowledge of those languages. So of the Hebrew, though in the seventeenth century Hebrew and Syriac advanced far beyond Greek, but retrograded again.

After Greek learning was lost in the western part of Europe, for some seven centuries it remained unknown, unread throughout Germany, England, France, Italy, etc. Not until the fall of Constantinople under the Turks, May 29, 1453, was it revived. The Vatican library was not founded till under Nicholas V, 1447. In 1445 it contained only five thousand volumes. Wycliffe's (1382) and the German versions (1460-1470) were from the Vulgate Latin. They knew nothing about Greek.

In the beginning of the fourteenth century only four classical manuscripts were found in the Library of Paris, and they were *Latin.* The Academical Library of Oxford in the year 1300 A.D. consisted of a few tracts. Greek was not introduced at Oxford nor in England till A.D. 1485 to 1509.* It was not introduced in France till 1458 nor in Germany till 1471. Even Latin was so little known in classical forms that in 1254 the names of Virgil and Cicero were unknown in Italy and France. In 1513 Garland said Greek could not be read in France. The first effort to teach Greek in England was under Grocyn (1485-1519). The first Greek grammar published (Lascaris's) in France in 1476. The first lexicon (Craston's) in France in 1480—"a very imperfect vocabulary."† "For many years" this "continued to be *the only* assistance of the kind to which a student could have recourse. The author was an Italian."‡

In 1521 the first Greek characters appear in England in a book at Cambridge.§ In 1533 "some Englishmen began to affect a knowledge of Greek."‖ In Scotland it was not yet pretended, but began to be studied in 1534. Not till 1550 was a Greek lexicon or grammar printed in England.¶ The first editions of Greek authors were very defective, and generally later writers, such as Ælian, Epictetus, Plutarch, or mere selections of Hesiod, etc., up to 1523. The *Etymologicum Magnum* of Phavorinus, whose real name was Guarino, published at Rome in 1523, was of some importance, while no lexicon but the *very*

---

* Hallam, Middle Ages, 548. † Hist. Lit., by Hallam, vol. 1, 130.
‡ Ibid. § Hist. Lit., I, 182, by Hallam.
‖ Ibid. 183. ¶ Hist. Lit., I, 184, Hallam.

defective one of Craston had been printed."* It is only a compilation.

Erasmus taught Greek at Cambridge where Tyndale, the first pretending translator of the Greek Testament into English, studied (1503-1514). These wretched and defective works were their only sources of information—Craston's their only lexicon. Vatable (Vatabulus) was the first Hebrew professor in France (1534 to 1545). He, in infancy of the study of Hebrew in Western Europe, is often paraded by immersionists as a *great* authority, even by such men as Gale, Ingham, etc.

With these encumbrances we are surprised at what Tyndale, Calvin, Luther, and others accomplished; but all can see what a miserable subterfuge it is to quote the opinions of these men as an ultimate authority, or on a primary meaning on *baptidzo* and *bapto*, when, however gigantic their intellects, yet the age; the very defective aids; the non-appearance as yet of the best Greek writers; the prevalence of the later and defective Greek writers over the earlier and better, as far as publications went, all show that *verbal* criticism was sadly defective and philology unknown. Of Luther, the Hebrew lexicographer "Simon has charged him with ignorance of Hebrew, and when we consider *how late* he came to the study of either *that or the Greek language*, and the multiplicity of his employments, it may be believed that his knowledge of them was *far from extensive*." Eichorn accounts for it "in the lamentable deficiency of subsidiary means in that age" (iii, 317). Yet "from this (Luther's) translation, however, and from the Latin Vulgate, the English one of Tyndale and Coverdale, published in 1535 or 1536, *is wholly* taken." †

* *Ibid.* 177.

† Hallam, Hist. Lit., I, 201; Simon, Hist. Critique, V. T., p. 432; Andrès, XIX, 169.

Such were the materials on which James's version is wholly based, such the aids of that age. Scotus, Aquinas, etc., also are paraded to decide *baptidzo* by Booth, Ingham, etc., when they never saw a Greek alphabet in their lives! Such is the treatment this question has received ever since it was mooted in the sixteenth century. Up to 1550 "no Greek grammars or lexicons were yet printed in England" (Hallam).* They were yet dependent mainly on such writers as Craston, Aldus, etc.; those works "generally very defective through the slight knowledge of the language that even *the best* scholars then possessed."† We ask now, of what value are the opinions of such authorities in *verbal criticism* as compared with those that are the result of a scientific and *exhaustive* examination of the facts involved? We constantly see the men who flourished in and about those times, Beza, Casaubon, Calvin, Zwingle, Luther, paraded on this question, with hosts of far inferior ones, when on such matters their opinions are of no more value than they would be on astronomy at that time. Many great and essential facts and principles in language, as essential to accuracy in philology as the microscope, telescope, and spectroscope are to science now, were wholly unknown to that age. Not till after Tyndale's New Testament was printed (1526), based on Luther's (1522), did the first effort at real lexicography appear—the *Commentarii Linguæ Græcæ*, Paris, 1529. "This great work of Buddæus has been the text-book and common storehouse of succeeding lexicographers ... His authorities and illustrations are chiefly drawn from the prose writers of Greece, the historians, orators, *and fathers*. [*Note that.*] With the poets he seems to have had a less intimate acquaintance" (Hallam.)‡ Yet this very class, poets, are the first by

* Hist. Lit., I, 184. † Hallam, Hist. Lit., I, 248.
‡ Hist. Lit., I, 178.

long centuries that use *bapto* or *baptidzo,* from whom we could best trace its *primary* meaning, being the first by many centuries that can give us light here. Only on words of jurisprudence, *legal* terms, did Buddæus bestow pains (Hallam). Hence a lexicon as late as 1537 abounds " in faults and inaccuracies of every description " (*ibid.* 178). In 1562 appeared Robert Constantine's Greek lexicon at Basle. Scaliger speaks of it and its author "in a disparaging tone " (Hallam). Yet he may have underrated it. The Quarterly Review observes, by one of its modern critics, that " a very great proportion of the explanations and authorities in Stephens's Thesaurus are borrowed from it" (Hallam).* As this is *the* lexicon whence so many others came to the world, its *make-up* is *all important*. Of Constantine's lexicon it is added, "The principal defects are, first, the confused and ill-digested arrangement of the interpretation of words; and secondly, the absence of *all* distinction between *primitives* and *derivatives*." He was assisted by H. Stephanus. Says Hallam, after Constantine's lexicon was improved, 1591, " It is *extremely* defective and *full of errors.*" † Yet Stephanus transfers " a very great proportion of the explanations and authorities" of this defective work to his own great work.

It was only in this way he could compile so enormous a folio work (now with additions making ten folio volumes) in twelve years. Buxtorf spent thirty years on

* Hist. Lit., I, 250.

† *Ibid.* 250. Since writing the above I have secured Max Müller's works, and in vol. 4, Chips from a German Workshop, p. 209, ed. 1876, where he says, "Even more pernicious to the growth of sound ideas was the study of etymology, as formerly carried on in schools and universities. *Every* thing here was left to *chance* or to *authority,* and it was not unusual that two or three etymologies of the same word had to be learnt, as if the same word might have had more than one parent." Gesenius is an eminent example of this error.

one lexicon, only *one* folio volume, and Castell's lexicon aggregates three hundred years' labor, two folio volumes. Stephen's *Thesaurus* (lexicon) appeared in 1572. Of it Hallam says truly (for *his* day, thirty to forty years ago), it "is still *the single Greek lexicon;* one which some have ventured to abridge or enlarge, but none have presumed to supersede." Scapula published an abridgment of Stephanus in 1579. After this age "for another century mankind was content, in respect to Greek philology, to live on the accumulations of the sixteenth; and it was not till after so long a period had elapsed that new scholars arose, more exact, more philosophical, more acute," etc. (Hallam).* Hedericus, Pasor, Schrevelius, etc. are only abridgments, while Donnegan, Dunbar (first edition), and many others are mere English translations and abridgments. Not till Schneider, Passow, Rost, etc., in the past fifty years, was there a real advance made in Greek lexicography. Passow made the first *real* advance toward science and accuracy. As Tyndale and Luther had to rest on such miserable help, and really, mainly, simply translated the *Vulgate Latin*, not the Greek, so James's translators adopted theirs with but little change, none on baptism, and had to rely on these helps alone. Hence they adhere so constantly to the Latin Vulgate. All these lexicons were for *classic* Greek, not a New Testament lexicon was yet produced. Indeed they knew not enough about Greek to know the facts now universally conceded, that the difference in restrictively religious words and those applied to ordinances is very great. Comparative philology is wholly a modern science. The discoveries of Grimm, Bopp, Max Müller, in philology generally (vol. iv, Chips from a German Workshop, etc.); the labors of

* Hist. Lit., I, 261.

Fürst, Ewald, Hupfeld, Delitzch, in Semitic tongues; Freund, Schiller, etc., in Latin; as well as Passow, Kühner, Rost, Palm, Pape, in Greek, have advanced these departments immensely, and the work is only fairly begun.

To return now: The lexicography of the past centuries, as well as all the English versions, were WHOLLY *by* IMMERSIONISTS—called *dipping* then—UNDER IMMERSION INFLUENCES AND LAWS. Yet have they not filled the land with the cry of pedobaptist lexicons, concessions, versions, as if they were AFFUSIONISTS?

Dr. Conant, Baptist (Baptizein, p. 138-9), quotes the statutes of England from Edward VI (1549) to Charles II (1662) for dipping as the law, save in cases where a *physician* certified that the child was too delicate to be dipped. A. Campbell quotes the same (Ch. Baptism, pp. 192-200). See Louisville Debate, pp. 522-3, and M. Stuart on Baptism, pp. 152-3, and Introduction by J. R. Graves, p. 24, where it is proved "that the English Church practiced *immersion* down to the beginning of the seventeenth century, when a change to the method of sprinkling gradually took place." But James's version followed the Bishops' Bible, both followed Tyndale's, on baptism in New Testament. It is a reprint of that of 1526 in *these* respects. At this time all agree *no change* in favor of sprinkling had been thought of in England or France. Tyndale was an out-and-out immersionist, as Graves, Conant, A. Campbell, etc. prove. A. Campbell quotes him to this effect, as well as Conant (Baptism, p. 140), and adds, "The translators of the common version were all, or nearly all, genuine Episcopalians, and at the very time they made the version were accustomed to use a liturgy which made it the minister's duty, in the sacrament of baptism, 'to take the child and dip it in the water' contained in the font. I have seen copies of James's version, printed in 1611, which contain the Psalms and service of the church, in which frequent allusions are made to immersion, all indicative of the fact that it was then [1607-1611] regarded as the primitive and proper baptism; consequently, these translators accepted the king's appointment and restrictions, to retain baptize and baptism rather than translate them,* and on no occasion favored the innovation of sprinkling by any rendering or note marginal in that translation."

Benedict, the great Baptist historian, quotes Ivimey's History of English Baptists (vol. 1, pp. 138-140) thus of the years 1616 to 1633, in England: "Immersion being incontrovertibly the universal practice in England at that time," etc. (p. 337). I presume this does not mean that individuals at that time were not *baptized* by pouring at least, but that immersion was practiced over all the kingdom—was general. It agrees with the facts of Wall (vol. 2, p. 581) and note there as to Dr. Whittaker's influence, beginning 1624.

Since the above was written Dr. Graves (Debate, p. 425) quotes Wall, part 2, chap. 9, and indorses it as saying, "As for sprinkling, properly called, it seems it was at 1645 just then beginning and used by very few. It must have begun in the disorderly times after 1641, for Mr. Blake, who lived in England in 1644, had never used it nor seen it used." Notice now the clearly-made-out facts:

1. James's version, so far as baptism is concerned, is Tyndale's, 1526—a real immersionist.

*There is no special restriction as to baptism in his instructions. The fact that *all versions in kindred tongues*, from the Itala, Jerome, Wycliffe, Tyndale, Coverdale to James's ALWAYS anglicised the word was sufficient reason for it.

2. Not till after the appearance of Dr. Whittaker's work (1624), fourteen years after James's version was completed and thirteen years after it was published (1611), did any one advocate sprinkling.

3. As late as 1645 sprinkling was only beginning to be practiced.

4. Still as late as 1662 the civil statutes re-enacted dipping, and Wesley, as a British subject and chaplain to Governor Oglethorpe, as late as 1736 rigidly adhered to it in the case of Mrs. Parker's child, Georgia being then a British colony.

5. James's translators were educated by immersionists altogether, used lexicons and notes wholly steeped in immersion prejudices, under immersion laws. Hence, truly,

6. They never favored sprinkling "by any rendering." No, they translate it that Christ went "straightway up out of the water" in utter violation of all Greek usage, and where in the Pentateuch it is "*wash with* water" repeatedly they render it "*bathe* in water," in utter contempt of the Greek, Hebrew, and common sense, as if it were a *medical* and not a *religious* rite, cleansing, washing, *bathing* not being the object.

Buddæus never studied the older and purer Greek writers at all. He only studied closely the law-terms of any. His is the great lexicon till Stephanus. He completes his enormous work in twelve years; copies large parts from Constantine, a work full of defects, blunders, errors. Many of the best Greek writers were not accessible, not edited yet or convenient to him. They came to their work and to *baptidzo* not as scientists, not as philologists should, but crammed with superstitious ideas of the "magical effect of baptism," looking at it largely as settled by ecclesiastics, carrying thus the huge bulk of the rubbish of the accumulating superstitions of a thousand years. Yet they are paraded as if prejudiced in favor of *affusionists!* They did the best they could. They are a marvel of success, considering their age and chances. On *baptidzo* or *bapto* Buddæus and Stephanus fall hundreds of years short of the *earlier* or literal earlier use of these words. This will come up in due time. The ignorance, the prejudices of centuries had to be overcome. All the talk of Casaubon, Beza, Suicer, Witsius, Vossius, etc., etc. about originals, etc. is based on the conceits of those times, overthrown by all parties since and rejected by all men. Yet these critics and lexicons are far more consistent and reliable than many such men as Lange, Conybeare and Howson, etc., who *assume* that Paul (Rom. vi, 3, 4) *dogmatically* settles a question of *philology* and *science*. But with all their prejudices and unripened knowledge of language, and unscientific processes, they overwhelmingly sustain our position, as will be shown when we quote them. We charge not them with *willful* conduct. Prejudices are often honest, and superstition is both sincere and terribly in earnest very often. The *facts they* saw were enough to convince them, and the facts were valuable as far as they went; but in *accounting* for the facts they were like the old astronomers— wild as to the *causes*, the laws of language.

CHAPTER IX.

CHANGES IN MEANING—CLASSIC AND NEW TESTAMENT GREEK—PRIMARY AND DERIVED MEANINGS.

The way in which classic Greek has been used in this controversy is not only unscientific and onesided, but persistently self-contradictory, as all will see. Were the parties appealing to it as *decisive* of the controversy consistent, they would abide their own decisions. Not one of them has ever done so; not one ever will do so. While classic Greek may and will prove a great help in determining the *philology* of the word, *the action*, the *meaning* of the word *as a secular* word, it can not aid at all in determining the religious force and application of *baptidzo* for reasons that will soon be presented. We will soon see Conant, Cox, Ingham, Carson, A. Campbell, Halley, Mell, Gale, the whole body of immersionists, shrinking from their classic proofs when they come to the New Testament. Their "drench," "sink," "overflow," "overwhelm," "intoxicate," "make drunk," "burden with taxes," "soaked," all give way. If classic Greek settles its *use*, *why* abandon these in carrying it into the New Testament? As for ourselves, we are perfectly willing to settle the force of the *action* of *baptidzo* by an appeal to classic Greek, but for its *use* and *design* as a religious ordinance classic Greek affords no help, gives no light.

Let us see the consistency of the other side. Of sixty-three occurrences in consecutive order Dr. Conant renders *baptidzo* "whelm" and "overwhelm" fifty-three times, "immerse" ten times. This sheds much light on the subject and will aid in discovering the primary meaning of the word. And that is the main aid afforded by classic Greek.

Granting, as we do, that "whelm," "overwhelm" are the prevailing meanings of the word in certain periods, whence sinking is the result, hence to sink (*immerse*); this clearly shows that *immerse* is *derivative*. It must be remembered that we have Greek literature centuries before we have *baptidzo*. We have *bapto*, its root, centuries prior to *baptidzo*. Both words may have been in use centuries in works that never have reached the days of book publishing or printing. Words are always changing their meanings. Who can tell what changes these words have undergone during those centuries? We have one way of learning—the laws of philology alone affording any help. The great body of words in all our European and Asiatic tongues so far as known are perpetually changing.

We must notice these two facts, viz. that, first, words constantly change their meanings, and second, the difference between classic and biblical usage. Noah Webster says, "Words which have been long retained have often lost their old meanings and taken on new ones. In the combination and construction of words, in phrase and idiom, the changes have yet been more numerous. . . . These differences are *mainly* LEXICAL and rhetorical rather than grammatical."* Again, "We must have respect chiefly

* N. Webster's Brief Hist. Lang., Dict., p. xxvii, ed. 1865. Those who wish to examine the subject more thoroughly may consult Planck, I, pp. 13-23; Tittman, Synon., I, 202; Hermeneutical Manual, by Fairbairn, 93; Ed. Robinson's Intro. (Preface) to Greek N. T. Lexicon, V-VII. Hist. Art. in Bib. Repos., Ap., 1841; Geo Campbell's Prelim. Dis., I, 30; Walton's Prolegomena on Syriac Versions, I, 92; Liddell & Scott's Greek Lex., Intro, xx, xxii; M. Stuart, Bib. Repos., Ap., 1833; Horne's Intro, vol. 1; Winer's Idioms, 26-34.

to the *usus loquendi*, the CURRENT *sense* or *established usage at the time,* to this more than to their *etymology.* . . . The *ultimate use* scarcely *exhibits a trace* of the *primal signification.*"

Carson, the Baptist, so often quoted says, "I maintain that in figures there is no different meaning of the word. It is only a *figurative* application. The meaning of the word is always the same" (Baptism, p. 57).

Since the above was prepared for the press Dr. Graves, in the Carrollton debate, was so pressed that he assumed the absurd and marvelous position that the current meaning was the *primary* meaning. Pages 253-4 he says, "The definition that all lexicographers place *first is the only real and proper definition.*" Again, page 254, "*There are no settled* principles of philology by which we can conclusively determine the *current* definition of terms by their *etymology.*" But at least *some* and the most essential "principles of philology" are now unanimously settled, namely, that we must trace *the history of each word* and find its earliest meaning—its "primal signification," as Webster says—then, by its later history, how it took on other meanings. All scholars are agreed on these principles since Passow's day. But why does Dr. G. become so alarmed at these principles? Truth can not suffer from them. He goes on worse still: "It is true that very often the *etymological* is the real physical sense of the term [it is the radical, primal meaning that applies first to 'physical objects,' objects of 'sense']; but then, *words* [hear that, will you] *so drift away from this that not a shadow of their etymological meaning* remains." He cites prevent, etc., and urges *once* its primary meaning was "to go before, precede;" "now its *primary*" is "to hinder, etc.!!" This is rich, racy, and rare. It is astonishing that a human could utter such ridiculous jargon as this. Fairbairn above uses the very words of Webster. Words so change—just as Dr. G. says, they drift away, etc.—" that the *ultimate use* [current usage] scarcely exhibits a trace of *primal* signification" (Her. Man., page 93).

PRIMARY MEANINGS.

Fowler, History and Grammar of English Language, says, "Words thus in *current* use sometimes escape *altogether* from their *original* meaning." Jahn, the great German critic, in his Introduction to the Old Testament, p. 95, sec. 31, says, "Etymology, that is, *the investigation of the primary signification of words* and of the manner in which other significations have arisen. [Italics his.] BY THE PRIMARY SIGNIFICATION IS MEANT THAT WHICH THE INVENTORS OF THE LANGUAGE ORIGINALLY AFFIXED TO A WORD." So Gesenius, Ernesti, Geo. Campbell, and Hävernick hold, *and every standard on earth*. Yet Dr. G. had to cut loose and drift out in a wild sea of breakers, a midnight of nonsense and absurdity, to evade the force of our facts, repudiating Carson utterly as well as all other authorities.

Dr. Ed. Robinson's Greek Lexicon, New Testament, 1865: "The scholar who would pursue the study of any language critically and philologically does not rest until he has traced each word to its origin; investigated its primitive form and signification; noted the various forms and senses in which it has been current in the different epochs and dialects of the language; and the manner and order in which all these are deduced from the primitive one and from each other," etc. (Preface, iv). He urges that only thus "is the scholar master of the word in question. This embraces the relations in which it stands to other words in construction and phrases and the various modifications which it has undergone in these respects."

Dr. Carson, Baptist, on Baptism, p. 23, justly says, "The just and most obvious method of ascertaining the meaning of a word is to examine its ORIGIN *and* use in the language." This is our method.

"For together with the primary signification of the act for the disciples its second universal, Christian, moral signification is established" (Lange on John xiii, 10, p. 409).

ROOTS AND THEIR MEANINGS.

Wm. H. Green's Hebrew Grammar, third edition, 1875, p. 92, sec. 67: "Roots do not enter in their nude or primitive form into the CURRENT use of language, but they constitute the *basis* upon which all actually occurring words, with the exception of the *inorganic* interjections *are constructed.* The second stage is the word itself in its simple *uninflected* state." This is "the *radical idea*" with the precise conception intended. The second stage is as "in the actual *utterances of speech,* so modified by inflections as to suggest the definite qualifications of the idea," tense, mood, etc., etc. First. In a word the root is not in actual current use. Second. The word is uninflected. All inflections modify the word, and in this stage the radical idea is brought into our precise conception intended, etc.

Dr. Carson, Dr. Graves's idol (p. 280) takes exactly the same view that these and all standards agree on.

Last and greatest of all on this subject we cite Max Müller (1876), a work issued since the preparation of these pages, since the debate at Carrollton—Chips from a German Workshop, vol. iv, p. 218, which settles it forever: "It is one of the fundamental laws of etymology that in tracing words back to their roots we have to show that their *primary*, not their *secondary* meanings, agree with the meaning of the root." This later meaning, current, he calls "the historical development of the meanings." See also page 216.

Fowler, the learned author of the History and Grammar of the English Language, sets this matter in its true light. He says, "1. The question may arise whether, in a given sentence, there is a rhetorical form? Now it must be conceded that it is not always easy to answer this question. . . . The number of *radical* words in a language is comparatively few, and are chiefly applied to PHYSICAL *objects*. As men found the stock of their ideas increasing, instead of inventing new terms to describe them they applied old words with an EXTENDED or CHANGED *meaning*; or, what is the same thing, used them figuratively. In this way the *great body* of words in a language, in one stage of their history or another, has been used tropically. The word *imagination*, derived from *image*, a term applied to its sensible object, was, on its *first* application to a mental faculty or operation, *tropical*. But it CEASED to be TROPICAL when it had been used so long that its *secondary* meaning became indissolubly fixed as THE PRINCIPAL *one*, or indeed to most minds as *its* ONLY ONE. IMAGINATION CAN NOT NOW BE CONSIDERED AS A FIGURATIVE TERM. It has *lost* its *tropical* meaning, at least to the mass of readers if not to the scholar. What is true of imagination is true of a vast number of words."

Fairbairn says in his fourth rule to interpret words of the Bible, "In settling the meaning of words, we must have respect chiefly to the *usus loquendi, the current sense, or established usage at the time"* (p. 93). Italics his. He then shows that words so far depart from their radical meanings "that the *ultimate use* scarcely exhibits a *trace* of the *primal signification"* (p. 93). *Villain* was once a dependent serf simply. *Sycophant* once meant only an accuser, then *false* accuser, now a *fawning flatterer*. Yet in Greek it originally meant *a big shower*.

Winer, a universal standard, without a superior in the department of New Testament grammatical use, treats the subject of classical use and grammatical rules with admirable judgment. Idioms, pp. 26, 27, he shows that in Alexander's time and on the Greek "underwent an internal change of a twofold nature," the Attic its basis, "and there arose a language of popular intercourse," this became prominently Macedonian. This, differing especially in the "provinces of Asia and Africa, constituted the basis of the style of the Septuagint and the Apocrypha as well as the New Testament." He shows that "the Jews in Egypt and Palestine learned the Greek first by intercourse with the Greeks, not from books." This was the case eminently as to "the LXX, New Testament writers, and the authors of many (Palestine) Apocrypha. A few of the learned Jews, who valued and studied Greek literature, approached nearer to the written language, as Philo and Josephus." Winer then says in a note, "That the style of the latter (Josephus) can not be accounted the same with that of the Septuagint or of the New Testament will be readily perceived by a comparison of the sections in the earlier books of the Antiquities with the parallel ones of the Septuagint" (p. 27). In the peculiarities of the New Testament Greek he shows with Planck, Sturz, and Lobeck that "entirely new words and formulas were constructed," of which "baptisma," baptism, is given as one (p. 30). Now how can classic Greek determine the meaning of a word *never* in use in *any* classic author? He then shows that into this New Testament dialect came "foreign intermixtures," and their Greek style took not only the general complexion of their mother tongue (Hebrew), which showed itself in monotony and circumlocution, but more especially its inflexions. . . .

Hebraisms and Aramæisms (Syriac shades) are more numerous in lexicography than grammar. Lexical Hebraisms soon became established, consisting in *extension* of meaning, etc. Hence originated a *Jewish* Greek, *which native Greeks generally did not understand, and therefore despised.*" So Hug., Introduction to New Testament, vol. 1, 137, Buttman, Kühner, Jelf, and *all* writers agree in all this. How absurd, then, to use a literature—classic Greek—as all immersionists do, to show the meaning of *baptism* in the New Testament when the very *word* never occurs in all their voluminous works, and go to its verb form in a language the apostles "did not understand."

After Alexander the Great "The Syrians and Hebrews spoke a more corrupt Greek than the native Grecians, and impressed on it more or less of the *stamp of their vernacular language*" (p. 32). Hence the dialect thus formed "which originated with them" ("this *Oriental* Greek dialect") "acquired the name of *Hellenistic idiom*" (Winer's Id., p. 32).* The learned Scaliger, not Drusius, gave it

* We feel like apologizing to any scholar for introducing such a world of evidence on such a subject, now universally acceded to by reasonable scholars (see on the Greek Language in the English Cyclopedia, etc.); but the bitterness of partisanship on baptism drives men to say very absurd things, and we have to waste much space to expose them.

this appellation. "It is well known that in the time of Christ the Syro-Chaldaic and not the old Hebrew was the popular language of the Jews of Palestine (*ibid.*, pp. 32, 33). Winer then shows that some carry these facts too far, stretch them into abuse.

From these facts we may readily see why the Jews used baptism in the sense in which it occurs throughout the Old Testament as a sprinkling and pouring on of water for religious purposes. Hence the Hebrew and Syriac or Aramæan languages will shed far more light on it than any other source of information, since as it occurs in the New Testament it was wholly by *Jews*.

We give these facts though and rules as to the difference between radical and metaphorical uses of words to have correct principles laid down, while at the same time we are not at all dependent on them to establish our principles, as the reader will readily see.

The twelve apostles and Christ being Jews (as well as all their converts for eight or ten years after the commission was given save one or two individuals) never read or spoke in classic Greek. Paul seems to have had some knowledge of the classics. But not one of the twelve to whom Christ gave the commission ever read classic Greek. This fact need not debar us from going to the classics, but should teach us *how* to use them. The Greek used in the New Testament, Apocrypha, and Septuagint was a different dialect altogether from that of the classics.* The difference need not here be noted only as applied to this word. The following facts are very important.

---

* And yet Dr. Graves (Graves-Ditzler Debate) says, page 527, "It is not true that any standard lexicon distinguishes between classic Greek and New Testament Greek in giving definitions of *baptidzo*." *Not one standard lexicon exists that fails to note a difference.*

CLASSIC AND NEW TESTAMENT GREEK.

While, therefore, classic Greek is essential to the science of language, its use could never determine the force *baptidzo* has in the New Testament, as the following facts sufficiently show:

1. Baptism, the noun *baptisma,* never appears in any classic before Christ. It first appears in the New Testament.

2. In classic (heathen) Greek *baptidzo* is never applied to a religious rite.

3. Nowhere is it, or any of its names, applied to religious washings, cleansings, or "initiations," etc.

4. Nor does *baptidzo* or its nouns in classic Greek ever apply to washing.

5. In classic Greek, after it came to imply immersion as one of its meanings, it always leaves the object immersed or submersed to whatever extent it put it into or under the element.

6. In the New Testament and Apocrypha it never has such force or use.

7. In classic Greek it often means to make drunk, intoxicate. It never has such meaning in the New Testament or Apocrypha or LXX.

8. In the classics it often means to drown, overwhelm,* submerge, leaving its object submerged always when it so occurs, but never has such force in the New Testament.

9. As a religious word immerse can not represent *baptidzo.* The English of immerse all admit is to "sink in."

---

* Some think *baptisma* means overwhelming sufferings once in New Testament *correct* Greek text; but all early fathers apply that to shedding His blood on the cross, and the water that came out of His side.

How can "sink in" or sink represent New Testament baptism?

10. As a *classic* word *dip* or even *baptize* in English can not represent *baptidzo* in the classics, since the latter means most generally to asperse, pour abuse upon, overwhelm, intoxicate, overwhelm with debts, taxes, confusion, drown. Dip does not represent any of these.

11. Every lexicon of any note and every Greek scholar of any rank make a distinction between *baptidzo* in the classics and the New Testament that is emphatic and pointed, unless we except a few Baptist writers who are governed wholly by their prejudices on the question.*

These facts settle the question, if facts, along with the authorities, can settle a question.†

As long as you hold an object under the water *it is immersed*, it is not baptized. As soon as you take the subject *out of* the element he *is baptized*, but he is *not*

---

* The fact that I presented these facts in substance in the Louisville Debate, 1870, pp. 405-6, and in the Carrollton Debate, pp. 371-2, and Drs. Wilkes and Graves never offered a reply, shows that they felt they could not explain away these difficulties.

† Yet Dr. Graves (Debate, p. 527) says, "It is not true that any standard lexicon distinguishes between classic Greek and New Testament Greek in giving definitions of *baptidzo*." Let the reader turn to our lexicons and see, as we cite them. There is not a standard Greek lexicon in existence that fails to distinguish the difference. His own Liddell & Scott, quoted correctly, in Prof. Drissler's letter, in the Debate, page 495, *the only fair report of a lexicon on his side in the* ENTIRE BOOK, notes the distinction, however feebly or imperfectly, as compared with Stokius, Schleusner, Passow, Rost, Palm, and Pape. He garbles, suppresses, mistranslates, translates the same entirely different in other places, and he has not copied in the Latin the whole New Testament definition of a single lexicon quoted. He has not copied the original or a translation of a single German lexicon in full, but has left out what they called the *general* meaning of the word. In a word, he has mangled every lexicon in the Greek, Hebrew, or Syriac that he has cited—not reporting a single one correctly.

immersed. Hence you can see the difference between *immersion* as a mere act and baptism.

Baptism implies that which neither *immersion, sprinkling, pouring,* nor dipping, *as mere actions,* imply. This is one of the constant blunders of immersionists—they look at and for *mere action* as if it were only a *secular* word.

12. As all immersionists agree that baptism is alluded to often in both the Old Testament and New by the term wash, rendered "*bathe*" sometimes; that *baptidzo* represents the *rachats,* and *louo, wash,* of the Pentateuch (Conant, Carson, Gale, Ingham, A. Campbell,* and all their writers do this in common, and we all concur, and they hold also that the *wash* of Titus iii, 5; Ephesians v, 25, 26; Acts xxii, 16, etc. refer to baptism), will they tell us *when* and *where* the *baptidzo* of classic Greek ever took such a meaning? If wash is derived from *immerse,* why does *baptidzo never* mean to wash in the classics? *They know they are dumb as an oyster here.* If a man can not see from all this that mere classic *usage* outside of philology gives us no light on *baptidzo* directly as a *religious* word, or word applied to the ordinance used in the New Testament, he would not believe though one rose from the dead.

13. The words immerse, sink, dip, often occur in the Greek of the Old Testament, and New Testament and Apocrypha; e. g. *enduo, pontidzo, buthidzo, dupto, katapontidzo, kataduo* (Ps. lxix, 2, 15; cxxiv, 4; Ex. xv, 4, 5, 10; 2 Mac. xii, 4; 1 Tim. vi, 9; Luke v, 7; Matt. xviii, 6; xiv, 13). Had the sacred writers intended immersion or dipping it would have been expressed by one or more

---

*Gale, Wall, ii, pp. 95-107; A. Campbell, Chris. Baptism, pp. 167, 173-4, etc.; Ingham, pp. 383-386, etc.

of these words. Not once is either of them used in the Bible for baptism, either in speaking of it or alluding to it in the various ways in which we find it alluded to in the Bible. Such are the indisputable facts in proof.

Dr. Conant (Baptizein, p. 159) says of *baptidzo*, "The word was a favorite one in the Greek language. Whenever the idea of total submergence was to be expressed, whether literally or metaphorically, this was the word which first presented itself." How utterly incorrect this statement is will be realized when it is stated that *baptidzo* never occurs at all in all the works of Homer describing sea voyages, storms, battles, loss of ships, etc.; nor once in Hesiod, not once in Æschylus, Sophocles, Herodotus, Xenophon, Thucydides; only once in Aristotle, twice in Plato, not once in Theocritus, Bion, Moschus, Tyrtæus; and only thirty-three times in all the voluminous Greek writers from Homer till the birth of Christ, Conant himself being the judge! In one of these cases it is compounded with a preposition.

Let us now call attention to another important canon.

Blackstone, the great standard in Europe and America on law, gives us such a correct and unexceptional direction here that we readily adopt it as the essence of all that can be said here:

1. Blackstone xx, vol. 1, §11, 59-61: "To interpret a law we must inquire after the *will* of the *maker*, which may be collected either from the words, the context, the subject-matter, the effects and consequence, or the spirit and reason of the law.

"First. Words are generally to be understood in their usual and most known signification, not so much regarding the propriety of grammar, as their general and popular use. . . .

"Second. If words happen to be still dubious, we may establish their meaning from the *context*, etc. Of the *same nature and use* is the comparison of a law *with* laws, *that are made by the same legislator, that have some affinity with the subject,* or *that* EXPRESSLY RELATE *to the same point.* . . . "

Here we are compelled to abandon classics, as *not* homogeneous with Bible Greek, to find the true force of the *purely religious* words of the Bible.

Before presenting our proofs of the erroneousness of all their assertions as to lexions, and having destroyed all their theories and so-called *axiomata*, we wish to notice two more favorite theories of the more humble and less learned writers on the immersion side.

They assume it as a rule that if *baptidzo* means sprinkle, pour, immerse, a person then is not baptized till *all* these definitions be exhausted upon him ! Such an assertion is too silly to be seriously noticed. We will simply answer, however, thus : If because we discover three meanings these three must all be exhausted on the subject ere he is baptized, how then can our *opponents* ever baptize any one, when A. C. himself gives to *baptidzo* thirteen or fourteen renderings, among them drench, intoxicate, drown; and putting all their great lights together, we have at least the following meanings: "Soak," " dip," "imbrue," "drench," " whelm," "overwhelm," "immerge," "sink," "plunge," "intoxicate," " lay," " endure," "administer," "drown," "overflow," "inundate," "plunge in a knife," "make drunk," "wash," "steep"—TWENTY meanings. This will do! When we see them exhaust *these* definitions on their candidates, we will all be besieged by the masses rather to exhaust only *one* definition on them. It will be seen at the same time how silly also is Mr. A. C.'s FIRST PRECEPT

FROM THE DECALOGUE OF PHILOLOGY (Christian Baptism, page 178), * viz. "*That the definition of a word and the word itself are always convertible terms.*" Italics his. He then urges that you "substitute it (the definition) in the place of the original word defined or translated," and "in *all* places the definition makes good sense." Otherwise it is incorrect. Let now the reader apply the above definitions, most of which are Mr. A. Campbell's, to the commission and places in the New Testament where the original is *baptidzo*, how will it do? "Go, disciple all nations, soaking them," etc. "John the *drunkard* came, preaching the intoxication of repentance." "He commanded them to be *drowned*" (Acts x, 46, 47).

Mr. A. C. then goes on: "The word sprinkle is *always* followed by the *substance* sprinkled, and next by the object. We can sprinkle ashes, dust, water, or blood, etc., because the particles can be severed with ease, but *can we sprinkle a man?* We may sprinkle something *upon* him, but it is *impossible* for any man *to sprinkle* another in a river" (Christian Baptism, page 178). "This text will hold to the end of the volume" (page 179). "Now, as John can not pour the material James, neither can he *sprinkle him*. . . It is *highly improper* and *ungrammatical* to use such a phrase" (page 179). "Some persons accustomed to a very *loose style* see no impropriety in the phrase 'sprinkle him—pour him,' because of the supplement in their minds. . . Now, while the abbreviation may be *tolerated,* so far as time is concerned, it is *intolerable* in *physical* and *grammatical* propriety, because it is physically impossible to *scatter a man into particles like dust,* or to pour him out like water," etc. (page 179, 180).

* We do not regard A. Campbell as a "lesser light" as an *intellectual* man. He was a man of wonderful resources and personal influence—a great man truly, but crude and defective in verbal criticism.

CHANGES IN MEANING. 103

If Mr. C., Dr. Graves, etc. were as loosely constructed as this so-called first precept in the decalogue of philology, certainly they could be scattered as dust and absorbed as water. They ought to have known—

1. That the Hebrew word mostly used for sprinkle, *nazah* (Arabic, *nazach*), not only took a direct accusative of the person, but meant *to moisten, to* make wet, irrigate; which words take direct accusatives constantly. And this is the Hebrew word they cite.

2. They should have known that *they* contend that *nazah*, to sprinkle, occurs in Isaiah lii, 15, where they insist on rendering as the LXX do—"*astonish*," which ruins his decalogue. No preposition can come between here.

3. He ought to have known that the two Latin words generally used for sprinkle, *perfundo* and *spargo*, take a direct accusative of the person; i. e. Ovid's Met. iii, 190-195, "And sprinkled his vile face, and sprinkling his hair," etc.* That *perfundo*, to sprinkle, also meant to *wet, bedew*, etc., utterly destroying his rule.

4. That *conspergo*, to sprinkle, meant "to stain," to "soil," etc., taking accusatives.

5. That the following quotations, which could be multiplied a thousand-fold, show the utter ignorance or intellectual obtusity of these men: "The demons ... caused those entering their temples to sprinkle themselves."† "Sprinkle one with songs," "sprinkle one with praise." ‡ The Greek, Latin, and Syriac of Psalm li, 9, reads "Sprinkle me with hyssop;" § 2 Maccabees i, 21, "Sprinkle the wood with water, etc." ‖ "He sprinkled me with a cloud of

---
* *Vultumque; perfudit; spargensque comas.*
† Justin Martyr: Ραντίζειν ἑαυτούς.
‡ 'Ραινέιν τινὰ ὑμνω—'ραίνειν εὐλογίας τινά. Pindar viii, p. 81, etc.
§ *Rusi*, ραντεῖς με—*asperges me*.
‖ 'Επιρρᾶναι τῳ ὕδατι τὰ τε ξύλα, etc.

dust" (Ovid's Met. ix, 35).* "Consult now Hebrews ix, 19, 21; xi, 28; xii, 24; x, 22; Latin of Isaiah lii, 15, as well as Syriac, German, etc. In the face of the fact that Webster, Worcester, all authors of most learning and taste in *all* languages, use as constantly that form as any form on earth whenever a subject is treated of that brings it up, it is absolutely amazing that any man however obstupified by prejudice or besotted with party spirit could make such blunders as the above, *followed* also by so many.†

* *Sparget me*, etc. So *perfudit caput;* Castell: Sprinkled the head.

† After the above was written, Dr. J. R. Graves, in the Carrollton debate, presses this silly rule with an earnestness that is astonishing, which shows how desperate is their cause.

CHAPTER X.

GREEK LEXICONS—FIRST ON BAPTO.

We now quote the lexicons. For forty years the immersion pulpits have rung with the testimony of the lexicons. As a sample of the many bold and daring assertions we quote a few specimens from Mr. A. Campbell. Remember that many of these authors are defining classic Greek; that their theories of *immersion* were built on the false assumptions we have refuted, and which Conant, Carson, Ingham, and others utterly refute; that Stokius, Schleusner, Suicer, etc. belong to that class; that all these lexicons, save Passow (Greek), Rost, Palm, Pape, were more or less translated from and based upon those lexicons made in the dawn of the *revival* of Greek literature, when immersion was the *enforced* law of the land, the general practice where they were made; affusion being allowed only in cases of parties too weak or ill to allow of "dipping." Though pedobaptists, they are all based on *immersion* sources and under its influence. We give the definitions of those recognized as the great masters of lexicography.

That the lexicons simply aim to present the *current*, not the primary, meaning of *bapto* is evident, for, first, the older ones, whom the rest follow—copy—did not discuss primaries at that time; second, the *first* citation Stephanus gives is Aratus, *seven centuries* later than its occurrence in Greek, four centuries later than we meet with it in other writers than Homer. If it be contended that such lexicographers *were* discussing *primaries* thus, it destroys their merit utterly and disqualifies them utterly as witnesses. See fully on this under *baptidzo* hereafter.

We present a few authorities on *bapto*, the root of *baptidzo*, not giving all they say, but a few; and we give the first meanings they attach, as our opponents contend these are the primary meanings.

A. Campbell says (Christian Baptism), "We have, then, *the unanimous* testimony of ALL the distinguished lexicographers *known* in Europe or America that the proper and every-where current signification of *baptizo* .... is to dip, plunge, or immerse, and that any other meaning is *tropical*, rhetorical, or fanciful" (§§ 126, 127, 147).

"They ALL (lexicons) WITHOUT ONE SINGLE EXCEPTION, give, dip, immerse, sink, or plunge, synonymously expressive of the true, proper, and primary signification of *baptizo;* NOT ONE of them giving *sprinkle* or *pour* as a meaning of it, *or any* of its *family*." "It never has been (Debate, p. 109) translated by either *sprinkle or pour* by *any* lexicographer for eighteen hundred years" (Debate, p. 139). "*Can not show one* (Greek dictionary) *that gives wash as its first* meaning" (Debate, p. 118).

1. Stokius: Βάπτω, *bapto*, tingo, *moisten, stain*.
2. *Cyrilli Philexeni Glossaria:* Bapto, to stain, moisten, imbue, wet.*
3. Faciolatus and Forcellini give *bapto* as the synonym of *tingo*, to moisten, wet.
4. Andrews's Latin Lexicon: *Baptæ, painters.*
5. Anthon's Classical Dictionary: "Baptæ. The priests of Cotytto. The name is derived from βάπτω, to tinge or

* Βάπτω, *inficio, tinguo, fuco, imbuo, tingo.*

dye, from their *painting* their cheeks and *staining* the parts around the eyes like women."

6. Kühner's Greek Grammar, § 143, p. 173: Βάπτω, *bapto*, to *tinge*.

7. Dalzel, Græci Majorum: Βάπτω (tingo), *tinge*.

8. Ursinus's Greek Lexicon: To stain, to dye, to wash or cleanse (*abluo*), to *sprinkle* (*aspergo*).

9. Groves's Greek Lexicon: To dip, plunge, immerse, wash, wet, moisten, sprinkle, steep, imbue, dye, stain, color.

10. Gazes: *Bapto*,* to cast or thrust down. To stain, to dye, and to sink. To pour any thing into or on any thing. . . . To shed forth, to wash, to wash the hands, etc.

11. Kouma, almost same as G., has *brecho*, shed forth, or sprinkle, wash, etc.

12. Stephanus, favoring immersion, gives "paint" (*fuco*), "stain," "moisten," "imbue" as by far the most prevalent meaning, and "pour upon." †

Although we have only quoted a few lexicons, several of the above not only being lexicographers but grammarians, annotators on classic Greek, etc., such as Kühner, yet his learning and accuracy are *far*, very far, above the great body of lexicographers, and he is aiming at the *primary* force, *they at popular classic use*, to aid students to *translate*. We give more, however, on *bapto* by far than A. Campbell and others. As immersionists appeal from lexicons in disgust, we give more space to "*authorities*" appealed to as more valuable.

---

* Gazes, a native Greek lexicographer of immense research and learning, defines βάπτω thus: 1. Βάλλω τι μέσα (εἰς τὴν βαφὺν) εἰς τι. 2. Κρωματίζω, βαφω, καὶ βυθίζω, χώνω τι μέσα εἰς τι . . . 4. Βρέχω, λούω, πλύνω. 5. Αντλῶ, γεμίζω.

† "*Superfusa*," this being by the great editor, Valpey. Buddæus, the older lexicographer, and ancient glosses do the same—give stain, paint, moisten, imbue, as the prevailing use of *bapto*.

Carson insists that "as to *totality of immersion*, the one (*bapto*) is *perfectly the equivalent* to the other," *baptidzo* (p. 23). A. Campbell, Gale, etc. fully adhere to the same.

Evidently a close inspection shows this to be utterly untrue; that *bapto* is far feebler than *baptidzo*, the former never being applied in the classics to such *bapting* or *baptizing* forces and elements as the waves of the sea, overflowing tides, great calamities, burdening debts, misfortunes, etc., or torrents of abusive epithets. But that is not *our* fight; if they admit what A. Campbell, Carson, Gale, Ingham, Ripley, Cox, Mell, etc. do, it is not our loss. Yet the truth requires this remark. But since all agree that *an appeal to original authors* is alone a settlement of the question, to them at once we will appeal.

Dr. A. Carson, Baptist, says of lexicons, "They are not an *ultimate authority*. . . *The meaning of a word must ultimately be determined by an actual inspection of the passages in which it occurs*" (p. 56). "The just and most obvious method of ascertaining the meaning of a word is to examine its *origin* and *use* in the language" (p. 23). Again, "USE IS THE SOLE ARBITER OF LANGUAGE" (p. 46). Capitals his.

President J. M. Pendleton, D.D., New York: "Lexicons indeed do not constitute the *ultimate* authority" ("Why I am a Baptist," p. 86). He repeats it (p. 96) and adds, "Lexicographers are necessarily dependent on the sense in which words are used, to ascertain their meaning. But it is not impossible for them to *mistake the sense*. If they do, there is an appeal from their definitions to the *usus loquendi*, which is the ultimate authority (p. 96).

A. Campbell's Christian Baptism, p. 122: "The meaning of a word is ascertained *by the usage of those writers* and speakers whose knowledge and acquirements have made them masters of their own language. . . . We, indeed, *try the dictionaries themselves by the classics*, the extant authors of the language." See 127, 130-133, also. To the same effect speaks Ingham (p. 43), and then quotes Carson as above at length. Conant writes his whole work on this assumption, appealing at once from the lexicons. So does Professor Ripley and all the rest. We fully acknowledge the justness of their position, though not their inconsistency in such wholesale repudiation of *lexical authority*. Yet we are bound to admit the principles they act upon, that lexicons are not "*ultimate authority*."

But in appealing to the "ultimate authority," and making an "inspection of the passages in which it occurs," knowing that words in all languages are always changing, as A. Campbell and others tell us, and as demonstrated in these pages so fully, we will not pursue the unscientific and strange method of Carson, M. Stuart, Beecher (Dr. Edward), Gale, and others of confounding and confusing *bapto*, the root, with *baptidzo*.

CHAPTER XI.

Bapto in Greek Writers.

Drs. Gale, Carson, A. Campbell, M. Stuart, E. Beecher, etc. confound *bapto* and *baptidzo* in a heterogeneous mass. They first cite a sentence with *bapto* in it, then a few with *baptidzo* in them, then a few with *bapto*, until only Greek scholars can tell the difference in the words. Their meanings are utterly confounded. Along with these, Conant, Dale, Ripley, Vossius, Sulcer, and all the rest have paid no attention to, first, the dates* of authors, so as to trace primary uses, trace developed meanings, and arrive at some conclusion that would be satisfactory, or at least give promise of such a result some day; second, the relative merits of writers in Greek; third, periods of the Greek language in which marked changes occur, as from Plato to Polybius. In a word, they seem never to have thought of the fundamental principle in all philology, that system, order, development of language, chronological order must be observed. As a sample of the reckless manner of treating this subject, Dr. Dale, in his late works on baptism, when treating on *bapto*, its primary meaning, to be determined by "inspection of the passages" in which it occurs, entirely ignores every rule or principle by which a primary could be discovered. He cites his *first* passage to

---

* Conant and others often give the age in which an author was born or wrote, but have no chronological order at all. That is the point of value.

find a primary from an author who flourished some twelve hundred years later than Homer! He inspects a passage nearly a hundred years later than Æschylus. And he uses the word primary in the sense we do and in that of all scholars on the subject of primaries. Such has been the unscientific method on this subject. Nor does he ever hint that between even Plato and his Iron-age author there had been a great breakdown in the language—a fact any lexicographer of note would have told him of in his introduction. Is it a wonder that no definite philological facts could be settled upon, but merely some surface facts discovered but not explained. We will see more of this under *baptidzo.*

To trace the primary meaning, then, of *bapto*, the universally admitted root of *baptidzo*, we will give all the earliest occurrences of the word that have been found, unless by accident some have escaped our observation, which would not materially change the question, though if it did it would likely be in our favor, since the other side has produced all they could, and we select mainly from them.

We will begin by giving a summary of Drs. M. Stuart and Dale, when producing all the texts they could on *bapto*, giving the ages in which they lived, and without any scientific order. And Dale at least wants to prove immerse as the primary of *baptidzo*, and dip as that of *bapto*. Dale begins with Ælian, A. D. third century.

I. DR. DALE'S SUMMARY ON BAPTO.

He renders *bapto* dip, fourteen times; dye, fourteen times; imbue, seven times; temper, two times; smear, one time; stain, one time; wash, four times; moisten, two times; wet, one time—forty-seven.

Of these forty-seven cases, as rendered by him, we have

1. Thirty-three against fourteen for dip.

2. Some of these cases are partial dips, a very slight and not a total penetration into the element by the object said to be *bapted*.

3. In no case was there an *immersion*, i. e. *sinking*.

4. All the oldest authorities fail to furnish a case of dip or plunge, when Dale was seeking for proof of dip as the primary meaning. We will give his renderings of the earliest occurrences of the word. In Homer, stain, temper. In Æschylus, temper. In Herodotus, wash. In Aristophanes, smear, wash, dye, dip. In Sophocles, stain, temper. In Euripides, stain. In Aristotle, moisten. In Plato, dye. This is a sample, though we may not have counted as accurately as in the other counts, where we took greater pains still, more being demanded.

5. For five hundred years after *bapto* appears no case of a literal dip occurs, but stain, where it is by affusion, temper, wash.

6. In the next two hundred years dip appears as a meaning only twice against a large majority of cases pointing to affusion, aspersion, as the modes by which the objects were stained, moistened, dyed, colored, washed, smeared, etc.

II. M. STUART'S SUMMARY ON BAPTO.

So strongly does Stuart favor the immersionists in their over-estimation that Dr. J. R. Graves, 1856, published his book on baptism, taunting the other side that they would not publish it.

1. Of fifty-six occurrences in classic and non-Biblical usage he renders it by dip, dye, color, smear (Dr. Carson and other Baptists render it "smear"), thrust, bathe, tincture, tinge, plunge, wash—ten renderings.

2. In these fifty-six cases he has seven full dips, nine where it was partial, not total—sixteen for dip. This gives forty-nine against seven total dips, or forty against sixteen for dip, partial and total. It is forty-nine against seven plunge—they doubtful, very. There is no immerse. He gives thirty-three against the sum-total for dip and plunge.

3. If, as our opponents assume at least that current usage determines the primary meaning, then dip is not the primary meaning of *bapto,* and immerse does not even enter court with a plea. H. Stephanus, though educated under all the prejudices of an education among immersionists, shows in his great Thesaurus that moisten, stain, paint (*fuco*), prevail by great odds over dip as a meaning.

BAPTO FROM ONE THOUSAND TO FIVE HUNDRED YEARS BEFORE CHRIST.

Two writers occur in this period who use *bapto* each twice.

Homer, before Christ one thousand years, by popular date, round number.

1. Batrach v, 218: Of a frog pierced and slain in battle he says, "He fell without even looking upward, and the lake (*ebapteto*) was tinged with blood."* Here the effusion of the blood from the delicate veins of a pierced frog is what *bapted* the lake. Small were the drops, delicate indeed was the stream from such a source. Yet the

* Ἐβάπτετο δ' αἵματι λίμνη.

lake is *bapted* with the affusion of the few drops of blood that spun out from its veins. Here, too, we have, first, a clear case of very delicate effusion, aspersion, from *bapto*. Second, it shows how stain, color, tinge, dye, came as a meaning of *bapto*.

2. Odyssey i, 302: "As when a smith tempers (*baptei*) a hatchet or huge pole-ax with cold water," or "in cold water." Here *bapto* may imply such a partial dip as we often witness in the shops where smiths temper "a huge pole-ax" or a hatchet. The edge is slightly dipped. But from the context this does not seem to have been the allusion. It was more likely the well-known process of putting some cold water on the anvil, placing the ax or hatchet on it, and striking a blow with the hammer, which makes an explosion or report louder than an ordinary gun. This is done constantly in tempering axes and hatchets.

1. We have in Homer no immerse for *bapto*.

2. We may barely have a case of partial dip, but it is extremely doubtful.

3. More likely in both cases it is aspersion.

4. Any way, one of them is a clear case of aspersion in this the first known Greek author.

ÆSCHYLUS ON BAPTO, BORN FIVE HUNDRED AND TWENTY-NINE YEARS BEFORE CHRIST.

1. "For the wife has deprived each husband of life staining (*bapsasa*) the sword by slaughter."* Here is a case easily determined. It does not say the sword was plunged into some penetrable matter—mersed or dipped. The sword is stained by slaughter—bapted by the blood of slain men in whatever way cut down.

* Premeth, v, 861.

2. The second case is thus given: "This garment, *stained* (*ebaphaen*) by the blood of Ægisthus, is a witness to me."

Here the blood spurts out from the wound and besprinkles or affuses the garment, staining it, and witnesses of the violent death of the victim.

1. Here again, in the next writer we have after Homer who uses *bapto*, *bapto* is used for a clear case of affusion.

2. We see again the mode of the staining, the coloring, the tinging, dyeing of *bapto*.

3. Notice well that in neither of the cases where *bapto* is used for staining is it a *dip*. The old process has always been to take the *later* cases of *bapto* after it took on the later meanings, and where the art of dyeing by dipping was discovered, or else at least where it from stain, color, came to apply readily to dyeing, then to dyeing by any mode; hence by dipping, then to dip in any object, and securing *this* meaning in late, Iron-age authors especially, they assume it as the primary meaning and explain all else from that! Even Dale adopts this process.

We have now traced *bapto* through five hundred years. It occurs four times. It is doubtful as to mode in one case. Three are cases of effusion and affusion. That is, the blood effused from wounds and affused or stained the objects besprinkled or affused. Hence its primary meaning is readily determined by all the established laws of language—SPRINKLE.

BAPTO FROM FIVE HUNDRED TO FOUR HUNDRED AND TWENTY-NINE YEARS BEFORE CHRIST.

1. Sophocles, born B.C. 495: "Thou hast well stained (*ebapsas*) thy sword (*pros*) by means of [or with respect to] the army of the Greeks."* This is a case like the above.

---

* Ajax, v, 95.

2. Herodotus, born B.C. 484, in Euterpe: (1) "Going to the river he washed (*ebapse*) himself." † Here he washed himself, not into, but at the river. He simply went (*epi*) to the river and washed. The word himself is merely added by us. Pharaoh's daughter (Ex. ii, 5) "washed herself (*epi*) at the river." We see this was the custom in Egypt. Herodotus is here telling of an Egyptian. Judith (xii, 7) "washed herself—baptized—(*epi*) at the fountain."

(2) "Colored garments" (*bebammena*, i. e. *bapto*). This is the first case of the application of *bapto* to garments colored or dyed in the ordinary sense, the others being as seen stained, sprinkled with blood, or the blood gushed out upon them. In what way the garments were colored does not appear. Let us suppose it was by dipping in dye. Then we have these facts. Six hundred years before this *bapto* applied to sprinklings of blood, that of course stained. Forty years earlier than Herodotus it is applied to affusions of blood, staining the object on which it falls. Here we see dye comes from stain, stain from effusions, from sprinkle. From applications of water come wash, a very rare meaning of *bapto*.

3. Euripides, born B.C. 480. Here is the first case of *bapto* clearly indicating a *dip*, a partial dip only, when a pitcher is dipped sufficiently into water to get water and immediately withdrawn. Hence, "Dip a vessel and bring sea-water." "Dip up with pitchers." He uses it for a more violent dip still. His sounding scimeter "he plunged (*ebapse*) into the flesh." Here in all cases notice the object dipped and the object "plunged" is immediately withdrawn, our word "plunge" not being the exact equivalent of *bapto* even in these cases. In later days Lycophron says, "Plunged his sword into the viper's bowels." Dion-

† Βάς ἐπὶ τον ποταμον ἐβάψε.

ysius of Halicarnassus, "Plunge (*bapsas*) his spear between the other's ribs." He "at the same instant plunged his into his belly." In these, and in all that the strongest immersionists can produce, there is no total immersion. Where the sword, the spear, the lance is bapted only a part, and in many instances only a small part, enters the object. It is in cases where the sword, the spear is at once withdrawn.

4. Aristophanes, born about B.C. 450. He uses *bapto* more frequently.

(1) Speaking of Magnes, an old comic writer of Athens, he says, "Smearing himself (*baptomenos*) with frog-colored paints" (*batracheiois*).

(*a*) Here *bapto* applies where there is no dip, no plunge.

(*b*) The coloring matter is applied to the object bapted. Putting coloring matter on his face bapted it.

(2) "Do not adorn yourself with garments of variegated appearance, colored (*bapton*) at great cost." Here the colors seemed to be the effect of needle-work, as often now occurred, taking different colors and working them into garments, thus bapting them. *Bapto* came thus to apply to nature's colors, to birds of color, precious stones of beautiful colors, etc. Hence Aristophanes—

(3) *Ornis baptos,* "a colored bird."

(*a*) Dipping, plunging is out of the question here.

(*b*) The variegated plumage was bapted thus as it grew. Thus *bapto* applies where no mode is specially involved, the coloring matter effecting the bapted condition by the most delicate touches. To put it nicely, here *bapto* by streams or parts of drops so small that only a microscope could discover them to our eyes effected a bapted condition. The birds and stones were bapted by these delicate affusions and infusions. Hence Greeks, Hebrews, and

Arabians used these phrases: "Sprinkled with colors," "Sprinkled with gray." Again, Aristophanes—

(4) A bully speaking says, "Lest I stain you (*bapso*) with a Sardinian hue (*bomma*)."* Here *bapto* occurs twice in its different forms.

(*a*) There is no dip, no plunge.

(*b*) The meaning, as all lexicons agree, is, that the bully would strike the other party on the mouth with his fist, give him a bloody mouth or nose. The blood issuing out would stain his face.

(*c*) Clearly enough the *bapto* here bapted the object by affusion.

(5) The next case is, "First wash (*baptos*) the wool in warm water." While the wool would in this case undoubtedly be dipped in the water to become saturated with the water, yet the word *bapto* applies to the process of washing the wool, which was effected by rubbing it in the hands or otherwise while saturated with water. Mere dipping into the warm water would not wash the wool.

(6) In his day already *bapto* was strengthened by a preposition to make a clear case of dip, *en* being employed for that purpose.

In this noted author, then, six times he uses *bapto*. In not a single case did he use it for dip, plunge, immerse. To make it mean dip he strengthens it by *en*, i. e. *embapto*, as Luke, the nearest to a classic writer of all New Testament writers.

6. Hippocrates, born B.C. 430. This noted Greek, quoted by Carson (Baptist) says of a dyeing substance, "When it drops (*epitaxœ*) upon the garments they are stained (*baptetai*), dyed.

Notice now—

* Acharn, act 1, scene 1.

1. We have had no case where a complete envelopment even for a moment has been effected by *bapto* from Homer to Hippocrates.

2. Herodotus used *bapto* for dyed or "colored garments," but how colored we did not see.

3. Hippocrates gives us *the mode*, the process by which the garments he names were bapted. The dyeing matter "drops upon the garments."

In this way, by this mode, "they are dyed" (*baptetai*). Is there controversy over the mode of this bapting? Yet immersionists tell us dyeing, coloring, is always by dipping. Justice requires that we say Dr. Carson is an exception, and admits it is effected by sprinkling, but thinks *bapto* primarily meant dip, then dye by dipping, then dye by any mode. But he, as all the rest, never took the matter up chronologically, but selected nearly all his proof-texts as Campbell, Dale, Gale, etc. do from later and Iron-age Greek, then explains the early use from the later! No scholar will now call that science or philology or good sense.

We have now gone over the period from Homer to Plato, who comes next. In all these periods of six hundred years among the most illustrious writers Greece ever produced, we find the following exhibit:

1. Not once does *bapto* mean immerse, i. e. sink.
2. Not once does it totally dip the whole object.
3. Only three times do we find it for a partial dip.
4. *In no instance does it apply to, or describe the act performed by Baptists when they baptize.*
5. *It frequently applies to the mode of those who baptize by affusion, and to the exact mode, effusion, aspersion,* though not any single, exclusive mode, and the application in any decent mode is what we require in baptism.

6. The prevailing action or mode involved in *bapto as yet* is aspersion, effusion, affusion.

7. The primary force of the word is aspersion.

BAPTO FROM PLATO TO ARISTOTLE, ETC.

1. Plato, born B.C. 429, uses *bapto* repeatedly, and uses it for dye and dip, and as we promptly grant this we need not quote passages.

2. Alcibiades, born B.C. 400, alluding to the offensive and opprobrious epithets applied to him by a comedian in the play called *Baptae*, says, "You aspersed (*baptes*) me [with the abusive epithets] in your play."

(1) Here *bapto* is used by both parties—the one calling his play *Baptae*, in a metaphorical sense, applying *bapto* to speech.

(2) All metaphorical use is based on a prior literal use of words, as no one will question.

(3) In Greek, as we see elsewhere, and elaborately, and in Arabic, in Latin, and in English, abuse is represented by words meaning to sprinkle and to pour constantly. "Foul aspersion," "base aspersion," is a common English phrase. "Pour abuse upon" is another. We never say that we "dip a man in abuse," "plunge him into abuse."

(4) Here is, therefore, a clear use of *bapto* by both parties, and by Greek comedians generally, that show sprinkle to be the primary meaning of *bapto*. And the writer uses the words "streams more bitter," as the means with which he, in a volley of words, would *baptize* him, not merely *bapt* him.

3. The great Aristotle, born B.C. 384, comes next in chronological order as using the word. He uses the word

where there is a partial dip, and where also objects are colored, and where dyeing is by dipping. Then also thus, speaking of a dyeing substance: "Being pressed, it moistens (*baptei*) and dyes (*anthidei*) the hand."

(1) There is no dip, plunge, immerse here.

(2) Like nearly all the cases cited, it is a *literal* use of *bapto*, not a metaphorical one.

(3) The fluid came out upon the hand—effusion, was the literal mode by which the object was *moistened*.

(4) It is such a delicate effusion that it merely moistens the hand.

(5) The effect of its being coloring matter that was pressed was to dye or stain the hand; and *bapto* does not express that, but *anthidzo* does, which primarily applies to sprinklings. See the word and the lexicons on it in the next chapter. *Anthidzo* is defined "to sprinkle," "stain," "color," "strew with flowers," "paint."

4. Diodorus Siculus, B.C. 69-30: "Coats (*baptais*) colored and flowered with various colors." "Native warmth has tinged (*ebapsen*) the above varieties of the growth of things [i. e. birds, precious stones, etc.] before mentioned."*

Omitting dates now, the writers of this period speak on this wise. Plutarch, vi, p. 680: "Then perceiving that his beard was colored (*baptomenon*) and his head." Ælian: "The Indians dyed (*baptontai*) their beards." Marcus Antonius speaks of the soul tinged (*baptetai*) by the thoughts. "Tinge (*bapto*) it, then, by accustoming yourself to such thoughts."

Here still *bapto* continues to be used where,

1. There is no dip, plunge, and immerse is never a meaning of the word.

2. It is applied where the coloring matter is applied to

* Tom. iii, 315; xi, 149.

the hair, to the beard, and in many cases to the cheeks, the eyes, as in the case of the priests of Cotytto, given elsewhere.

3. In only two cases yet have we found it applied to simple water, and no immersion was found; and we have come down to the period after Christ.

BAPTO IN DANIEL.

In the Greek version by Theodotian, second century after Christ, *bapto* occurs several times, as follows:

1. Daniel iv, 33: "And his body was wet (*ebaptae*) with the dew (*apo*) from heaven."

2. Daniel v, 21: "And his body was wet (*ebaptae*) with the dew (*apo*) from heaven. Here,

(1) Nebuchadnezzar's body was *bapted* with the falling dew—a clear case of gentle affusion.

(2) It is a case where water pure is the element, not blood or coloring matter, paint, etc., as so often we found.

(3) To parade, as Gale, Carson, and others do the copious dews of that country, is simply ridiculous. What do we care for the copious fall of dew? Was his body dipped into it, covered up by the process, or did the "copious dew" fall upon him "from heaven"?

(4) Jerome and other ancient writers translate two of these passages by "*sprinkled*" with the dew of heaven."*
(Dan. iv, 20).

(5) The Arabic translates it sprinkled. The Latin version in Walton on Daniel v, 21, *perfusam*, "sprinkled with the dew of heaven."

---

*Conspergatur and *infunderis*, sprinkled, besprinkled. Chaldee, chap. iv. 21, וּמִטַּל שְׁמַיָּא יִצְטַבַּע; Vulgate, *Et rore cœli conspergatur*, v. 22, Chal. יְטַיִּל, from the dew; מִצְטַבְּעִין. *infunderis*.

(6) The Latin version in Origen's works renders Daniel iv, 22 (*bapto** in Greek), by "his body shall be sprinkled with the dew of heaven" (chap. iv).

BAPTO IN NEW TESTAMENT AND SEPTUAGINT.

Bapto occurs three times in the New Testament, *embapto* twice. Of these three cases

1. Two are very partial, very slight dips for the purpose of moistening the object. It is simply *one* case reported by the writers Matthew (xxvi, 23), John (xiii, 26), Mark (xiv, 20)—"He that dippeth his hand with me in the dish;" "I shall give a sop [morsel] when I have dipped it;" "And when he had dipped the sop"—morsel.† As Luke uses *embapto* in the dip of the tip of the finger in the case of Lazarus, it being compounded with a strengthening word *en*, it does not come in for discussion, though we do not object to it on any other ground, of course.

These may all be held, then, as just *one* case in the New Testament where *bapto* is used.

1. In this case no immersion occurs.
2. No plunge occurs.
3. The dip was only a touching of the morsel of food to the element to moisten it for eating.

The other case is Revelation xix, 13, "And he was clothed with a vesture [garment] (*bebammenon*) sprinkled with blood." In our version the immersionist translators

---

* Greek τὸ σῶμά σου βαφήσεται, *et de rore cœli corpus tuum aspergetur.*

† In Exodus xii, 22; Leviticus xiv, 16, 51; iv, 17; ix, 9, etc., *bapto* occurs in the Greek version made third century before Christ. 1. In no case was it immersion. 2. In most cases the object was merely *touched to* or *by the* bapting fluid. 3. In no case was there envelopment. We will examine the cases under the Hebrew *tabhal*, which see.

of James render it "dipped in blood." How untrue and absurd!

1. The Syriac renders this case by "sprinkle." That part of the Peshito was made later than the rest, yet by the close of the second century or dawn of the third.

2. The old Itala, made undoubtedly by the close of the apostolic age, renders *bapto* here by "sprinkle"—*aspersa*.

3. The Coptic, third century, translates it "sprinkle."

4. The Basmuric, third century, renders it "sprinkle."

5. The Sahidic, second century, renders it "sprinkle."

6. The Æthiopic, fourth century, renders it "sprinkle."

7. The Lutheran, sixteenth century, renders it "sprinkle" (*besprengt*).

8. The Lusitanian has it "sprinkle" (*salpacado*).

9. *Bapto* is translated *sprinkle* by the learned Greek, Irenæus, born by common chronology four years before John the Apostle's death; some put it later. Irenæus was bishop of Lyons and a great defender of the purity of the church. He cites Revelation xix, 13, where in the Greek it is *bapto—bebammenon*—and translates it, "And he was clothed with a vesture SPRINKLED with blood."*

10. Origen, the most learned father and commentator the world produced in sixteen hundred years, born some eighty-six years after John's death, translates *bapto*, in the same passage, "SPRINKLED† with blood."

11. Hippolytus, the learned Greek archbishop, A.D. 220, copies the common reading of Revelation xix, 13, *bapto*, thus: "And he was clothed with a vesture [*bebammenon—bapted*, in our version *dipped*] in blood," and adds "See, then, brethren, how the vesture, SPRINKLED with blood, denoted," etc.‡

---

* Against Heresies, b. iv, chap. 20; c. xi.
† Ερραντισμένον, *errantismenon*.
‡ Against Noetus, chap. xv.

12. The oldest and best copy of the Bible in the world, Tischendorff's manuscript, made about A. D. 325, translates it *besprinkled*,* thus: "And he was clothed with a vesture BESPRINKLED with blood."†

In the light of these records we see the following facts made patent:

1. That many lexicons, being deeply steeped in immersion prejudices, selected their texts on *bapto* from the few cases, mostly in Dark-age Greek, where it also meant dip, stain, dye, and gave not one of those cases which we have presented above.

2. The utter unreliability of the parties who tell us that *bapto always* means to dip, immerse, etc.

3. That from the earliest use of the word it applied to sprinklings, even the most partial and delicate, and continued to be so applied in later Greek.

4. That it constantly applied to effusions, to cases "merely touched in part or in whole," by the fluid.

5. That sprinkle was the primary import of the word.

6. That dip is a late and a derived meaning.

* Περιρεραμένον, *perireramenon,* besprinkled.

† To those who seek to evade the force of this by saying as Gale did, when it was only known that Origen thus rendered it till we brought out the rest, that Origen had a copy (codex) with sprinkle in it, which A. Campbell indorsed in the Rice debate, and Tischendorff's being found with besprinkled in it, and that Origen merely copied that, we reply: 1. Tischendorff's MS. dates about one hundred and ten years *later* than Origen—how could Origen copy him? 2. Irenæus so translated it long before Origen did. 3. Origen's was not copied from Tischendorff's copy, for it has *the word different*—one is *errantismenon,* the other *perireramenon;* very different in form—one *raino,* other *rantidzo;* and a compounded word. 4. Hippolytus *copies bapto,* then translates it.

CHAPTER XII.

Bapto—Primary Meaning Continued.

It is remarkable that the root of *baptidzo* should mean, in addition to sprinkle, moisten, imbue, wash; also to stain, color, dye. It seems more so when we learn that the leading word in use among Latin Christians of the earliest ages—Tertullian, Cyprian, etc.—for baptize, when not using by transfer the word itself, was "TINGO," which primarily means to moisten, make wet, where it is by tears, by dew, drops of liquid, etc., yet comes to mean to stain, color, dye, dip. *Tabhal* (in Hebrew, baptize) means to stain, but rarely; while the Syriac and Arabic *tzeva*—baptize—means to stain, to dye, or color, and applies to colored birds, animals, etc. It will be seen that all these words, save *tingo*, mean primarily to sprinkle, to shed or pour forth, applied to liquids; they mean also to moisten, make wet.

From this substantial agreement of all these words in meaning—defined alike by lexicons generally, vindicated by an inspection of original sources—we have a clue, a key to some great and essential philological principles. By these we can arrive at a correct conclusion.

We have examined BAPTO from the standpoint of scientific investigation. We saw sprinkle as the primary force of *bapto*. In a future chapter we will see a great number of words primarily meaning to sprinkle coming to mean all that *bapto* means and lapping over all that *baptidzo* means. Let us here trace the process by which all these meanings are derived from *bapto*. It must not be forgotten that *bapto* appears in Greek literature as early as Homer but only a very few times in centuries, being a rare word; that *baptidzo* does not appear for quite five hundred years later, the incautious writer, like Ingham, not telling the reader that the Orpheus, Æsop, etc. he quotes are spurious and of a late date. Conant shows that fact. We have it demonstrated from the inspection of cases and dates that *bapto* applied to cases of affusion, effusion, many centuries before it meant dye. It meant to stain centuries before it meant to dye. It meant to wash as early as it meant to color in any way beyond a stain effected by slight aspersion. These being historic facts are way-marks to help us.

BAPTO AND PHILOLOGY.

Now, no one believes that the art of dyeing was suddenly invented and practiced. Such arts are always the result of accidental discovery from seeing the effects of the elements in nature. Though many saw apples fall and tea-kettles boil and lift their coverings, it was centuries before a Newton applied the suggestions of the one or a Watt or Fulton the power of the other.

A person from breaking or bruising a weed, herb, or shell that had coloring matter in it; from an incision in the bark of a tree causing a spurting out of juice, sap; from bursting a grape or berry on the hands or clothes, would thus earliest discover the staining qualities of the attaching liquid. Seeing the effects, it might be such a color as would please some parties very much, and it would be natural to go to work to apply the matter to color their faces, beard, hair, or garments. *Bapto* applies earlier to staining by centuries, we saw, than by dyeing. When they had used it thus for a time it would sooner or later turn out that parties would extend the discovery, and get enough of the coloring element to prepare ornaments, adorn their clothes, and finally dilute the coloring matter in water, or collect enough to dye their garments. They would learn to dip the garments; first no doubt parts of it in one dye, parts in another, so as to have the "variegated garments," or, as in some cases, resort to needle-work. Whatever the word applied to the first stain, where it was by the slightest aspersion or dropping of the matter, it would remain the word through all the varying fortunes of the art. In the case under consideration BAPTO was the word. It must not be supposed that *bapto* was the favorite word. As late as the fourth century before Christ that learned and careful writer, Aristotle, when speaking of the dyeing substance even, does not use *bapto* for dye but for moisten—if pressed "it moistens (*bapto*) and colors (*anthidzci*) the hand"—showing that *bapto* represented moisten of the slightest kind much more correctly than color or dye. That speaks volumes. It demonstrates additionally from the historic order that color, dye, is derived, and derived from it as meaning to moisten, not from to dip. Thus history, philology, and common observation all harmonize. All the historic light we have sustains these facts. The earliest colorings we read of, save one or two soon to be noticed, occur in Exodus xxv, 4; xxvi, 7, 31, 36, etc., which were purple. The Scriptures give no light whence these colors came. 1 Maccabees iv, 23, calls them "purple (*apo*) from the sea." It is agreed that the colors were obtained "from

BAPTO—PRIMARY MEANING CONTINUED. 129

the juice of certain species of the shell-fish" (Kitto). "The majority" of ancients ascribe the discovery "to the Tyrian Hercules, whose dog, it is said, instigated by hunger, broke a certain kind of shell-fish on the coast of Tyre, and his mouth becoming stained of a beautiful color, his master was induced to try its properties on wool, and gave his first specimens to the king, who admired the color so much that he restricted the use of it by law to the royal garments."* The Tyrians practiced coloring thus for ages. As the Hebrews, Syrians, Arabians, and Chaldeans were all of kindred blood, language, and habit, their habits of coloring most likely began there. It is worth note that one of the leading words for baptize in Arabic, occurring often in the New Testament (*tsava-tsevagha*) in its noun-form, means the juice of a vine. But all this aside, we prefer and rely on the development and science of language, along with the record of facts.

Facts now. First, *bapto* applied to sprinkling, to effusions. This was its first primary force. Second, it meant, consequently, both to moisten and stain; for to sprinkle or effuse with staining elements, blood, juices, etc., both moisten and stain result. Yet it does not necessarily apply to staining; it always implies moistening or wetting. It may be assumed that there is no case of *bapto*, a verb, without moisten. This is the only meaning or idea that never forsakes it in a single instance. Third, it never means to dye where it is by dipping till the last half of the fourth century before Christ, so far as facts go. Its corresponding Hebrew *tabhal*, in earlier Hebrew only corresponding, the stain—*molunein*, in Greek; *tingo*, Latin; *tabhal*, Hebrew—is even in Genesis xxxvii, 31, better rendered with the Syriac sprinkled.

* Pollox Onom., i, 4; Kitto, sub. v, purple.

Now *baptidzo* is a derivative of *bapto*. When was it formed—when first used? We can no more tell than we can as to *bapto*. Like *bapto* it was but seldom used. It first appears in a writer of the close of the sixth century before Christ. Immersionists all assert that *baptidzo* derives the *primary* meaning of *bapto*, but not the *derived* meanings (see A. Campbell, pp. 119, 120, Carson, etc., etc.) or figurative meanings of *bapto*. That will do us very well. But truth, and philology as its aid, we want. *Baptidzo* comes into use in the sixth century before Christ, we know. But *bapto* never meant *dye* nor applied to dyeing by dipping till Plato and Aristotle, so far as records go. It never applied to *colored* clothes till a hundred years after *baptidzo* appears in literature. *Baptidzo* not only antedates dye as a meaning of *bapto*, but *dip*, even a partial dip, as a meaning by a century.

When *baptidzo* took its departure from *bapto*, it carried no stain, no dip, no dye with it. All agree that *baptidzo* never means to stain, color, paint, or dye. Drs. Gale, Carson, Stuart, A. Campbell, etc., etc. dwell on this marked difference between the two words. Indeed they all make that the only difference. In that they greatly err, but we have no interest in that here.*

Now the facts we have adduced account for the whole phenomena, so inexplicable to philologists. Had *baptidzo* been derived—been an extension of *bapto*—an intensification or frequentative of it after *bapto* meant stain, color, dye (Liddell & Scott, A. Campbell, etc.), or put the object into the condition indicated by the root *bapto* (Kühner, etc.), then *baptidzo* would have meant all that *bapto* does, only perhaps much intensified. All know and agree that this is not the case.

* Dr. J. R. Graves, since the above was written, over and again notes the same fact in the Carrollton debate.

But supposing *baptidzo* to have been formed long before it appears in the literature that has survived, as we know it did (for it first appears in a highly figurative form in all its earliest occurrences, Pindar, Aristophanes, Plato, Demosthenes pointing to an earlier literal meaning long in use), we can see why it never means color, stain, dye. It was formed as an *intensive* from *bapto* when *bapto* had but one meaning—*to sprinkle*. When we come to examine *baptidzo* philologically this will appear with overwhelming force. It was when *bapto* meant no more than *sprinkle* that *baptidzo* was formed. Let any one examine the passages where *bapto* occurs throughout all ages, especially for one thousand years from Homer to Christ, then *baptidzo*—the difference in use is almost *infinite*. The one, *bapto*, constantly occurs in respect to a slight contact, especially the element generally applied is small. It never applies to *bapting* with great billows, waves of stormy seas, wars, and calamities, etc., etc. It even appears in contrast with *baptidzo*, sometimes both in classics and the Greek fathers. Yet at times both words apply to one and the same kind of operation late in their history, not early. We refer to cases where each equally applies to cutting or piercing with a sword. Both are so used, and we present a number of cases. *Baptidzo* implies a more copious affusion primarily than *bapto*. Hence we will see it much more naturally coming to mean *to wash*, as the effect of descending water, then also overflow, overwhelm, and from thence to *sink*. Hence, really we will find that *baptidzo* never means to dip at all, but sink, *immergo*, when it does put the object into or under the element.

On the contrary, neither A. Campbell, Carson, Gale, nor Stuart ever found an example where *bapto* meant immerse. They can't find an example of *baptidzo* meaning to dip in any true sense of the word in classic usage. We named the fact parenthetically that *baptidzo* first appears in a highly metaphorical form. This will appear when we come to the word. This points to long use when it had its proper literal meaning. Both chronology and philology show clearly that *baptidzo* was in use before *bapto* took on the later meanings, dip and dye; the dip being derived from dye, not dye from dip; the dye from color, stain; that from moisten, sprinkle.

Herein we see clearly why *bapto* at times means to *dip* simply, but does not apply to *immerse,* a slight contact with the element being its general later use; whereas *baptidzo* being primarily intensified, a stronger form, implying intenser force, early passed over into *pour,* that into *wash;* also into overflow, overwhelm literally and metaphorically; thence from overwhelming and overflowing—burdening by such heavy affusions—*sink* was taken on. Hence it can not mean dip—never means dip. A careful examination of the few passages in classics will show this, the strongest case being one in Plutarch, but clearly *baptidzo* (*ek*) there does not apply to dipping, but to drinking—becoming intoxicated out of the wine-jars, etc. If dye is derived from *dip,* as immersionists all assume, and *baptidzo* inherits "dip" as the *primary* meaning of *bapto,* why did not *baptidzo* mean dye also? If dye comes from *dip,* why does not *dupto,* dip, and *kolumbao,* dip, immerse, mean dye? And if dip and immerse are "synonymous," why do not the Greek verbs *buthidzo, katapontidzo, kataduo,* which definitely mean to immerse, and Hebrew *tabha,* immerse, mean to dye, stain, color—have the real meanings of *tingo* and of dip also?*

---

* Since the above was written, several years ago, 1870-72, the Graves-Ditzler debate occurred, and Dr. G. says, page 322, "As *tingo* once pri-

In a future chapter the mass of facts will be presented and the science of philology applied, putting all beyond a doubt, and, like the full-orbed sun scattering the mists and shadows of night, the dark night of false philology and assumption will be dissipated before the dawning of a better day.

IS STAIN, DYE, FROM DIP?

As Dr. Graves (Debate, 323), since all our facts were written, reiterates the old theory, not giving a word of proof, about dye, color, coming from dip, we now further add, in demonstration of our philological position, the words that generally mean to stain, color, dye—meanings all agree to give to the root *bapto*—and see if color, stain, dye came from dip, as has been universally assumed by immersionists, admitted by too many of their opponents.

1. *Moluno.* Stephanus says, quoting another, its "primitive meaning is to sprinkle."* Yet Liddell & Scott define it "to stain, sully, defile, to sprinkle."

Groves: "To dye, stain, discolor, tinge," etc.

2. *Tenggo* (τεγγω). Liddell & Scott: "To *wet, moisten, to bedew with*, esp[ecially] with tears (*dakrusi*), *to wash, to shed tears. Ombros etengeto,* a shower *fell.* (2) *To soften* (properly by soaking, bathing, etc.). (3) *To dye, stain;* Latin, *tingere.*" "Dye, stain," he puts as derived meanings.

Groves: *Tengo,* to moisten, wet, water, sprinkle, bedew, to soften, soak, steep, relax, to tinge, dye, stain,

marily meant to dip; second, to dye, now it has lost its first, and its *secondary* has become its *primary*" signification. It is difficult to say what this means, but it shows confusion worse confounded, under only a few of the above facts. On page 323 he reiterates all the old jargon about "dye" from dip, but not a fact, text, or argument offered!

* *Adspergere.*

color, etc. So Donnegan, Pickering, Dunbar, Pape, Passow, etc.

3. *Palasso.* Liddell & Scott: "To besprinkle, to stain, befoul, defile." The staining, defiling, was from sprinkling blood, etc., etc.

4. *Anthidzo*, to sprinkle.* Liddell & Scott: "To strew with flowers, to deck as with flowers, and so to *dye* or *stain* with colors. Passive, to bloom, to be dyed or painted, sprinkled with white, browned."

Groves: "To bud, blossom, etc., to strew with flowers, to color, tinge,† dye."

5. *Chraino.* Liddell & Scott: "To touch slightly. Hence to smear, to paint, to besmear, to anoint, to stain, spot, to defile."

Groves: "To color, dye, stain, smear, daub, paint," etc.

6. *Miaino:* "To paint over, to stain, dye, defile, soil" (Liddell & Scott).

Groves: "To stain, dye, color, to polish, defile," etc.

7. *Chrodzo:* "To touch the surface of the body; generally to touch, to impart by touching the surface; hence to tinge,† stain," etc. (Liddell & Scott).

Groves: "To color, paint, tinge,† dye, stain," etc.

Chrotidzo: "To color, dye, tint" † (Liddell & Scott).

8. *Spilō:* "To stain, soil" (Liddell & Scott).

Graves: "To spot, stain, blot, defile."

9. *Deuo:* "To wet, water, moisten, bedew, sprinkle, to tinge,† dye, color, to soak, soften" (Groves).

Stephanus: "To wet, moisten, imbue, stain (tingo),† pour, besprinkle, infect, stain, *baphaeus.*"

10. *Poluno:* "To strew, scatter upon, to besprinkle,

---

* Stephanus . . . *adspergo.*

† Notice here how often *tinge, tint,* is used; *tingo* where the processes or modes are by sprinkle, touch, etc., and not dip.

snow sprinkled the fields, to sprinkle with flour" (Liddell & Scott).

Here now are ten words, counting *chrotidzo* as one, not one of which ever had dip as a primary or general meaning. Every one accomplished the coloring, staining, tinging, dyeing *by application* of the coloring element. Yet they tell us dyeing, coloring, etc. are effected always by dipping. There is now one more Greek word that means to dye, stain, color, tinge as well as to sprinkle, wet, etc. Liddell & Scott, the favorite immersionist lexicon, gives *bapto* these meanings among others: "To color," "to dye the hair," "to steep in crimson." Groves gives, "Dye," "stain," "color," as well as "dip," "sprinkle," "wet," "moisten." Is it not governed by the same laws of language? All the other ten words that have the meanings it has have either sprinkle or bedew, the same, "touch slightly," "to touch the surface of the body," "to shed tears" as the primary meanings. (1) In all the primary meaning was either sprinkle, shed, as tears, dew, or touch. One was by sprinkling flowers. This forever settles the question about dyeing, coloring, coming from dip. (2) As words meaning dip (*dupto*), immerse,* never mean to dye, color, it shows *bapto* never primarily meant to dip.

It has now been demonstrated—

1. That *bapto* primarily applied to sprinkling, to effusion, where liquids were the elements, either blood, or water, or juice, sap, staining, or moistening elements.

2. That it applied where the slightest possible aspersion occurred, even a few drops—Homer, Hippocrates, Aristotle, Aristophanes.

3. That dye, stain, color do not come from, are never meanings of words that properly and generally mean to

---

* Βυθίζω, καταδύω, etc. See them all elsewhere immerse.

dip, as *dupto, kolumbao* in Greek; *tauchen, tunken* in German; dip in English; or from immerse—*pontidzo, en,* and *kataduo, buthidzo, katapontidzo* in Greek; *mergo, in, de,* and *submergo* in Latin. So of Hebrew, Arabic, Persic, Chaldee, Syriac. In no case does color, stain, dye come from dip or immerse.

4. But in scores of cases stain, color, paint, dye come from words primarily meaning to sprinkle, and from words primarily meaning to moisten, where it is by sprinkling, dropping upon, etc. Even *molunein,* stain, primarily meant to sprinkle. The full list of such words will be given under *baptidzo.*

5. Immersionists are unanimous in the assertion that immerse and dip can never come to mean to sprinkle or to pour. We agree to this. It is unquestionably true. But we see *bapto* used where *dropping,* sprinkling, pouring, touching with the element occur, as well as falling of dew on the body. So overwhelming is the evidence that Dr. Carson is compelled to admit, and the rest concur, that "*Use is the sole arbiter of language. Bapto* signifies *to dye* BY SPRINKLING as properly as by dipping, though originally it was confined to the latter" (Baptism, 63). The latter remark has been shown to be utterly incorrect from chronological facts as well as from philology. As immersionists so pointedly assert that dip can never come to mean to sprinkle—a word properly meaning dip—and yet are compelled to admit *bapto* does so apply, it shows that sprinkle, and not dip, was the primary meaning of this word. But,

6. When it is known, as will be exhibited under *baptidzo,* that great numbers of words primarily mean to sprinkle, others to moisten, wet, where the mode was sprinkling, dropping, yet come to mean derivatively all

that *bapto* and all that *baptidzo* are admitted by all parties to mean, then it becomes as perfectly demonstrated that *bapto* primarily meant to sprinkle, as that things equal to each other are equal to the same.

7. That *dip* is later, rarer, a derived meaning of *bapto*.

8. That immerse is unknown as a meaning when "inspection" tests the matter, themselves being judges.

9. That in the Bible it clearly retains sprinkle as one of its meanings still, while it never implies immersion.

10. That the fathers of the earliest ages—Irenæus, born only a few years before John's death, Origen, and Hippolytus, all learned Greeks, translate *bapto* sprinkle.

11. That the versions from apostolic times till the sixteenth century render *bapto* sprinkle as well as by other terms.

12. Over and again A. Campbell asserts that *bapto* and *baptidzo* are the same in meaning. So does Drs. Carson, pp. 19, 18, and 23, and Gale, quoted also by Carson. See Carson also, p. 315. While we do not sanction this, we produce it to show how they regard it.

CHAPTER XIII.

Lexicons on Baptidzo.

We will now cite the most critical, the most popular and authoritative and universally-recognized standards of Greek lexicography known. In the list we give the entire body of native lexicographers who define this word.* Writers on this subject have skipped from *bapto* to *baptidzo* in lexical citations, and bounded to and fro in classic citations, and Mr. A. Campbell, not to be outdone, doubles down the lexicon into defining " *bapto et baptidzo* " as one word, on several occasions, when no lexicon on earth ever made such a stupendous blunder. Booth, and my good friend Dr. G. W. Brents, of Tennessee, string out long lines of theologians small and great, historians read and unread, authorities learned and ignorant, and lexicons good, bad, and doubly indifferent, together with private letters partisanly written, glossaries on single books or authors—all confusedly mixed and jumbled together into a strange, crude, and indigestible mass, heterogeneously mixed up, till confusion is confounded, and, in nine tenths of the cases words and sentences enough left out to defeat all hope of accuracy and analysis. In many cases, also, the real lexicons cited are some Arabic, some Hebrew,

---

* Following others, we once quoted Suidas on *baptidzo*, but he does not define it at all. Hesychius and Suidas give to *bapto* only its *rare* meaning, wash, *pluno*, and are not cited for that reason under *bapto*. Dr. Graves still keeps up the old blunder of quoting Suidas on *baptidzo*, all *apocryphal*.

some Syriac—all quoted as if Greek, and on *baptidzo!* We have carefully avoided all these absurdities.

Yet, on account of their early period and great advantages, and because they define and translate the word, acting from the standpoint of lexicography, we do cite four authorities who never compiled lexicons. But they translate the word used by Messiah in the commission to baptize, and for that reason we quote them at once. They are the only authors of all antiquity we have found that define the word. Hence they are too valuable to be omitted in this place.

1. Julianus, fourth century after Christ: "*Baptidzo* means to sprinkle."*

Julianus† was one of the most acute and profoundly

---

* Βαπτίζω *perfundere interpretatus est.* Beza's *Annotationés Grecœ Nou. Test.*, Matt. iii, 11, ed. 1598, folio. Dr. Graves, since the above, Debate, p. 258, tanslates *perfundere* "besprinkle."

It is a painful fact that after all the exposures we have made, had made in the Louisville Debate, and in various papers, of misquotations, suppressions of essential points in lexical citations as well as of authors, and the severe chastisement we gave some authors at Carrollton, Mo., 1875, that still partisans and mere controversialists will not agree to be governed by a spirit of fairness. Dr. Graves, e. g. professing to quote forty (40) Greek lexicons (Graves-Ditzler Debate, pp. 322, 529), in the list puts down a number of mere glossaries, mere lexica; a private letter reported as a lexicon (!); one as Trommius's lexicon, when it is also a glossary, and not made nor published by Trommius; and a long list of authors reported as *lexicons* whom he never saw, whose works he never consulted, and whose relative merits are never distinguished—all thrown together in a heterogeneous and undigested mass, without analysis, order, or accuracy. And to make bad worse, *only one lexicon out of the so-called forty is correctly reported!!* In every lexicon cited, save one, most essential definitions are suppressed, and essential words left out in all cases save the single exception!

Then after the rebuke we gave Dr. Judd and him at Carrollton, which he never resented *there* (pp. 146-7), Dr. Graves in his last speech —*not as delivered,* but as *rewritten* by him after I had returned to Kentucky (p. 530) — repeats the shameful untruth, and says, "*Amad* in

versed opponents Augustine had, and was in that early day thoroughly acquainted with these questions.*

2. Augustine, fourth century, next to Jerome the most illustrious of Latin fathers, admits Julianus's definitions, and seeks to limit or distinguish already between Bible and classic use.

3. Tertullian, A. D. 190 to 220, renders *baptidzo* by sprinkle. †

Syriac, AS ALL STANDARD LEXICOGRAPHERS TESTIFY, PRIMARILY SIG- NIFIES TO IMMERSE"!! A more willful falsehood was never uttered by any perjured, oath-bound member of a robber clan on earth. These, with hosts of other statements in these last speeches on Mode, and all subsequent parts of the so-called debate, account for their not sending to me a single proof-sheet after my sixteenth speech on the First Proposition, though I requested it, and gave them my address. (For Castell's definition and "primary" force of the word, see the Debate, p. 147, with the original given.) In the same strain he defies decency on page 531, from XIV on to XX. Here he pretends that all these Methodist, Presbyterian, and eminent pedobaptist scholars, "full one hundred," embracing Terretinus, Witsius, Beza, Wesley, A. Clarke, Vossius, Lightfoot, Stier, Walæus, M. Stuart, as the most noted, held that "immersion was *the only act of* Apostolic or primitive baptism"!! Dr. Graves as well knew that every word of the above was without any foundation or truth as he knew he held his pen in hand, and that *every one of the above* writers maintained *just the reverse*. (See them all quoted in this work, as well as in that debate.)

Adversus quem eruditissimos libros scripsit Augustinus; Beza, *ibid.*

† *Perfudit.* Thus: *Illi quos Menander perfudit,* "those whom Menander baptized"—sprinkled. De Anima, c. 51. Irenæus, A.D. 160, uses "baptized" of them instead of "*perfudit.*"

We have known partisans who tried to evade the force of *perfudit,* as if it implied a very copious pouring all over the person, which, though it changes not our argument, is not true, as the following use of it shows:

1. Stokius: Ῥαίνω, *raino* [sprinkle], *perfundo, adspergo.*
2. Ed. Leigh, *Sacra Critica:* Ῥαίνω, *perfundo, aspergo.*
3. Schleusner, O. T. Lexicon: Ῥαντίζω, etc., a ῥαίνω, *perfundo, . . . sic usurpatur de sanguine* (Heb. ix, 13, 19, etc.): sprinkle, "from *raino,* to sprinkle. Thus it is used of the blood, etc. (Heb. ix, 13, 19, etc.).

4. Euththymius, fourth century, besprinkle * [sprinkle].
5. Codex Sinaiticus, besprinkle † [sprinkle].
6. Codex Vaticanus, besprinkle ‡ [sprinkle].
7. Kouma, a native Greek of this century, the lexicon written at great length in modern Greek: "*Baptidzo*, from *bapto*, to sink, to put frequently into water; to besprinkle,§ shed forth (or sprinkle). 2. To draw or pump water. 3. In an ecclesiastical sense, to baptize." ¶

4. Stephanus, *Thesaurus Græcæ Lin.:* 'Ραίνω, *perfundo, aspergo* (p. 8175).

5. Schrevellius: 'Ραίνω, *perfundo, aspergo*. Thus all the lexicons define the Greek *sprinkle* by *perfundo*, and as equivalent to *aspergo*.

Scores of texts in Latin could be cited to the same effect; the following samples suffice: Ovid, in the apostolic age, "She took water, and—*perfudit*—*sprinkled*- it on his face (Met. iii, 190); "And—*perfudit* —sprinkled the wide ditches with blood" (Met. vii, 245); Castell uses *perfudit caput, perfudit aqua*—sprinkle the head, sprinkle with water, often; as well as Schindler, Buxtorf, etc.

* 'Ραντισῶνται, in Mark vii, 4. Alford's and A. Clarke's Notes on, and the Tischendorff Sinaitic manuscript.

† 'Ραντισῶνται, in Mark vii, 4.

‡ 'Ραντισῶνται, in Mark vii, 4. Eight others rendered it sprinkle.

§ In the light of this chapter, how does the language of A. Campbell and others appear, when they so boldy asserted that "It never has been translated by either sprinkle or pour by any lexicographer for eighteen hundred years."

Dr J. R. Graves, followed by swarms of others, says, in The Baptist, Nov. 6, 1875, "Not one of them [thirty-two Greek lexicographers claimed] defines it [*baptidzo*] to pour or to sprinkle." He modified it thus in his *unspoken*, written speech, where he knew I would not see it till in the published book, too late to be exposed in the work (p. 526). In *capitals* he says, "No standard lexicon in the world gives 'to sprinkle,' or 'to pour' as a literal and real signification of *baptidzo*." If Baptists are edified by such reckless dealing we ought to be satisfied. He then *pretends* to call on me "to produce one Greek lexicon of acknowledged authority, or an authoritative quotation from one, that gives 'to sprinkle' or 'to pour' as a PRIMARY meaning of *baptidzo*." HE HAS NOT DONE IT." Capitals his own in this line. He well knew he never said that *in the debate*. Such hypocrisy is contemptible.

¶ Kouma: Βαπτίζω M. ἴσω ἐκ τοῦ βάπτω; βυθίζω, βουτῶ συχνάκις εἰς ἴργον, καταβρέχω, βρέχω. 2. 'Αντλῶ. 3. Βαπτίζω . . . εκκλης. Σ.

8. Sophocles, restricted to the Iron Age or later Greek, is an immersionist, and a favorite with them. "*Baptidzo*, to dip, to immerse; sink, to be drowned [as the effect of sinking]; to sink. Trop., to afflict; soaked in liquor; to be drunk, intoxicated. 2. Mid., to perform ablution; to bathe; bathed [baptized] in tears; to plunge a knife. 4. [Ecclesiastical in Dark Ages]: *Baptizo, mergo, mergito, tingo* (or *tinguo*), to baptize; New Testament, passim."* Baptism with tears is hardly a clear case of dipping or immersing.

9. Schætgennius. "*Baptidzo:* First, properly (i. e. in classics) to plunge, sink in (immerse); second, to wash, to cleanse (Mark vii, 4; Luke xi, 38); third, to baptize, in a sacred sense. Metaphorically it means, first, to pour forth abundantly (Matt. iii, 11; Acts i, 5, etc.); second, to be subjected to great dangers and burdens"† (classic reference to Diodorus Siculus, etc., as well as one to Matthew xx, 22, of Christ's sufferings).

10. Wahl. He has two editions. In the first the New Testament meanings are given thus: " First, to wash (classic, to sink down, submerse); second, to immerse; third, metaphorically, overwhelm any thing with any thing; to imbue plentifully, as with the divine Spirit," etc.

In his second later edition it reads, Wahl, *baptidzo* (1831)—

---

* Where it is "baptized" in tears, he cites the Greek thus, Βαπτίζεσθαι ταῖς δάκρυσι, which is, " baptized with tears." The word occurs in Eusebius's Greek History, where John the Apostle "baptized" a penitent who had backslidden "as if a second time with his tears," as well as in other writers.

† Βαπτίζω—1. *Proprie mergo, immergo*; 2. *Abluo, lavo* (Marc. vii, 4; Luke xi, 35); 3. *Baptizo, significatu sacro, metaphorice accipitur et significat.* 1. *Largitur profundo* (Matt. iii, 11; Acts i, 5); 2. *Multis periculis et oneribus subjiceo* (Matt. xx, 22); *eadem sensu apud profanos occurrere*, etc.

1. "To immerse (Josephus, Ant., ix, 10, 2; Polyh. i, 51, 6, classic use), (*a*) properly, also, of the sacred immersion, then by immersion; (*b*) with the idea of overwhelming included; to sprinkle,* followed with the dative of the instrument, etc., with water. Metaphorically, for to imbue largely; (*c*) to plunge in or overwhelm with calamities. 2. "For *nipto*, wash, i. e. Mark vii, 3." Later he erases sprinkle.

11. Grimshaw. *Baptidzo:* To wash, dip, besprinkle.†

12. Ewing, 1827, Glasgow. "*Baptidzo:* I plunge or sink completely under water, I cover partially with water, I wet; third, I overwhelm or cover with water by rushing, flowing, or pouring upon . . .; fourth, I drench or impregnate with liquor by affusion; I pour abundantly upon, so as to wet thoroughly; I infuse . . .; I wash."‡

13. Ed. Robinson's Lexicon of the New Testament (classic use he gives first, as), to dip in, to sink, to immerse; in Greek writers, spoken of ships, galleys, etc. Polyh. i, 51; Diod. Sic., Strabo, Plut. . . . In the New Testament, first, to wash, to lave, to cleanse by washing; second, to wash oneself, i. e. one's hands or person, to perform ablution;§ third, to baptize, etc. He then adds in a note to the word:

* *Perfundo*, sq. dat,; etc. . . . pro νίπτω, *lávo.* In first edition, in brackets, he has demergo, *submergo* (Polyb. i, 51-6; Diod. Sic., etc.).

† This is the only lexicon we have accepted from other than the original on the lexicons on *baptidzo.*

‡ This wild definition, so labored and strange, is the only one given that really gives a meaning that exactly suits immersionists—"sink *completely under water.*" Water no more inheres in *baptidzo* than oil, honey, mud, or filth, as Conant, Carson, A. Campbell, etc , show.

§ Dr. Graves (Debate, p. 281) cites him thus: "To immerse, to sink; 2. To wash, to cleanse by washing," etc., and leaves out the note. He carefully leaves out also the words "*In New Test.*" preceding the words "to wash, to lave, cleanse," etc., after asserting that no standard lexicon makes *a difference* between classic and New Testament use!

["Note.—While in Greek writers, as above exhibited, from Plato onward, βαπτίζω is every where to sink, to immerse, to overwhelm, either wholly or partially, yet in Hellenistic usage . . . it would seem to have expressed, not always simply immersion, but the more general idea of ablution or affusion." Ed. 1854.]

14. Stokius. We next take up this author, old school of philology, and for years paraded by immersionists as having no superior!*

"*Baptidzo:* To wash, to baptize; passive, to be washed, to be cleansed."† He then gives the current classic use and the old-time philology in his usual note to a word of any extended use in the New Testament, thus: "Generally, and by the force of the word, it obtains the sense of dipping or immersing.‡ Specially (*a*) properly it is to immerse or dip in water; (*a*) *tropically* (1) by a *metalepsis*, it is to wash (*lavare*) or cleanse (*abluere*), because any thing is accustomed to be dipped or immersed in water that it may be washed or cleansed, *although also the washing or cleansing can be, and* GENERALLY IS, *accomplished by* SPRINKLING THE WATER (Mark vii, 4; Luke xi, 38).

* That you may see how much importance is attached to the opinion of Stokius, I will read you from A. Campbell's works: "Has he produced a lexicon, of the eighteen centuries past, giving *sprinkle* or *pour* as the *proper* or as the *figurative* meaning of *baptidzo*? . . Let him produce any modern dictionary, English, French, Spanish, German, etc., thus expounding the Greek words *bapto* or *baptidzo*" (Debate, p. 181).

Of Stokius: "This great master of sacred literature" (Debate, p 60); "One of the most learned rabbis in the school and learning of orthodoxy" (Debate, p. 206); "The two still more venerable names of Schleusner and Stokius" (Debate, p. 208). "Schleusner, a man revered by orthodox theologians, and of enviable fame" (Debate, p 58).

A. C. (Debate, p. 208) declares Stokius and Schleusner "are still more decidedly with us [them] . . . than *any one* or *all* of the *classic* dictionaries."

† Βαπτίζω, *lavo, baptizo, passivum* βαπτίζομαι, *luor, lavor.* Lavo is to wash, wet, bedew, besprinkle, by all lexicons.

‡ It might equally well be dipping and immerse, but I prefer to follow immersion translations, unless they grossly depart from the original.

Hence it is transferred to the sacrament of baptism. . . . 3. Metaphorically it designates (*a*) the miraculous *pouring out* (*effusionem*) of the Holy Spirit upon the apostles and other believers, as well on account of the abundance of the gifts of the Holy Spirit, since anciently *the water was copiously poured* upon those baptized, or they were immersed deep in the water," etc.*

Here Stokius adopts the old theory held by Suicer, Vossius, Beza, Terretinus, etc., that *baptidzo* came to mean to wash derivatively, then to wash by sprinkling. And he cites two New Testament texts where it refers to Jewish baptisms thus effected, for in *both* it is *baptidzo* (Mark vii, 4; Luke xi, 38). Then as *Jewish* baptism (*lotio, ablutio - baptidzo,* and *baptismos*) was effected generally "by sprinkling the water," "*hence* it is transferred to designate the sacrament of baptism." Then he tells us metaphorically it designated the pouring out of the Spirit. Why so? He tells us, "Since anciently the water was copiously poured upon those baptized," etc.† Because

---

* Βαπτίζω, *lavo, baptizo, passivum, luor, lavor*. Then he adds a note: 1. *Generatim ac vi vocis intinctionis ac immersionis notionem obtinet.* 2. *Speciatim,* (*a*) *proprie est immergere ac intingere in aquam;* (*b*) *tropice,* (1) *per metalipsin est, lavare, abluere, quia aliquid intingi ac immergi solet in aquam ut lavetur, vel abluatur quamquam et* ADSPERGENDO *aquam, lotio vel ablutio fieri queat et soleat* (Mark vii, 4: Luke xi, 38). *Hinc transferetur ad baptismi sacramentum,* etc. . . . *Per Met. designat* (*a*) *miraculosam spiritus S.* [*sancti*] *effusionem super apostolos, aliosque credentes, tum ob donorum spiritus S., copiam, prout* OLIM AQUA *baptizandis copiose* AFFUNDEBATUR, *vel illi penitus in aquam immergebantur,* etc.

† Dr. Graves (Debate p. 354) says. "Stokius says that properly it means ONLY 'to immerse,' 'to dip into,' " etc. Where is the "*only*"? He cites the Latin from my lexicon, which he borrowed, as he borrowed Leigh, Castell, etc., at Carrollton; but there is no "only," nay *he* has him translated, but *no* "*only.*" He admits he says it "was by sprinkling," as above, but that was merely Stokius's "opinion." All he said was simply "opinion;" all as to "immerse" or "dip in water," to wash,

the water was thus poured on those baptized in the apostolic age they metaphorically applied the word to the Spirit's influence, etc. How plain and simple.*

15. H. Cremer, second edition, 1878. This is a "Biblio-Theological Lexicon of the New Testament Greek," from the second German edition, by W. Urwick. "*Baptidzo*: To immerse, to submerge; often in later Greek, Plut., etc." After "immerse and submerse," as "later" classic meanings, he urges that *rachats* [wash], *louo* [wash], and *niptesthai* [wash the hands] (Matt. xv, 2), for which Mark vii, 4, has *baptidzesthai* are all one. Then he says, "Expressions like Isaiah i, 16 ["wash you"], and prophesies like Ezekiel xxxi, 25 ["then will I sprinkle clean water upon you"], xxxvii, 23 ["cleanse them"] ff., Zechariah xiii, 1, are connected with the Levitical washings, etc. . . This is the reason also why *baptidzein* in itself was not a thing unknown to the Jews." On Luke iii, 16, John i, 33, and Matthew iii, 11, he urges that "it makes no material difference whether *en* [in, with] be taken locally [i. e. in water] or instrumentally [*en hudati*, with water]. It is the former, if in *baptidzein*, with the meaning to dip, we main-

and a very erroneous opinion at that, against all facts and the science of language. But that is *Stokius*.

*To ward off Stokius's testimony, the immersionists quote him on *baptisma*, where S. *abridges* his language, and refers to baptism, "in which those to be baptized were *formerly* immersed into water; though at this time the water is only sprinkled upon them," etc. I copy Dr. Graves's own version of it (Debate, p. 353). Now of this—1. Stokius is not defining *baptidzo*, but *baptisma*, a word *not used once* in all the gospels for Christian baptism. 2. No Scripture text, *not one*, is cited by Stokius. He cites a host where the sprinkle water—and pour apply—after his *hinc*—hence, because the water was sprinkled, etc.—hence transferred to the sacrament of baptism. 3. He is talking of its use by the fathers *after* the apostolic age. Hence his word, "They call it [the sacrament] of initiation"—"first sacrament." Where is it so called in the New Testament.

tain the idea of immersion; it is the latter [with] if we maintain the idea of a washing or a pouring over." He had said already, "That the meaning 'to wash in order to purification from sin,' is metaphorical, and not that of "immerse,' is clear from the contraposition of *en hudati* and *en pneumati* [baptize with water—with the Spirit], by which the two baptisms are distinguished from each other. Both in the case of John and of the Messiah the question was one of purification from sin, which the former effected by means of water, the latter by means of the Holy Spirit and fire. Cf. [compare] Ezekiel xxxvi, 25-27; Malachi iii, 2, 3; Isaiah vi, 6, 7." Then follows the above extract beginning "It makes no material difference," etc. Cremer, like Hävernick, Ebrard, and hosts of others, holds Ezekiel xxxvi, 25, "sprinkles," to be baptism. That baptism is not immersion.

As my exposures of immersion quotations of these authors stung them into madness, they have resorted to the most astounding dodges and bold and most reckless accusations in order to draw off attention from their bad use of these authors. Hence we give the full text both in the original and the translation, with the exposure of their reckless criticisms and assertions appended, that all may see the simple desperation of their leaders in the West.

16. Schleusner. *Baptidzo:* Properly,* I immerse or

* Βαπτίζω. 1. *Proprie, immergo, ac intingo in aquam mergo, a* βάπτω, *et respondet,* Hebrew טָבַל [*tabhal*]—2 Reg. v, 14; in vers. Alex. et טָבַע [*tabha*], *apud symmachum* (Ps. lxviii, 5); *et apud incertum* (Ps. ix, 6). *In hac significatione nunquam in N. T. sed eo frequentius in Script.* Greek *legitur, v. c.* (Diod. Sic. i, chap. 36), *de Nilo exundente* [text of land animals submersed, etc.]—Strabo, Polyb, etc. . . . *Jam, quia haud raro aliquid immergi ac intingi in aquam solet, ut lavetur hinc.* 2. *Abluo, lavo, aqua purgo notat. Sic legitur in N. T.* (Marc. vii, 4), καὶ ἀπὸ ἀγορᾶς ἐὰν μὴ βαπτίσωνται (*in quibusdam codd.,* ῥαντίσωνται), οἰκ ἐσθίουσι [Latin rendering—*et res sq.*]—Luc. xi, 38 [texts in his Latin—*aqua*

dip, I plunge into [or in] water, from *bapto,* and answers to the Hebrew *tabhal* [i. e. translates *tabhal*], 2 Kings v, 14, in the Alexandrian version [LXX], and to *tabha,* in Symmachus, Psalm lxviii, 3 [really], and in an unknown [uncertain as to its translator] Psalm ix, 6. But in this sense it never occurs in the New Testament, but very frequently in Greek [classic] writers; for example, Diodorus Siculus, Strabo, etc., of the overflowing of the Nile, etc., Polybius, etc. . . . .

"Now, because not unfrequently [rarely] a thing is immersed or dipped in water that it may be washed; hence, second [it means], to cleanse, to wash, to purify with water. Thus it occurs in the New Testament.* Mark vii, 4 [translated by him], Luke xi, 38 [copied likewise and translated in Latin]. [He notes that in some texts—codices—it reads sprinkle (*rantisontai*) instead of "baptize themselves"]. *Baptidzesthai* not only means to wash, but to wash oneself, etc. Eccles. xxxiv, 30; Judith xii, 8. Hence transferred to the solemn rite of baptism. [Detailed comments follow.] Fourth, metaphorically, as the Latin, to imbue, to give to largely and copiously, and to administer, TO POUR FORTH abundantly (Matt. iii, 11), etc".

Here this great lexicographer gives immerse, dip, *oblutæ et purgatæ fuerint—se non lavasse*]. Βαπ, *non solum lavari, sed etiam se lavare significare multis locis probare potest* (Sirac. xxxiv, 30) [text.]; Judith xii, 8 [text]. 3. *Hinc transferetur ad baptismi ritum solemnem,* etc. [Detailed comment and texts—not on mode, follow.] 4. *Metaphorice: ut Lat. imbuo, large et copiose do atque suppedito, largiter profundo* (Matt. iii, 11).

*After all this pains by Stokius, and more still, if possible, by Schleusner, to distinguish between the classic and New Testament use of *baptidzo,* Dr. Graves (Debate, 527) says, "It is not true that any standard lexicon distinguishes between classic Greek and New Testament Greek in giving definitions of *baptidzo*"!! Was ever mortal so reckless who believed in a God?

plunge, in which sense it often occurs in classic Greek, as he holds, and in the sense of sink it does often so occur, and of overflow, overwhelm; but he adds, "In this sense it never occurs in the New Testament." In what sense, then, does it occur in the New Testament? In the sense of "cleanse, wash, purify with water." In certain ancient codices it reads sprinkle for baptize. In what other sense does it occur in the New Testament? Among others, "to pour forth abundantly." *

* As might be expected, garbling the text, suppression, and the boldest dealing have distinguished some of the western immersionists on this author. It has been assumed that " in this sense it does not occur in the New Testament," means in the sense of *tabha*, as distinguished from *tabhal* [!!], but by no scholar. We translated it as it is. Our views are supported—

1. By the very language itself. Schleusner says expressly of these meanings—cleanse, wash, purify, "*Thus it occurs in the New Testament.*" He cited the well-known passages Mark vii, 4; Luke xi, 38, which were Jewish baptisms, and renders them "wash."

Then he cites the fact that in certain ancient manuscripts of the Bible it read, instead of baptize themselves, *sprinkle* [-*rantisōntai*] themselves. Nine of them thus read. The two oldest copies of the Bible known in the world read "sprinkle" for "baptize." He cites Judith xii, 7, where she baptized—ἐπὶ τῆς πηγῆς τοῦ ὕδατος—at the fountain of water, washed; and Ecclesiasticus, "He that — [*baptidzo*] baptizeth—*washeth* himself from a dead body," etc., and he translates them all "*wash*." Then he tells us—since he showed it applied among the Jews to washing, and so many ancient copies had it *sprinkle*, that hence the word is transferred [i. e. from this Jewish use for ages by the Jews] to the solemn rite of baptism.

2. It is perfectly evident further from the fact that he defines its New Testament use to be "*imbuo*," *largitur profundo*—"to imbue, to pour forth abundantly." These are not meanings of *tabhal* or *tabha* in any case.

3. The words "*in hac significatione*" can not refer to *tabha*, "but in this sense" of *tabha* as distinguished from *tabhal*, for the punctuation unites them, and the *et—et*—"to *tabhal* AND to *tabha*." To evade this, Dr. Graves absolutely suppresses the *et*—throws it out in translating it (Debate, p. 347). Nor again, because of the absurdity implied; for *tabhal* occurs with blood the first time it appears in the

It may be that we do not know how to sympathize with our good immersionist friends, but they must bear these exposures.

world (Gen. xxxvii, 31, and Ex. xii, 22; and in other passages in Leviticus); with oil also. Dr. Graves, and others whom he follows, makes Schleusner say *baptidzo* does not occur in the sense of *tabhal* in the two verses given; but it *does* occur in the sense of *tabhal* (2 Kings v, 14)— "dipped himself." But is that its New Testament sense? Do they dip themselves in the New Testament. If it is used only for "dip himself," and only in the sense of *tabhal*, whence comes S.'s " wash, cleanse, purify, pour forth abundantly"? *Tabhal* in Bible use never means wash, cleanse, purify. It occurs in connection with blood, oil, etc. oftener than any thing else, as Dr. Graves's own citations show (Debate, pp. 487, 489).

4. Dr. Graves, in his blundering way (Debate, p. 348) says, "And that it also corresponds to *tava* [*tabha*] in Psalm lxviii, 5, 'Thou hast *overwhelmed* (i. e. *destroyed* by an overwhelming) cities,' and in an unknown writer, a gloss; or (Ps. ix, 6) 'Their memorial is *perished*' (by an overwhelming that covers it out of sight). But in *this* sense it is never used in the New Testament. In what sense? Unquestionably the latter, as *tava* is used *in these two passages.* In the sense, then, of to destroy by immersing it is never used in the New Testament." Again (Debate, p. 412) he says the same, in brief, thus: "Undoubtedly [it refers] to the last, *tava, which is used in* the two Psalms referred to, in the sense of to destroy by overflowing; and Schleusner declares that *in this sense*, i. e. *to* DROWN, to perish by *the* submersion, it is never used in the New Testament." He tells us of Baptist doctors sustaining this!!

Does it not occur to their minds that this absurd theory destroys their position on several other points?—e. g. where Dr. G. insists that no standard lexicon distinguishes between classic and New Testament use (Debate, p. 527).

Also, that Dr. G. himself cites classic cases where *baptidzo* destroys by drowning, and that Conant points out many such places? But let us examine him in detail to see how reliable are Baptist criticisms here.

Dr. Graves and his backers make *tabha* (*tava*) apply to overwhelmings. It never so applies in any passage in the Bible, and no lexicon that ever was made translates it "overwhelm" or "overflow," or by any like word. But let us read the two passages cited by Schleusner (Ps. ix, 6—in the Hebrew, ix, 16; in James, ix, 15). "The heathen are *sunk* —*tabha*—down in the pit that they made." Now where is the overwhelm of Dr. G.? Where does the "overwhelming," "cover" them

17. Stephanus, 1572. *Baptidzo:* I plunge or immerse, as we immerse things in water for the purpose of wetting [washing?] or cleansing them; plunged, i. e. I submerse, "out of sight"? It is such an "overwhelming" as results in causing the subject to perish, says Dr. G. Not a word of it. Not one perishes here by *tabha.* It shows they sunk down in the pit, were taken in their own net; not one is overwhelmed, not one perishes. Take the other passage (Ps. lxix, 3—misprinted 5 in S.); in James it is Psalms lxix, 2, "I sink—*tabha*—in deep mire." Where is the "overwhelm" or "destroy" there? Not a word of it. Where he names waters and overflow he changes both the verb and noun, the manner of getting into the element and the element. *Mire* is not *water.* Dr. G. most shamefully slips out, quotes not a word of the real and expressed elements into which the *tabha* sinks them, leaves them *out,* and runs to other figures, other words, and slips them in the place of the suppressed words!

But after we exposed (Debate, p. 256) his blunders, and we had left Memphis for Kentucky, he then writes (Debate pp. 484-5) that *tabha* in Psalms ix, 15 (English version), the Hebrew word translated *baptidzo,* is from a word that means "to settle down, as Proverbs ii, 18: 'Her house sinks down—*shubat*—into death [*el maveth*].' In *this sense* the great Schleusner wishes to say, and does say in his lexicon, that *baptidzo* is never used in the New Testament." Here is a change and going back on his former dodge completely. Where is now "overwhelm"? Where are the floods? To sink down, to settle down into a thing, is not for the thing to come, as a flood overwhelming it. But we will not allow this shameful deception. It is "mire" in one place, a "pit" in the other into which *tabha* sinks them.

His repeated blunders, adding more still (Debate, p. 484), we need not consume time with, where he writes as if it were in the LXX, this *tabha* was rendered *baptidzo,* instead of *Symmachus* and the unknown version.

5. Finally, as *tabha always* means immerse—nothing in all the Bible but immerse—and is so defined by every and all Hebrew lexicons we ever saw, and yet Dr. Graves says *baptidzo* is not used, does not occur in the New Testament in the sense of *tabha,* in the places where it does mean immerse, it is destructive of their own position. He makes Schleusner say directly, "In the sense of immerse *baptidzo* NEVER *occurs in the* New Testament." So I believe with all my heart.

The fact that S. refers to overflowing of the Nile as the very example he cites to show *baptidzo's* classic use, demonstrates that he could not mean to say that *tabha* was used in that sense, as it never is so used. In the *r*ewritten debate (p. 412) he says, backed, he urges, by several

I overwhelm with water; overwhelmed. ‖ *Baptidzo,* to cleanse, to wash (Mark vii, 4; Luke xi, 38").*

18. Gazes. "*Baptidzo:* To put frequently any thing into any thing, and thence upon it; to shed forth any thing; to water; to pour upon; to wash. 2. To draw or pump water; to put a vessel into a place of water that I may pour out. 3. To wash the hands or to wash oneself.

Baptist doctors, that "*hac*" refers to *tavha!* "Undoubtedly to the last *tava which is used in the two Psalms referred to in the sense of* TO DE-STROY BY *the overflowing*"! Is it not amazing that sectarianism can go so far? In neither case was the party destroyed that was *tavhœd*. One was *tabhœd*—"sank" in "deep mire." Was that to "overflow" him? In the other he sank in a pit.

* Βαπτίζω *mergo S. immergo ut quæ tingendi aut abluendi gratia aquæ immergimus.* Plut. (6, 633) Sic. Alex. Aphr , *pro immersus.* He then says Buddæus interprets or renders it "*intinctus* also," "*etiam intinctus,*" but he does not sanction that. Strabo uses it for "*mergo, submergo,*" etc ; of others later. ‖ "Βαπτίζω, *abluo, lavo* (Marc. vii, 4)," etc.

Mr. A. Campbell, Drs. Graves and Booth all render the Latin of Stephanus and Scapula thus: *Mergo, seu immergo, ut quæ tigendi, aut abluendi gratia aquæ immergimus. Mergo,* i. e. *submergo, abruo, aquæ.* "To immerse or immerge, as things which we immerse for the sake of dyeing or washing in water" (Graves, Debate, p. 281).

Dr G , p 282, has Scapula saying under *baptidzo* "*item tingo.*" It is a false reading, copied from an error of Dr. Rice in debate with A. C. Dr. G renders Scapula "to immerse or immerge." "Also to immerse, as we immerse things for the sake of dyeing or washing them in water!" No dip. But after we exposed his blunders he at least after that slips in dip for "*immergo*" repeatedly! He leaves out their New Testament "*abluo, lavo.*"

We append the definitions of these lexicons, all copied from the originals directly.

1. Scapula, 1579, ed. 1820, *Londoni:* "*Baptidzo, mergo, seu immergo, ut quæ tingendi, aut abluendi gratia aquæ immergimus.* Plut., etc. *Item mergo, submergo, abruo aqua. Item abluo, lavo* (Marc. vii [4]; Luc. xi [38].

2. Hedericus, ed. 1825: " *Baptidzo, mergo, immergo, aqua abruo;* (2) *abluo, lavo;* (3) *baptizo, significato, sacro.*" The first classic cited for "immerse" is Helidorus, a *late* author; second one is Plutarch—long after Christ.

4. Among Christians, to baptize."* Here "shed forth" (*brecho*) pour upon [*cheo* to, pour, *epi* upon], etc. are given by this great author, a native Greek.

3. Schrevellius, ed. 1814: "*Baptidzo, mergo, abluo, lavo; Angl. baptize.*"

4. Pasor, xvi, 44: "*Baptidzo, immergo, abluo, baptizo* (Matt. iii, 11)," etc. He shows it applies to sufferings in New Testament also.

Here we have these few old abridgments of Stephanus and Morell showing that *Baptidzo*—

1. Never meant dip any where.
2. Never meant immerse till in late Greek.
3. Never meant immerse in the New Testament any where where the rite occurs.

4 Had only the force of cleanse, wash, baptize, without regard to mode in the New Testament.

* Gazes was a native of Melias, Thessaly. He was educated at Venice, traveled over Europe; was one of the most learned of Greeks; was a member of the committee that framed and signed the Declaration of Grecian Independence. He put forth his lexicon, founded on Schneider's, with changes and improvements, at Venice, three volumes quarto, which the learned Hilarion followed, who, with the approval of his archbishop, revised the translation of the Bible by the British and Foreign Bible Society. Here is his definition in full: Βαπτίζω: M. σω (βαπτω). Συχνὰ βουτῶ τι μέσα εἰς τι καὶ ἐντευθεν ἀνὰ τον. Βρεχω τι, ποτίζω, ἐπιχυνω, λούω. 2. Ἀντλῶ βουτῶ εἰς τὸ νερὸν ἀγγεῖον τι διὰ νὰ ἐκβάλλω. 3. Πλύνω τὰς χεῖρας, ἡ λούομαι. 4. Βαπτίζω, παρα Χριστιανοῖς, etc.

Dr. T. J. Conant, with Gazes and Kouma before him, suppresses all their definitions that were in serious debate, thus, as published by Elder Wilkes in Louisville (Debate, pp. 478-9).

NOVEMBER 18, 1870.

To WM. H. WYECHOFF, LL.D , *Cor. Sec'y of Am. Bible Union:*

MY DEAR SIR—Your friend asks, "What is the definition of βαπτίζω and of βαπτισμα, as given by each of the following lexicographers, viz. Hesychius, of the fourth century; Suidas, of the tenth; Zonaras, of the tenth or twelfth; and Gaze of the seventeenth?

Suidas has only *baptidzo*. He gives no definition of the word, and only says it is used with the accusative case. Gaze defines it, 'to dip repeatedly'; hence, for, to drench, to wash, to bathe."

Very truly yours, T. J. CONANT.

How can a man act thus? Yet Dr. Graves (Debate, p. 528), after I had expo-ed Dr Conant, suppresses all the above facts, by pretending

19. Parkhurst.* *"Baptidzo:* To dip, immerse, or plunge in water," etc. He supports immersion, then says, "3. To baptize, to immerse in, or wash with, water in token of purification from sin," etc. Then, "V. In a figurative sense, ' to baptize with the Holy Ghost.' It denotes the miraculous effusion [pouring out] of the Holy Ghost upon the apostles and other believers, as well on account of the abundance of his gifts (for anciently the water was copiously poured on those who were baptized, or they themselves were plunged therein)", etc.†

20. Walæus: "Indifferently, sprinkling or immersion."‡

21. Vossius gives immerse, etc., then, "III. To sprinkle."§

22. Arst gives as a proper New Testament meaning, "sprinkling" (*perfusionem*).

Vossuis above cites Matthew iii, 11, as a place where the baptism was by sprinkling. Alas, when immersion requires such a defense!¶

that such meanings as "shed forth," "besprinkle," "pour upon" are "figurative and secondary meanings"!

* We would not quote so ordinary a lexicon as this, but that immersionists quote him so often, and, like **Dr. Graves** (Debate, p. 281), suppress the very point in issue. He leaves out all that we cite above.

† Dr. Graves, A. Campbell, etc., always cited Parkhurst as supporting the Baptist view.

‡ *Aspersione an immersione* (Leigh's *Crit. Sacra*).

§ *Adspergere* (Leigh's *Crit. Sacra*).

¶ I went to the pains and expense to send to New York and Cambridge both, and secured exact copies of these two great lexicons, as they had been so incorrectly quoted on all sides. Dr. Conant professed to give the definitions of these authors, and suppressed all the very definitions in controversy! Dr. Graves tries to excuse himself for doing the same by shamelessly calling them figurative meanings! When can we settle a question if authors act thus?

In Carrollton debate, 1875, *rewritten* by Dr. Graves in April and

23. Liddell & Scott (classic), ed. 1850. "*Baptidzo:* To dip repeatedly, dip under; middle [voice] to bathe. Hence to steep, wet. Metaphor[ically],* soaked in wine; to pour upon, drench, over head and ears in debt, overwhelmed with questions. II. To dip a vessel to draw water. III. To baptize (New Testament)."

This work being professedly a translation of the great work of Passow, though much abridged really, was prepared especially, like Donnegan, Pickering, and Dunbar, for popular school use. But the Baptists raised such a roar of disgust over the words "poured upon," that the publishers to appease their fury erased them in subsequent editions in England and the United States. Drisler has tried to deny this (Carrollton Debate, p. 494-5), but the very fact that they also erased "pour [water for washing"] out of their edition under the word *louo*, though still retained in the English editions and quoted by the Baptist Ingham, on Baptism, p. 445, the work most relied on by Dr. Graves in his quotations, shows that it was the Baptist pressure that did it. On *louo* and its connection with baptism see the laver argument, and our chapter on Wash.† But we must in a note be-

May, 1876 (Debate, p. 283), he copies Suidas on *baptidzo* thus, "To immerse, to immerge to dip, to dip in," after Dr. Conant had told him Suidas does not define it at all, and I had so told him. He copies the errors of hosts of old citations in this way. It is shameful.

* Note here, "bathe" and "wet," as well as "steep," are not put as metaphorical meanings. Yet Dr. Graves always treats such as metaphorical—e. g. in case of Gazes.

† Dr. Graves (Carrollton debate) eulogizes this work so much that it is proper to add more than its character entitles it to at our hands. No one denies its excellence, for it is only an abridged translation of a great work, with, of course, a few additions on a few unimportant words, comparatively speaking. Liddell & Scott first define *baptidzo* as we quote it, and boast of their lexicon in a way soon to be quoted. 1. The first definition is "to dip repeatedly." Is that the *primary* meaning of *baptidzo?*

low give some facts on Liddell & Scott's Lexicon that will not only throw light upon its claims on this point, but also shed much light on the history of this word and philology. If it was the scholarship of Europe and America that forced Liddell & Scott to erase "pour upon," why all these other changes—at least eleven on

Do immersionists dip people repeatedly for baptism? O, but he took that out! Well, then, if he blundered on that point so seriously, may he not blunder on others? 2. He now has that part thus, "To dip in or under water (Aristoph. of ships), to sink them" (Polyb. ii, 51, etc.). Well, this is the last edition. Is it better than the first? If it is only "dip in" water, it never means that, nor does he cite a case where it does. It is "of ships, to sink them." Do ships that only dip sink? Never. If they sink, it is not dip, for to dip is to put in, partly or wholly, and immediately withdraw, take out. He cites *the same passage* to support *this* definition that he cited for the former. 3 He then gave "(2) to draw water." Where does it mean "to draw water"? He cites no case of *baptidzo* for that. But he erased that also. Did he? Wrong again, then! Mark that four changes. Well, he had "steep" in that edition. 5. O, but he took "steep" out! Did he? That makes five changes. 6. But he had "wet" as a meaning. But he took *that* out. That makes six changes! Pretty good, this; surely he is reliable! He has taken out so much good Baptists will sleep soundly now. As he professed to follow Passow's correct method, and "make each article a history of the word," surely he will stop now; for if he did this he could hardly blunder much. 7. But he had "drench" as a meaning. O, but he took that out. Indeed! Then Baptists can nod refreshingly, for this marks eight changes on one little word. But he does not stop. 8. In the first edition it was "overwhelmed with questions." In the second edition that meaning is changed [!!] to "a boy drowned with questions"! Nine changes, and worse still. "Drowned with questions"! That ought to do. Lexicons always render it, as a rule, either "confused" or "overwhelmed with questions." But in the last edition he changes that to "seeing him drowned with questions." *Ten* changes, and the same one citation in Plato given to sustain these changes! Will not ten changes do? No! 10. In the first edition it meant (2) "to dip a vessel, to draw water." Now he has "to draw wine from bowls in cups" (of course by dipping them).. In the Greek of this passage it is simply that they baptized, i. e. became drunk. out of [*ek*] the great winejars," etc. (See the passage examined under classic citations.) There is no dip in *baptidzo*—never. It is due to Liddell & Scott to say they

one word? Why did not that scholarship force Suicer, Swarzius, Stokius, Schneider, Schaetgennius, Schleusner, to take out pour, sprinkle, etc., found in all their editions, or words equivalent to both? And why allow the still later Passow, Rost, Palm, and Pape, late as 1874, to put in both "sprinkle" and "pour upon" in lexicons used universally by the great scholars of all countries?

24. Swarzius.* "*Baptidzo:* To baptize, immerse, to overwhelm, to dip into, to wash by immersing. Sometimes to sprinkle, to besprinkle, to pour upon," etc.

apologize for their lexicon by saying, "For the most part we had only *spare hours* to bestow" on the work—"time was limited" (Preface, xvii). But they say they "*always* sought to give the *earliest* authority for its *first*" meaning. Yet the earliest they give for immerse, i. e. "sink," is Polybius, one hundred and fifty or hundred and sixty years before Christ. The earliest for "dip" is long after Christ, and a false rendering. They tell us that there are few words that do not change their meanings in the downward course of time (2 Preface, xx). Also that a word occurs in Homer often only in a metaphorical sense that occurs in a literal sense first in Plato. This is correct, and is well said. *Baptidzo* meets us first in metaphorical use in Pindar, and never occurring in an extant author in a literal sense till *once* in Aristotle. All these things will be given in due time. But hear L. & S. (Preface, xx): "After the Attic writers, Greek underwent *a great change*." This change he notes as complete in *Polybius* and all later writers. Note well, then, that NO LEXICON IN EXISTENCE GIVES IMMERSE OR DIP AS A MEANING OF BAPTIDZO EARLIER THAN Polybius, Diodorus Siculus, AND PLUTARCH, Polybius being the earliest. Liddell & Scott do not give "immerse" in theirs at all, while Stephanus, Scapula, Pasor, Hedericus. do not give dip at all, as either a classic or Bible meaning. Liddell & Scott give a catalogue of their authors, that we may know the century and age in which they wrote; that we may "determine the time of a word's first usage, and of its subsequent changes of signification." This shows what they mean by primary meaning. Hence dip being supported by no early authority in L. & S.'s estimation, it is no "primary" meaning.

* See this lexicon, a large one indeed, and of high standing, quoted correctly, and word for word as above, in Ingham's Hand-book on Baptism (Baptist work, p. 40); and in Booth's (a Baptist) Pedobaptist (in Baptist Library, p. 351-2).

25. E. Leigh's *Critica Sacra* (Lexicon) New Testament. "*Baptidzo:* To baptize (occurs thus often), from *bapto*, to wet, to plunge, etc., and primarily may signify any kind of washing, or immersion, which may be in water-vessels in which we immerse linen. Yet generally and very frequently it is taken also for any kind of washing, cleansing, or purification, even of that where is no immersion, as Matthew iii, 11, 22; Mark vii, 4, etc., etc."* He, then, quoting a number of texts in support of this, quotes Vossius where it is, "III. To sprinkle or cleanse the body of any one sacramentally (Matt. iii, 11)." †

26. Suicer, whom Dr. Smith thinks the best lexicon ever prepared for the interpretation of New Testament words, and certainly for its purpose the ablest extant, elaborates the word through a series of large folio pages in its patristic use. He tells us *baptidzo* is stronger than *epipoladzo*, to swim lightly, and " less than *dunein;*" but as Conant and Carson ‡ crush this silly theory of Beza, Vossius, Suicer, etc., we need not quote it so often in the old writers. Then, pursuing the view of the old school, he says, as Beza does in substance, " But because any thing is accustomed to be mersed or dipped that it may be washed and cleansed, hence it occurs as *taval* [*tabhal*] in the Hebrew, which the Seventy translate (2 Kings v, 14)

---

* Βαπτίζω, baptizo, *sœpe* . . . *a* βάπτω, *tingo, mergo,* etc., *et primario significet istiusmodi lotionem seu immersionem, quœ in vasis aquariis sit, quibus lintea immergimus; tamen largius et latius etiam sumitur pro quocunque genere ablutionis, prolutionsi seu mundationis, etiam illius, cui nulla immersionis species adest; ut* Matt. iii, 11, *et* xx, 22; Marc. vii, 4, etc., etc.

† III. *Aspergere seu abluere corpus alicujus sacramentaliter* (Matt. iii, 11). To cite the number of times that Dr. G. misquotes Leigh would be a waste of paper. Leigh, after the above, cites a number of authors *on both* sides of the question up to his time, and Dr. G. cites the immersionists invariably, *as Dr. Leigh!!*

‡ Carson on Baptism, 64, 66; Conant, *Baptidzein*, 104, 156-9.

by *bantidzo*, and is taken for *rachats*, which is to wash; similarly in Greek 'to *baptidzein*,' by a metalepsis is used for the same [*lavare*, to wash], as Judith xii, 8 (?) [7]; Sirach xxxiv, 30; Luke xi, 38." He then shows the fathers use it for immerse also in vast numbers of cases after the fourth century. Then " the thing signified is represented by immersion or sprinkling."*

27. Schneider, the next best classic lexicon issued, Leibzig, 1819. *Baptidzo*, from *bapto*: I dip under; thence as *brecko* [i. e. moisten, shed forth, sprinkle.] Also metaphorically to be thoroughly drunk, overwhelm with debts, etc. [classics given]; . . . to wash," etc.

28. Wolfius: "This word [*baptidzo*, Luke xi, 38] means washing done by sprinkling." †

29. Passow. The great Passow, the master critic of all classic lexicons, to whom Liddell & Scott, Pickering, and all others now profess to look for aid, we reserve as the last Greek lexicon quoted, next to the Thesaurus of Stephens the largest—three large volumes, the first containing eighteen hundred and eighty-four double-column pages, fine print—thus deposes: " *Baptidzo*, from *bapto*: 1. Oft and repeatedly to immerse, submerse, with *eis* [into] and *pros ti*, in respect to any thing. . . Thence to moisten, to wet, sprinkle, *hoi bebaptismenoi*, translate, made drunk, *vino madidi* [Latin, soaked with wine]. Generally to besprinkle, to pour upon, to overwhelm, to burden with taxes, with debts (oppress), to confuse with

* Thesaurus Eccles. E. Pat. Græcis, 2 vols., folio, 1728—*Res significata, quæ per immersionem aut aspersionem adumbratur.*

† Ed. 1841, p. 489, vol. 1.—Βαπτίζω (βάπτω), oft u. wiederhalt eintauchen, undertauchen. Εἰς *u.* πρός τι Plut. auch ἔντινι dah. Benetzen, anfeuchten, begiessen . . . betrunken, *vino madidi*, uber, übergiessen, uberschutten, uberhaufen, mit Abgaben, mit schulden überladen mit fragen überschuttet (2 Schöpfen, 3 taufen, med.), sich taufen lossen; auch baden, waschen.

questions. 2. Pump water. 3. Baptize, suffer oneself to be baptized, also to bathe, to wash."*

30. Rost and Palm, in three volumes, the latest save Pape. "*Baptidzo:* †Oft and repeatedly to immerse, to submerse. . . . To moisten, to wet, to sprinkle, made drunk, *vino madidi.* Generally to besprinkle, to pour upon,‡ to overwhelm, to burden with taxes, with debts, to oppress. (2) Draw [or pump] water. (3) To baptize, to suffer oneself to be baptized; also to bathe, to wash." We close this illustrious list with the latest and distinguished lexicographer, Prof. W. Pape, of Berlin, 1874, in three volumes.

31. Pape. "*Baptidzo:* § To immerse, to submerse, Plut. [extracts and renderings given to sustain this all from late Greek]; to moisten [or wet], to besprinkle [or pour upon, to besprinkle¶]; [*hoi bebaptismenoi*] those drunk, Plato. To overwhelm with debts, Plutarch."

* *Verbum hoc lationem inferat, aspersione. factam.* Conf. . . . Doylingii—Observat. Sacr. Wolfii Philol. et Crit., editio tertia, i, p. 658. A semi-lexicon and expositor of vast learning.

† German same as in Passow, last quoted, which see. Lünemann's Lat. Deut. Hand-worterbuch, 1831, defines *perfundo*, begiessen, oder benetzen. *Fundo* [pour] by giessen oder ausgiessen, etc.; auch schütten, etc.

‡ Ingham, Baptist, in his Hand-book on Baptism, London, recently issued, says, page 94, "Thus Professor Rost, in his German Greek-Lexicon, revised with the assistance of a native Greek, . . . under the words *wash, wet, pour,* and the like [has] *waschen, benetzen, giessen, begiessen* . . . (Chris. Rev. vol. iii, p. 97.)" So here they agree that *giessen, begiessen* is used for "*pour,*" not "pour *over,*" as Dr. Graves's friend Toy rendered it to conceal the truth, and by Rost in the above lexicon.

§ Βαπτίζω. 1. Eintauchen, undertauchen; Plat., Quæst. Nat. 10; Πλοῖα schiffe, etc. (Pol. viii, 8, etc.), scheint βαπτίζεται er wird auf dem Meer herumgetrieben — anfeuchten, BEGIESSEN. Οἱ βεβαπτισομενοι, die betrunkenen Plat. mit schulden überladen Plut. da ich den knaben schon gantz tzeigedeckt sot, durch die Sophisterein des Gegners, Plat. 2. Ἐκ πίθων (Schöffen, Plut. iii, N. T. u. K. S.), taufen. Med. sich taufen lassen, βάπτισμα die Taufe, N. T.

¶ Like the Latin *perfundere* " begeisgen " means both to pour upon and to besprinkle—perfuse. See the word in Passow, Rost, and Palm.

2. "To draw water" [out of any thing], etc.

3. "In the New Testament and ecclesiastical historians, to baptize. Middle voice, to suffer oneself to be baptized. *Baptisma*, the baptism, in New Testament."

In the light of these facts what are we to think of the cry that no lexicon, ancient or modern, ever gave sprinkle or pour as a meaning of *bapto* or *baptidzo?* Notice well—

1. That every one of these lexicons, save two, and the great authors among the fathers who speak lexicographically, out of the thirty-one, give either sprinkle or pour or (Schneider and Robinson) words equivalent to both, as meanings and uses of *baptidzo.* The two exceptions are Sophocles, who gives "perform ablution, to bathe, bathed in tears," where it is "baptize with tears"—surely not immersion; and Stephanus, who never gives dip as a meaning at all, who never gives immerse as a New Testament meaning, but expressly gives the New Testament meaning thus: "*Abluo, lavo*"—only that, "to cleanse, to wash." Whenever *lavo* is modal it is "besprinkle," and every Latin lexicon we ever saw gives that as a prominent meaning. Baptize "with tears" is certainly affusion. Hence, thus—

2. Every one of the thirty-one authorities sustain affusion as baptism.

3. Scapula, Pasor, Schrevellius,* Hedericus, Morell, etc., etc., mere abridgments of Stephanus, all give "*abluo, lavo*," from Stephanus, as the only meanings it has as an ordinance in the New Testament, not one giving dip or immerse as a New Testament meaning. *Abluo* is "to cleanse"—no special mode. *Lavo* is to wash, bathe, besprinkle—never dip or immerse. If our opponents insist

---

* Schrevellius giving simply immergo for classic usage. *Baptize* and *lavo*=wash, bathe, besprinkle, as its N. T. meaning.

on the classic lexicons as proper authorities here they must abide their decision, that in the New Testament *baptidzo* is never modal save when it is by sprinkling—never dip, never immerse.

4. Not a lexicon on earth gives *abluo, lavo* as a classic meaning of *baptidzo*.

5. If six men testify in court that A killed B, using a generic or general term, and twenty-one good witnesses testify that A killed B, shooting him through the head, will not all say there is no discrepancy, that what the six meant by kill the twenty-one mean by their terms? And in view of the fact that kill embraces shoot as one of its modes of destroying; that shooting effects killing; that in that case they mean to agree with the twenty-one? So these lexicons, Scapula, Stephanus, Pasor, Schrevellius, Hedericus and many more mean by "*abluo, lavo*," what these others do by sprinkle, pour, etc., etc. Hence,

6. The great school of lexicography is unanimously with us on this question.

7. If Blackstone, Coke, Kent, Greenleaf, Chitty, etc. all agree on a point of law, sustained by the Pandects and Cicero; if Johnson, Walker, Richardson, Worcester, and Webster all substantially agree in the meaning of a word, would not that end controversy on that point? We would hang, convict a president, go to war, all on such testimony, if the case depended only on whether it were so or not, and such testimony were adduced that it was so. Note again—

8. Those lexicons were all made either, first, by immersionists (though they dipped their infants) when immersion was the law of the land, and the only popular mode—Buddæus, 1529; Stephanus, 1572; or, second, by those who merely abridged the work of Stephens, copying

him word for word generally throughout, but leaving off references that so fill up the space—Scapula, Pasor, Hedericus, Schrevellius,* etc., etc.; or, third, by those who abridged and diluted in translating Stephens's Latin into English liberally—Donnegan, Dunbar, Pickering, etc.; or, fourth, by those who still felt their influence and did not wholly start out scientifically—Schneider, Passow, Kouma, Gazes, etc.—yet made a great advance.

9. Not one shows that dip or immerse was the primary meaning. They do not treat of primaries, but aim at popular, current meanings. The very fact that nearly all their citations of proof-texts are from the later classic Greek, and not one cites the earliest nor takes note of it on either *bapto* or *baptidzo* in order, nor on the latter at all, demonstrates that point. Had they been treating of primary meanings common decency would have compelled them to take the primal occurrences of *baptidzo*, and that first, whereas not one of them cites the earliest cases of it at all.

10. That this was so, further appears from their entire want of harmony in defining *bapto* and *baptidzo*. Not one of the great body of old classic lexicons gives dip. as a meaning of *baptidzo* — NOT ONE, including Stephanus, Scapula, Hedericus, Pasor, Schrevellius, Robertson, nor Ewing, Wahl, Schaetgennius, Arst, Morell, and many others. But Carson says it means nothing but dip. Of all the above not one gives dip. Arst gives "overwhelm" first; Schrevellius and others give baptize first; Ewing gives "cover" first—a meaning it never has. Schleusner gives definitions wholly different in his two great lexicons; the one for the Greek of the old Testa-

* A. Campbell tells us originally Schrevellius had only *mergo*, sink, and *lavo*.

ment, the other for that of the New. They may be said to define *baptidzo* radically different—being wholly unlike. Wahl, a learned contemporary of Schleusner defines it in his first edition, first, *lavo*, wash, then in brackets, classic use, demerse, submerse; then, "second (New Testament use), immerse." In a second edition the same year, 1829, he reverses that, adds "*overwhelm*," "*imbue*," takes out "demerse, submerse," adds its New Testament use as equivalent to the νίπτω (*nipto*) of New Testament (Mark vii, 3, e. g.). But in 1831, only two years later, he brings out an edition, changes it again, takes out "immerse" from one place of New Testament usage, heading a list of references, and puts in its place sprinkle (*perfundo*). He is the strongest immersionist of all New Testament lexicographers. Yet how can we rely on such changes as these? If scientific accuracy and philological laws were his guide this could not be. Liddell & Scott defines it "dip repeatedly," "wet, moisten, pour upon," etc. Under Baptist pressure they erase wet or "moisten, pour upon" from later editions. Baptists feel delighted at this. Now they have a lexicon that suits them. What a shout they raised! They declare, then, that no definition is reliable that is not supported by one or more references to Greek writers where it has the meaning given. Alas for that, for the first definition by Liddell & Scott can not be supported by a single citation in the whole republic of letters. It no where means "to dip repeatedly."* Yet this is his first definition. Through a number of editions there it has stood, a living falsehood stalking down through the years to tell what blunders can be committed where no scientific method is adopted on the word. They are all equally wild on *bapto*, equally antagonistic, untrue as to

* See new Graves-Ditzler Debate, p 527, 401-2.

method. Clearly and evidently the lexicons never aimed at tracing primitive, but current meanings, as exhibited especially in later writers. Nay, the fact that Wahl, Schleusner, Liddell & Scott, Swarzius, etc., etc. do all begin with the later Greek writers, not a lexicon in the world beginning with the earlier—not to say earliest, as they all ought—shows the immense influence Buddæus, Stephanus, and Robert Constantine exerted on our lexicography through their ignorance of earlier writers.

11. To the thoughtful scholar it is a most important matter that no lexicon has yet given Aristotle's use of *baptidzo*, the first literal use of it known, nor that of the Greeks before Plato. It shows that where Stephanus and Buddæus stopped on that word their successors in the lexical work tarried.

It is a favorite dodge of immersionists that wash, cleanse (*lavo*, *abluo*), as well as moisten, sprinkle, pour, are metaphorical meanings of *baptidzo;* so meant by the lexicons. To this we reply—

(1) By the whole body of the old lexicons, Buddæus, Stephanus, Scapula, Hedericus, Pasor, Schrevellius, Morell, etc., *lavo*, *abluo* (wash, cleanse) were the only New Testament definitions given. Hence were literal, real meanings. Whether held as derived meanings or not—and they did so hold—derived meanings, all others agree, are as literal and real as the primary meanings, the latter often becoming actually obsolete. Derived meanings are not to be confounded with metaphorical uses of meanings.

(2) The "sprinkle" and "pour upon" are as literal meanings as the immerse in those lexicons, so meant by them. As stated, not one of them was discussing primaries, and the fact that they all date immerse as a late meaning shows that clearly enough.

12. By the rule Dr. Graves lays down since these papers were prepared, wash, cleanse, sprinkle, pour, as the modes of the wash, cleanse, are the primary meanings of *baptidzo*. Not only so, but by his rule they are the only meanings. Debate, p. 322, Dr. Graves says, " As derivatives sometimes lose the last shade of the signification of their primitive or root-origin—as *tingo* once primarily meant to dip, second, to dye, now it has lost its first, and its secondary has become its primary—we are compelled to go to standard Latin authors and learn the signification they attach to it."

By this rule, along with his other, that the first meaning attached by lexicons (Debate, p. 253) is the primary and current meaning, wash, cleanse, effected by sprinkle, pour, is the only New Testament meaning of *baptidzo;* for nine tenths of all the lexicons give these as the first and only New Testament meanings. We pass by the absurdities of the above as well as its untrue assertion on *tingo*, as it is fully treated elsewhere.

13. Our position harmonizes all the facts and all the meanings of *baptidzo;* is in perfect harmony with the laws of language, the principles of philology in all languages, whether Semitic or Aryan (Indo-European), and hence can not be wrong.

14. We will see that the lexicography of Hebrew and all the languages of the earliest versions will overwhelmingly support affusion as the apostolic mode of baptism. We reserve them till we treat of classic use.

15. Hence we see the force of Carson's noted words, " My position is, that it [*baptidzo*] always signifies to dip; never expressing any thing but mode. Now, as I have all the lexicographers and commentators against me in this opinion, it will be necessary to say a word or two

with respect to the authority of lexicons. Many may be startled at the idea of refusing to submit to the unanimous authority of lexicons as an instance of the boldest skepticism" (pp. 55, 56). Yes; we should think so. He then urges that lexicons "are not an ultimate authority." "Actual inspection" of the places where it occurs must settle its meaning. This is true; but had not they done this as well as Dr. C.

CHAPTER XIV.

PHILOLOGY.

There is something, as already shown, inhering in the Bible use of *baptidzo* which purify, wash, sprinkle, immerse, dip, separately or all combined, can not represent. Had purify or sanctify merely been meant, *kathairo, katharidzo, hagiadzo* would have been used. Had *wash* merely been meant, *louo, nipto, pluno, apokludzo* would have been used. Had *immersion* been meant, *kataduo, buthidzo, pontidzo, katapontidzo, enduo* would have been used. Had *sprinkle* merely been meant, *raino, rantidzo, katapasso,* or *proscheo,* etc. would have been used. No other word than *baptidzo* itself does or can represent the ordinance in its full and true import. No other word perfectly translates it as it habitually occurs in the New Testament. Wash, far more properly sprinkle, more perfectly represents it in Mark vii, 4, and Luke xi, 38, because it is not there used as a heaven-sanctioned rite, and it was a mere sprinkling of water for traditional baptism. Immerse, dip, plunge, sprinkle, pour are but actions, not implying necessarily any religious idea or fact, nor the unity, power, or effect of religious truth; nay, not the element itself—water. When, therefore, we show that primarily *baptidzo* has this or derivatively another meaning, as a word applied to express an action, it does not follow that either of these meanings will fairly represent it when applied to a rite. Such a thing never occurs as to any word. The original

PHILOLOGY. 169

Hebrew for circumcise, paschal feast, etc. are illustrations.

People are immersed, dipped, plunged in oil, in blood, in mud, in filth, in trouble. These words imply merely actions or modes of doing, and are but parts of the whole accomplished. As sprinkle, pour upon, dip, immerse, plunge are but actions by which some fact may be accomplished, and hence are but a part of the thing done or fact accomplished, they are only a part thereof and can not be equivalent to the whole.

Let us now examine the philological foundation of all the assumptions of immersionists. It assumes—

1. That immersion is a primary idea, which is impossible and absurd.

2. That immersion and dip are exactly the same.

3. That immersion is the primary meaning of *baptidzo* and its root, *bapto*, without a word of proof offered.

4. That wash, cleanse, is a philological effect of immersion, which will be found to be against all the facts and science of language, and utterly unhistoric besides.

Immersion is itself a compound in form and meaning and a derivative in thought. The English of immerse is "sink in."*

1. The idea of sinking in is not a primary. To sink in implies pressure and a yielding element. Hence it is not a primary or simple idea. In different languages immersion is often a derivative from press, burden, overburden, and it always implies that. Whatever falls upon, pours upon, rolls upon, presses down, and if the objects receiving such elements are in a condition to sink, that ensues of course. Whatever may fall or pour upon an object, there-

* *In*, put "im" for euphony, and *mergo*, to sink. This fact, meaning "sink in," will be duly elaborated and proved. A. Campbell, Conant, Wilkes, Graves, all support it.

fore, is liable to immerse it. Hence the hosts of words we shall find meaning sprinkle, pour, etc. that come to mean immerse.

2. Mersion, immersion, is so far from implying washing, cleansing, as a sequence, that it does not involve or imply any particular element, and as often applies to filth, to mud, etc. as to any other element.

3. Indeed immersion constantly occurs in Latin, in Greek, Hebrew, Syriac, Persic, Arabic, German, and in English, etc. etc., where just the reverse of wash, cleanse, is to be found. Persons and things are immersed in mud, in filth, in blood, in dye, in vats, in stenchy pools, in slime. Hence in many languages it means to contaminate, defile, make filthy. Gesenius, Castell, and Schindler thus define *tama*.*

4. In no language of which we have any knowledge does any word that properly and primarily implies mersion, dipping — that is, used generally and properly for mersion, immersion, or dipping — mean to wash, cleanse, or purify. In no lexicon, and in no writer in Latin, Greek, Hebrew, Syriac, Arabic, Persic, Æthiopic, Chaldee, Italian, Spanish, German, or Portuguese, did we ever find a passage where immerse, dip, or plunge meant to wash or cleanse or purify. No lexicon we ever saw defines any word that properly and strictly meant immerse, dip, or plunge by to wash or cleanse or purify. The Hebrew *tabha*, immerse,† the Greek *enduo, kataduo, pontidzo, bu-*

---

* טָמֵא, *tama*, Arabic, to immerse, "defile, to contaminate" (Gesenius). "The primary idea is that of immersing" (Gesenius). Yet "unclean, defiled, polluted" (Lev. xv, 32; xxi, 4; Hos. ix, 4).

† טָבַע *tabha;* Hottinger, *immersus;* Gesenius, *immersit;* Castell, *immersus;* Schindler, *immersus;* so Buxtorf, etc. Not one begins *tabhal* with immerse. טָבַל, *mersit, submersus fuit, demersus fuit, im,* and *submersus aquâ.* Castell, Freytag, Schindler.

thidzo, katapontidzo, immerse, *dupto, kolumbao,* to dip,* often occur, and are rendered in our Bible by the English of immerse—"to sink," e. g. Exodus xv, 5, 10; Psalms cxxiv, 4; lxix, 2, 15; liv, 9; Ecclesiastes x, 12; Jeremiah ii, 2; Matthew xviii, 6; xiv, 30; 1 Timothy vi, 9; Luke v, 7; 2 Maccabees (Apoc.) xii, 4.

PRINCIPLES OF PHILOLOGY.

The following words in Arabic definitely mean to immerse, never sprinkle, rain, or pour: 1, *gamasa;* 2, *gamara;* 3, *amasa;* 4, *dala;* 5, *atta* (עט); 6, *gara;* 7, *gautsa, guts*†—seven words all meaning repeatedly to immerse; most of them mean to immerse in water. Yet not one of them ever means to wash. Not one of them ever means to intoxicate, to overflow, overwhelm, inundate, intoxicate, make drunk, moisten, wet, rain—never have those meanings that so perfectly inhere in *bapto* or *baptidzo*—never mean stain, dye, color. Notice by the Latin below that often immerse comes from *depress, oppress,* and words that mean to immerse or dip never mean to wash, etc. ONLY where sprinkle, pour, moisten, etc. are the primary meanings, and immerse a derived meaning. The Æthiopic has a word (*maab*) for immerse; but it never means wash, cleanse, wet, intoxicate, etc. The Persic has a word

---

* Δύπτω, *tauchen, undertauchen;* Passow, Rost, Palm, Pope, Pape — *dupto, undertauchen, kephalas eis hudor.*

† Arab. חמם, *demersit eum in aquam, demersit semet in aquam, mergantur,* etc. גמר (*gamara*), *mersit, submersus fuit, demersus fuit, im-, submersus aquâ;* ראל (Heb. רול), *depressit immersit ve in aquâ;* עט, *atta, oppressit, demersit, depresserunt . . . merserunt,* vii *demersus in aquam fuit, semet immersit, compressio;* עור, Arab. *gara, descendit, depressus fuit, demersus fuit* (three times repeated), *depressus;* עוץ, Arab. *gautsa, se demersit sub aquam, submersit.* Castell, Schindler, Freytag.

ghuta, to immerse in water;* yet it never means to wash, cleanse, etc. The Hebrew words for immerse properly and strictly mean primarily to impress, depress, then immerse. Thus *tabha*,† which in the Bible always means immerse, *kaphash*,‡ to depress, impress, immerse; *shaqah*,§ to submerse, depress into the deep, compress, demerse. The German dip, dip under, immerse,¶ no more mean to wash, to cleanse, than does our dip, sink. First, it is remarkable too from the standpoint of immersionists that not one of all these words for immerse is ever used in all the ancient versions translated from the original for baptize. It is well to notice, second, that dip never comes from immerse in all these words; third, that all words that properly and certainly mean to immerse, submerse, not only never mean dip, but are not defined by *tingo*, *intingo* as is *tabhal* and *bapto*. They are never used by any lexicon to define *tabha*, immerse. In Arabic *dahaka* means "to depress or immerse with violence" or force, while *yachal* means "to demerse, and make filthy."

Is it not astonishing that men of learning should base their main arguments on supposed laws of language assumed to be fundamental, being the foundation on which all their superstructure rests, so absolutely vain and a pure delusion? They assume that wash, cleanse, is the effect of immersion, a philological effect based on fact, and proceed from that standpoint to make their arguments, when not an instance has ever been adduced to vindicate the bold

---

* *Maab, maba;* Æthiopic, *submersit* (Castell); *Ghuta*, Persic, *in aquam immergere, demersio in aquam* (Castell).

† טבע, *tabha, figi, infigi, immergi demergi* (Buxtorf, Castell).

‡ כבש, *kaphash, depressit . . . immersit* (Castell).

§ שקע, *submersus, in profundum depressus, compressus est, demersit* (Castell).

‖ *Tauchen, untertauchen, sinken.*

assumption, and not a fact in the whole babbling earth can be adduced to support it. Nay, so far from it being supported, there is every reason why the reverse should be true, since immersion is so far from philologically implying washing that there is no necessary connection between the two ideas, immersion applying as readily to soiling, staining, defiling, and corrupting elements as purifying ones. Indeed Dr. Conant and Prof. Mell, of Georgia, tell us truly that *bapto* and *baptidzo* take as the elements into which they "put" the subject, "honey, wax, . . . gall, oil, vinegar, soup, moist earth, broth, fat, filth" (Mell, pp. 13, 14, on Baptism, replying to Dr. Summers). Here every element named defiles, unless the vinegar be excepted. Surely, as these are the elements, save water, into which *baptidzo* (for it takes them all; *bapto* takes "dirt;" both take "the human body," and often "blood") introduces its subjects when meaning to immerse, it argues poorly for wash as a consequent meaning. Note well, in not an author or place where *baptidzo* does mean to immerse does it ever mean to wash, cleanse, or purify.

PHILOLOGY, OR SCIENCE OF LANGUAGE.

While on the one hand immerse and dip, i. e. the proper words for dip or immerse, never mean to wash, cleanse, it will be found that in various ancient languages, especially in all those in which the Bible was originally written and its earliest versions made, the words for wash, both as to the body and the hands and face, the proper words for wash, cleanse, never mean to dip, immerse, but do in most cases radically mean—some of them, to sprinkle, others to moisten where it is by falling rain, dew, or slight aspersion of liquid; or as in other cases, words are used meaning to pour, shed forth, drop, as of water; or as in others still they mean wash, pour, sprinkle, as *louo, nipto*. In Hebrew we have *rachats*, wash, pour; *kabas*, wash; while *matar*, to rain, wet with rain, sprinkle,* is rendered by *nipto*, to wash, and in Arabic is "to sprinkle, pour, rain, wet," yet to wash, to cleanse.† In Arabic *gasala* is to wash, sprinkle, perfuse; never dip, immerse. It is the word most constantly used for wash. In German *waschen, baden*, wash, bathe; in Latin *lavo, abluo;* their corresponding words in French, Spanish, Italian, Portuguese never mean dip or immerse. On *nipto, pluno* (from *pluo*, to moisten, wet, rain),‡ to wash, sprinkle, *louo*, wash, pour, sprinkle,§ see the fuller facts in the separate chapter on Wash. In Æthiopic *rachats*, wash, means primarily to sweat, perspire, and then in Arabic next it means to wash, to cleanse, because perspiring profusely cleanses. We see wash derived from pour, rain, sprinkle, sweat, moisten—never from immerse.

The English Liddell & Scott's Greek Lexicon gives under "*louo*, wash, pour [water for washing"]. Many other authorities support the same, none against. See chapter on Wash.

There is another word we may notice in Greek that means to wash as well as to wet, moisten, rendered "wetted" by Dr. Conant and Elder Wilkes (Louisville Debate, p. 619). It is used by Clemens Alexandrinus, A.D. 190, and Theophylact as defining *baptidzo* as to mode. It

* *Pluviâ rigatus, depluit, pluviam demisit.* Arabic, *fluit, perfudit, perfusus, fluit,* etc.

† *Lavando urgeni et mundando* (Castell, 2043). Other words in Hebrew, etc. of affusion meaning to wash, cleanse, etc. will be given in abundance soon.

‡ Benetzen, anfeuchten. Latin, *pluo* v. *fluo*. Passow, Rost, Palm, Pape.

§ Galen, Stephanus, Hippocrates.

means to wash. It is compounded of *hugros*, liquid, water, same as *hudōr*, water, and *raino*, to sprinkle. Here the word *raino*, the root of *rantidzo*, to sprinkle, comes to apply to washing, as well as other words of like primary force.

The Hebrew word wash (*rachats, louo, nipto*, etc. in Greek) primarily means "to bubble up, to flow, pour out, to drip." It is translated pour (*cheo*) in the Septuagint also. For more details on wash we refer to a future chapter in this work on Wash. See the index. We see that wash is not derivable from immerse; it is from sprinkle and pour.

CHAPTER XV.

Philology, or Science of Language.

Having shown now beyond question that immerse is not the primary of wash, or purify, or cleanse—that wash does not and can not philologically be derived from immerse, and that it is derived constantly from words that both primarily and constantly mean to sprinkle, to pour, and to wet or moisten simply, where words are used mostly applicable to water (*kludzo, hugros, hudor* with *raino*, sprinkle)—we proceed to show a number of words that primarily mean to sprinkle, in some cases; to pour in others; to moisten, wet, in others, where it is by affusion, that derivatively come to mean to dip, to overflow, overwhelm, drown, immerse, showing that immerse is philologically derived from affusion, affusion never from immerse.

Immersionists are settled in nothing more securely to their own satisfaction than in this: If a word means to sprinkle or pour it never can mean, or come to mean, to immerse or dip. Hence as pedobaptists acknowledge that *baptidzo* in classic Greek often means to immerse as well as to whelm, etc., why, it can never include any other mode or action than immerse.

1. Dr. Fraser (Baptism, p. 70): "It must remain an impossibility to reconcile such opposite modes of application as dipping and sprinkling."

2. Prof. Wilson speaks of "The absurdity of attaching opposite meanings to the same term." "The false

principle that the verb denotes the two distinct acts of sprinkling and bathing" (184, 185).

3. R. Ingham (Hand-book on Chris. Baptism, London, 1865, pp. 184, 185): "We deny not that a copious sprinkling may approximate to pouring; yea, that a sprinkling might be so abundant that one person would call it pouring and another would call it sprinkling. Nor do we deny that in any language there is a word which may not sometimes be used in the sense of pouring and sometimes in the sense of sprinkling. Our belief is that in no cultivated language under heaven does one word mean definitely to immerse and also to pour and to sprinkle. . . . Between immersion and either of the other two there is an impassable gulf. . . . The explicit testimony of lexicons that *baptizo* signifies to immerse, we regard as evidence that it does not signify to pour or to sprinkle. . . . We hesitate not to appeal to any man to find a word which definitely signifies to immerse in the English, or Latin, or Greek, or Hebrew language, and which also signifies to pour and to sprinkle. We might now leave this subject," etc. (109).

Dr. Fuller: "If it means to immerse then it does not mean to sprinkle or to pour." "Indeed if it means immerse it can not mean to sprinkle or pour" (pp. 15, 25).

4. Hinton and Pres't Shannon: "Now if baptism does indeed mean immerse, as all admit, it must (to say the very least) be doubtful whether it can also mean to sprinkle or to pour. Immerse, sprinkle, and pour are three distinct ideas, expressed by different words in all languages" (H. quoting S., p. 44).

5. Dr. Carson (Baptism, p. 52): "But if the word originally signifies to pour or to sprinkle, no process can be supposed by which it would come to denote **to dye**.

. . . . The two meanings can have no consanguinity."
"7. I will state another canon equally self-evident, and equally fatal to the doctrine of Mr. Ewing and all our opponents. A word that applies to two modes can designate neither. . . . Without reference, then, to the practice of the language, on the authority of self-evident truth, I assert that *bapto* can not signify both to dip and pour or sprinkle. I assert that in no language under heaven can one word designate two modes. Now, we have the confession of our opponents themselves that *baptizo* signifies to dip. If so, it can not also signify to pour or sprinkle" (p. 90).

6. A. Campbell (Chris. Baptism, pp. 147-149): "The force of this argument recognizes only a concession which no man can refuse, namely, that *baptizo* once signifies to dip or immerse. This point conceded, and, according to the law in such cases, it must always signify to dip." "If, then, *baptizo* once means to dip, it never can mean sprinkle, pour, or purify, unless these actions are identically the same."

Yet Carson admits *bapto* is applied to sprinklings.

CAN A WORD MEAN TO DIP AND TO SPRINKLE?

To strengthen this they quote Leviticus xiv, 6-8, 15, 16, where the priest pours (*yatsak*) [χέω, *cheo*], dips (*taval*) *bapto*, and *sprinkles* [*nazah*, ραίνω, *raino*], the blood. Now, says the immersionist, this shows "a clear distinction made in English and Greek betwixt dipping, pouring, and sprinkling." Ingham, p. 109; see Louisville Debate also, p. 540; Mell, pp. 10, 11. This is regarded as a Gibralter of immersion power. Let us see how readily it crumbles before the batteries of truth.

1. If these be the invariable words for these specific actions it utterly annihilates our opponents and leaves us untouched; for the word dip in the corresponding Greek is not *baptidzo* but *bapto*, which is only the root of the word, and they say it has nothing to do with the ordinance.

2. It is only a partial dip and does not imply submergence. They demand a complete covering of the subject.

3. As dip occurs fifteen times in the Old Testament and several times in the New, why is *bapto* used every time in the Greek where any dip occurs in reality in the original? for all ancient versions render 2 Kings v, 14, by wash, not by dip, i. e. *lavo, secho, waschen*, etc.

4. Neither dip, immerse, sprinkle, nor pour as mere actions can represent *baptidzo* in the religious sense it has in the Bible. In the above passages the dip and pour are mere subordinate actions, not words of ordinance. Purification was the ordinance; these actions were to aid in accomplishing it; hence mere words of action alone.

5. Only one of these words is here meant to be *modal*, that is the word sprinkle, nor is it necessarily so. The mode was not involved in the pour and dip. The one was to put the element in the left hand—the log of oil. The bird, only in part (see Jamieson, *in loc.*), cedar, hyssop, and scarlet wool were to be baptized with (*taval*) the blood of the slain bird, and mode was not involved, and its head and wings were not even wet with the element, though the bird was baptized.

6. The word *yatsak* (יִצֹק) pour, is translated sprinkle repeatedly in the various Greek, Latin, and English versions, while the word *nazah*, sprinkle, is rendered wet, moisten, overflow . . by the highest authorities.

7. Yet, our opponents assume that each of these words

has a single, definite, specifically-settled meaning in the Bible, never departing therefrom, albeit they demand *nazah*, sprinkle, shall be held to mean "*astonish*," in Isaiah lii, 15, "So shall he sprinkle many nations," not allowing it to refer to the commission, "baptize" all nations. They say *cheo* being used in Greek for pour, *raino* for sprinkle, *bapto* for dip [Hebrew *yatsak, nazah, tabal*], these words can mean nothing else, because here set in such contrast. Yet when Christ poured water in a basin, and on various occasions when pour occurs, not only did he use a different word (*ballo*) altogether, but when the people were sprinkled that word for pour is often used. Nay, the Greek has thirteen different words meaning to sprinkle, and several more being quite equivalent, as *tengo* (τέγγω), a number for pour, while the Hebrew has between seventeen and twenty for pour, eighteen for sprinkle. See the list of some of them at the end of the chapter on Wash. To fasten on one of each of these as if it alone was and could be used to express the idea demanded, and deduce thence a fundamental law in philology, is the extremity of weakness.

Let us now put these canons or laws, so implicitly relied on as the pillars of the immersion theory,to an actual test on words, many of which are not related to this question, and see whether or not the same word may not mean to sprinkle and to dip, to pour and to overwhelm, to sprinkle, to pour, and to immerse. We will test it in every language that entered into the original composition and earliest and best versions of the Bible.

1. [נָקַע, *naka* or *naga*]. The primary force given by Fürst, Gesenius, Schindler, and Castell is to rend with violence, break off, be violent. In Arabic it means, "to sprinkle, to soften (by application of water), to moisten,

PHILOLOGY, OR SCIENCE OF LANGUAGE. 181

to make wet, to wash, to dip, to penetrate. Schindler.*
In Æthiopic the root is traced clearly to effervesce, bubble
or sparkle up of water, break off,† gush forth, applied to
a fountain of water breaking forth. See Psalms xxxv, 10;
lxxvii, 49. So in Arabic it means "to pour together,
flow-over, soften, saturate." But not only does Schindler
make it mean to dip, penetrate into, but Castell also, "to
be immersed in water, ... collection of saliva in the
mouth, to immerse oneself in water, descend, be immersed." ‡

2. [שָׁטַף shataph]. Gesenius defines this word "to
gush or pour forth, to flow abundantly; (2) overflow.
The rain pouring out."§ Fürst gives the primary meaning "drop," "let fall," noun-form—"an outpouring, raingust." Yet Schindler gives it also plunge, overflow,
overwhelm. Buxtorf gives it the derived force of "immerse." Castell gives it overflow, overwhelm, immerse.
Æthiopic, to plunge, submerse. ¶ Primarily it means to
drop, of rain. Then in Leviticus it always means wash.
Later, in 1 Kings xxii, 38, it is to wash, where it is by
affusion. Later, in Ezekiel xxxviii, 22, it is a pouring
rain. Later still it came to mean overflow, overwhelm,
from its application to pouring rains. It never means
immerse in the earlier books of the Bible—never in
the Prophets or Psalms. In the latest Hebrew writings
it nearly always applies to overflowing, overwhelming.

* *Infudit, maceravit, humectavit, madefecit, lavit, intinit, intrivit.*
† *Hiscere, debiscere, scindi, scaturire, ebullire, de aqua . . . fons vitæ*
‡ Castell: *Immersus fuit aquæ, . . . collectio salivæ in ore, . . . immergere se aquæ, . . . descendit, immersum materiæ penitus* (2405-6).
§ *Effudit, largiter, pluvit,* 2 *inundavit—n. effusio,* etc. (Thesaurus Heb. Lin.)
¶ Castell: *Supra—exundavit, inundavit, immersit.* Æthiop., *Mersus, submersus est, submersit, demersit* (p. 3737). שָׁטַף is rendered in LXX, by κλύζω, ἐπι, and κατακλύζω, νίπτω, ἀπονίπτω, πλύνω, καταποντίζω, etc.

Later still the Hebrews used it for immerse, and in the third century after Christ it came to apply often to immersion. Here is not only a full refutation of the immersion canon, but a great key to this controversy. But let us multiply proofs.

3. We have seen that *bapto*, the root of *baptidzo*, means to stain, color, applied to birds, to stones, etc. So *zarak*,* to sprinkle, besprinkle, pour out, in Hebrew, Chaldee, and Syriac; in the latter means also to color, "to color blue," "golden," and "various colors," while in Arabic, from this meaning, it applies to variously-colored birds, wet.

4. *Nuph, noph*,† to sprinkle, be sprinkled, pour out, shed drops, agitate, etc. Arabic means the same; to move, agitate, hurl, throw. Kindred roots, e. g. *nug*, agitate, commotion; *nuts* (same root), to agitate, move, to moisten, motion of water, then, washing, cleansing with water or any liquid.‡

5. *Naphuts*, to sprinkle, in Hebrew and Chaldee and Arabic, and in the latter to pour means "to cleanse thoroughly."

6. *Zarak*, often applied to rain, means also to make wet, to cast down, thrust down; then to rush forth, to press, oppress; the very meanings that often lead to immerse, submerse; next it means "to overwhelm." § Hence—

7. *Dachas*,¶ to press, oppress, impress, immersed, immersion.

* *Zarak, sparsit, aspersit, conspersit . . . infudit, cærulareus, sparsus, sparsio, effusio*,—color *cæruleus, acribus*, etc., *madefactus* (Castell).

† *Nuph, noph*.

‡ *Lotio, ablutio, sine aquâ sine alia re liquida* (Castell).

§ *Rejecit, projecet, dejecit* — noun form—*pluvia tempestivia, pluvia . . . obrutus est* (Castell).

¶ *Dachas, pressit, chal, compressit, impressit, . . . oppressio, . . . immersus, . . . immersio* (Castell).

8. *Matar*, to rain, wet with rain, sprinkle, is translated by the LXX *nipto*, to wash; and in Arabic it is to rain, to sprinkle, pour, then washing, cleansing.*

9. *Nataph*, to shed drops, drop [as of rain]; Æthiopic, to cleanse; Arabic, shed drops [as of rain], sprinkle, pour out, to rain, to cleanse oneself, to purify.†

10. *Natal*, Arabic, the same (*natala*), to press out, besprinkle the head with rain, pour water, etc., . . . pouring out, wet, bedewed, . . . irrigated; in Chaldee, to wash, cleanse, especially the hands. . . . for it is necessary that the water be poured upon the hands before eating.‡

11. *Zakhak*, or *zaquak*, in Hebrew means to pour, shed down, moisture, purify, make pure, shed forth, cleanse, and the same in Chaldee.

First, in all these words we see the connection between sprinkle and pour on the one hand, and wash, cleanse, purify or the other; second, every lexicon gives wash, cleanse, as the prevailing meaning of *baptidzo* in the New Testament, many confine themselves to those two meanings; third, we fail to find any connection between immerse, even when "in water," and wash, cleanse, purify; fourth, the Arabic words for immerse, four or five of which mean immerse and have no other modal meaning, never mean, as *baptidzo* does, to wash, cleanse, nor as it does in the classics often, whelm, overwhelm, overflow, intoxicate.

12. *Nazah* is the Hebrew word that most commonly

* *Matar pluvia rigatus, depluit, pluviam, demissit.* Arabic, *pluit, perfudit, perfusus, pluit,* etc. (Castell).

† Hottinger, Schindler, Castell, on *nataph.*

‡ *Natal.* Arabic, *natala, expressit, impluvio perfudit caput, fudit aquam, effusio.* Chaldee, *lavit, abluit, pec. manus . . . necesse est enim effundebatur aqua ante prandium super manus,* etc. (Castell). This is the word often used by Jonathan Ben Uzziel to translate *rachats,* wash (Targum on Exodus).

means, like the Greek *raino*, to sprinkle. It is translated sprinkle in the Septuagint every time it occurs, save once, and always in the Vulgate. Yet Schindler renders it not merely to sprinkle but to press out, bedew, make wet, to flow, overflow, distill. Fürst renders it moisten, water, besprinkle, imbue, etc. In Arabic it means to sprinkle with water, pour out, make wet. In Æthiopic, to make clean, purify, cleanse. It applies to "the water of purification" (Num. viii, 7), then "to thrust down, to submerse."*

These words cover all that *baptidzo* means save to intoxicate, and we will find words that primarily mean to sprinkle, to moisten, that cover that meaning amply, though wholly unnecessary.

13. *Ruk* [as if *ruke*], in Chaldee and Arabic, to expel, throw out, spew out, to pour out, poured out, pour down, rain, a shower. The same root in Arabic (*ruga*), "spew out, to strike, sprinkle, to immerse."†

14. *Kechal*, a Semitic word for stain, paint, Schaaf renders paint, stain, dip, sprinkle.‡

15. *Natsacha*, Arabic, to pour out, sprinkle with water, besprinkle with water, copious rain, sprinkling (Num. xix, 9, 13, 20; 1 Pet. 12), sprinkled, yet to make wet, to wash the members [i. e. of the body, limbs].§

16. *Mattatha*, Arabic, expansion, . . . to moisten with

---

* *Nazah, sparsit aquam vel sanguinem, aspersit, expressit, rogavit, humectavit, . . . asperus fuit, defluxit, inundavit, silivat.* Arabic, *natzad, sparsit, aquâ consperit, effudit, rigavit* . . . (Num. xix, 9, 13, 20, etc.). Æthiopic, *nazad, mundus, purus fuit mundavit; aqua purificationis, purgavit, dejecit, submersit.* Castell, Schindler.

† *Ruga, spuma, percussit, aspersit, immersit,* etc. (Castell). *Ruts, same root,* sprinkle water, *aquam infudit.*

‡ *Kechal, . . . intinxit, aspergit* (Syriac Lex. N. T.).

§ *Natsacha* in Arabic—*effudit,* etc., *sparsus fuit, . . . rigatus fuit. . . . abluit membra.*

ointment or paint, wet with water, to sprinkle oneself copiously with ointment, to immerse oneself in water, mixing, immersion, commotion, confusion, or agitation. *

17. *Lathav,* to wet with tears, to be given to tears, to stain a garment, as with sweat, dew, immersion . . . in water or blood. It applies to drops of gum oozing out of trees, moisture, bedew, tree-dropping juice or moisture, make wet.† We will see that one of the Arabic words for baptize applies to juice dropping from trees, from juice, etc.

18. *Ravah,* to moisten, make drunk, irrigate. In these senses this Hebrew word occurs many times; e. g. Isaiah xvi, 9, "I will water thee with my tears." On drunkenness as a meaning see 1 Samuel xxv, 36, "Very drunken;" 1 Kings xvi, 9, "Drinking himself drunk" (xx, 16; Jer. xlviii, 26; John ii, 10, Arabic). It means irrigation (Is. lviii, 11). It applies in Arabic to the "agitation of the earth, to drink, draw water, imbue with water, to irrigate"—often thus it occurs; then pouring rain, dew, dewy. ‡ Here a word applied to sprinklings, pouring rains, dews, like *baptidzo,* means to be drunk, intoxicated, and, like *bapto,* to moisten, bedew, draw water, and, like both words, to imbue, make wet, moisten, pour water, etc.

19. *Letash,* Chaldee, to sprinkle, in later days comes to mean "to sprinkle or immerse;" and Buxtorf and Cas-

---

*Mathath, expansio, . . . imbuit . . . unguento vel pinguedine, . . . humore imbutus fuit, . . . saturavit, miscuit, unguento se abundi perfudit; mersit in aquam, . . . mixteo, mersio, etc. (Castell).

† *Lathav madita sive irrorata fuit, manavit lachrymâ succo ve arbor, . . . diditus lachrymal conspurcavit uti sudore, vestem, demersio,* etc

‡ *Ravah madefactus, inebriatus, satiolus est potu, irriguus . . . Chal. i. q. Heb. ib ebrius . . . irrigatio. Syr. e. q. Heb. Arab. agitata fuit aqua per faciam terræ; conturbatio aquæ supra terram . . . hausit aquam, potavit, . . . imbuit humore, . . . irregavit . . . imbrem fundens, . . . effluens, . . . ras, roridatus* (Castell, 35, 42-3).

tell show that the word that means to make white, to glitter, means to wash, to cleanse.*

20. Arabic *garaka*† primarily applies to bedewing, dropping water, distilling rain, rain, dilute gently with water, rain wetting herbs, comes to apply to a garment dyed, like *bapto*, to objects "submersed in the sea," "to be submersed," "to immerse," "immersed in water," as well as "simply to pour water upon the head" as well as irrigate. Schindler's lexicon (folio) defines it to perspire, sweat, decorate, color, pour (*fudit*), and yet gives it the meaning of immerse, demerse, twenty times. Does this look as if the same word could not mean in some places to sprinkle, in others to pour, to pour water upon objects, on the head, and to immerse?

21. *Chamats, chamuts*, means, Gesenius, Castell, etc. tell us, to be sharp, acid, violent, to ferment. Hence to scatter in drops, to sprinkle. Hence Buxtorf, "To be sprinkled, stained, infected, made wet."‡ Schindler, "To sprinkle with water," etc. Yet it comes to mean "to stain, to dip, to immerse."§ It is applied to water thus, "They dipped them in the water."¶ It meant to oppress also.

22. *Gamas*, in Arabic, Schindler renders "dipped, immersed," as well as "sprinkled."

23. *Tomash* is applied to wetting objects with tears (Ps.

* Chal. *letash, sparsit, aspersit* (*p*. 1918). In later Talmudic days, "*aspergat vel immergat*" (Lex. Tal. et Rab. J. Buxtorf, 1140). *Chava*, white, etc.

†*Arak*. Arabic, *garaka*, ... *leviter, aqua diluit*, ... *gutta, aquæ, pluvia valida*, ... *imbris guttæ, imber herbes madefaciens, herba pinguefaciens mublieres*, .. *gutta aquæ*, etc. *Curcumá tincta vestis*, ... *in mare submersæ, mersum in corpore, submersus*, ... *immersio*, ... *capiti semel affudit aquam*. Castell and Freytag.

‡ *Conspersus, tinctus vel infectus, madefactus*, etc.

§ *Tingere, intingere, immergere* (Castell).

¶ *Intingunt eos in aquam*, as well as *aqua perfudit* (Schindler).

vi, 7—6 in Hebrew), to staining a mountain with human blood (Is. xxxiv, 3), yet is rendered " merse, moisten, dip, wash," etc.

24. Persic, *pharav*,* " poured, pour out water, . . . descend, go down and into the water, to immerse oneself, to flow down." Often " to depress, swallow, penetrate."

25. *Shabal* has the same root in Hebrew that *tabhal*, baptize, has—*bal*—and means primarily to pour, to rain, to flow. It is the same in Arabic, and means also " to overflow, overwhelm," as *baptidzo* in the classics.

26. *Shapha* is kindred with *tsevha*, baptize, in Arabic and Syriac, "to flow down, to pour out, sprinkle, pour forth, . . . to depress or sink, to overwhelm."†

27. *Tsuph*, " to pour upon, to moisten," " to overflow," " to inundate," " to overwhelm " ‡ are meanings.

28. *Ratab*, "to bedew, to wet, moistened, sprinkled, irrigated, dipped." §

29. *Nataph* [root *tab*, as above in *natab*], to drop, flow in drops, flow down, distill, fall in drops, to cause to overflow. ||

30. *Phuts*, sprinkled, dispersed (after), poured, pour out, scattered abroad, flow down, flow out, overflow, overwhelm, poured out, etc.¶

* פרו, *fundus, aquam effundere*, . . . *descendere, accidere et in aquam* . . . *se immergere, defluere*, etc.

† *Affluxit, defluxit*, . . . *effudit, declinavit, descendit, depressit* (Schindler). *Effudit, profudit—inundavit, profudit* (Castell).

‡ צוף, *tsuph, supereffundo*. Trommius, *manare, fluere, irrigare, inundere*, . . . *superindet*, etc. (Fürst and Castell).

§ רטב, *maduit, humidus, humectatus, perfusus, irrigatus, intinguntur* (Schindler).

|| *Guttavit*, etc. *Stellavit*, . . . *inundavit* (Schindler).

¶ פיץ, *phuts, sparsus, dispersus* (repeated, etc.) *fusus, effusus, diffusus fuit, defluit, effluxit, inundavit, exundavit*, . . . *effundatur*, . . . *inundarunt torrentes rivi, et Nilus*, etc. (Schindler).

31. *Chalal,* in Arabic, "to moisten, . . . to pour," yet in Chaldee it is to wash, cleanse, applied to the washings of Leviticus, e. g. chapter xvi.

32. *Barad,* to sprinkle hail, to hail. Æthiopic is the same. In Arabic, to pour forth water, wash with cold water, to wash oneself with cold water; then it is applied to coloring various colors of garments, etc.

33. *Motz,* "primarily, to pour out" is "to wash," applied to washing out the mouth, "moist, damp," yet applied to "wash oneself with a sacred washing."*

34. *Nasak,* to pour, pour out. Syriac, pour out, Arabic, wash with water and purify, . . . wet with rain, of the earth.

35. Arabic *gasa* is to rain, make wet with rain, pour out, yet applies to painting, coloring, etc.†

36. *Badar,* Hebrew, to scatter. Syriac, to sprinkle, scatter. Arabic *badara* is the same, to sow, sprinkle, scatter, yet it comes to mean "to impart a yellow color," and just like *bapto,* applies to coloring and adorning the eyes; then, like *baptidzo,* in the classics, "to sprinkle with words," a talkative man; then to "cause to enter," repeated often; then it comes to mean "to submerse." ‡

37. *Nazal,* "to sprinkle, dip, or distill water, rain; then to depress, or press down, descend, let fall; compress in Arabic. Here is the idea of immersion.

38. *Shakah* in Semitic languages is "to water, drink, irrigate, moisten, water," yet "to paint," to "impart bright golden or red colors," imbue, just as *bapto.*

39. Words meaning to press, impress, compress come to

* *Prim. infusa, etc. . . . lavit . . . ablutio . . . lavit se sacrâ lotione.*
† *Compluit, rigavit terram pluviâ, . . . effusus, etc —pluviâ rigatus, . . . pinguescit, pinguendo* (Castell, 2750).
‡ *Badar, semnavit, sparsit, dispersit, . . . verbum sparsor, . . . penetrare fecit. . . . submersit* (Castell).

mean immerse very naturally and constantly. Yet the same force of the word causes it to mean sprinkle often. Pressing an object may sink, immerse it. Pressing an object may cause juice to stream out of it, sap, moisture. A grape, many objects pressed, causes the juice to be sprinkled. In cases where there are many as in a wine-vat, or a large object full of moisture, it pours. Hence Arabic *atsara* means "to press, compress."* Next it comes to mean "shed drops, distill," applied to water; then to "enter into"† being pressed "to flee," from being oppressed; "rain" (*pluvia*), "juice" (*succus*); often it means juice, sap, "oil" pressed out, "clouds forcing out rain," "hail, snow, cold water" forced or thrust down, "sprinkled with water," or dew,‡ "immersed in water."§ In the above order all these with other kindred meanings belong to this one word, and it occurs in each of these senses.

Let us test the Latin language on these principles of philology.

40. *Conspergo*, to sprinkle, is not only applied by Ovid and the Latins to staining, polluting; but White's late Latin lexicon gives "to cover" as a meaning, while *aspergo*, to sprinkle, means "to defile, spot, stain, fill," and the root *spargo*, to sprinkle, means to be "spotted, covered, covered over," alluding to the colors, etc. It will be remembered that *tabhal, bapto, tseva,* have those meanings, spotted, colored, as of birds and garments thus colored.

41. *Tingo* ¶ is from the Greek *tengo*, "to moisten, to

* *Pressit, compressit* (Schindler). *Pressit* (Castell).
† *Ingressus fuit* (Castell).
‡ *Rore perfusum* (Castell).
§ *In aqua immergitur* (Castell).
¶ *Tingo*, Greek τέγγω [*tenggo* or *tengo*], to moisten. As this word figures extensively in some parts, we refer to another place for a full

make wet," where it is by tears, dew, rain, all cases of sprinkling, shedding forth, etc. Yet it comes to mean to wash, where it is by affusion, to stain, color, dye by any mode or process, then to dip, to plunge.

42. *Madeo*, to be wet, bedew, besprinkle, is thus defined by Bullions's Latin Lexicon, 1869, "*Madeo*, to be wet, to be moist, dripping wet, . . . intoxicated, . . . sweat, perspire; *madidus*, wet, moist, metaphorically, full of water, soft, ... intoxicated, . . . a drunkard; 8. soaked, dipped, dyed." How like *bapto* and in part *baptidzo!*

The Greek language follows the same laws.

43. *Pluno,** primarily to rain, flow (of water), to moisten, sprinkle, pour, in early use. In Aristophanes it came like *baptidzo* to mean "to abuse, revile, reproach"— i. e. besprinkle with abuse, pour torrents of abuse on one. *Plunos* was a lover. See Pickering's Lexicon. In Demosthenes *pluno* meant to abuse. It meant to wash, to cleanse, and that became its general meaning in Greek.

44. *Raino*, to sprinkle, is defined by Pickering "to sprinkle; passive, to be submerged."

45. *Diugraino*, sprinkle with water, wet. Groves defines also by "wash," by "soak, overwhelm."

46. *Katantleo.** Dunbar defines it "to pour upon, to bathe with water, . . . to soothe with eloquence, to over-

discussion of it. (See on Tingo.) Hesychius defines it by βρέχεις, σταλάζεις, πληροῖς, shed or sprinkle water, moisten, bedew, trickle down, as tears. Stephanus: *Tengo madefacio, humecto;* then Hesychius, as above. *Lachrymarum guttis rigare genas*—wet the cheeks with drops of tears. Pape: Τέγγω—benitzen, anfeuchten. Thränen: Vergiessen— moisten, wet, shed tears.

* Passow, Rost, and Palm: Καταντλέω, drüberher giessen oder schütten, daruber ausgiessen, met. einen womit überschutten, überhäufen, etc. 2. Begiessen ubergiessen, überschutten. Galen cited. See their definitions of *baptidzo* now in German—same words in large part.

whelm with or pour ridicule upon one." Pickering, "to pour on; to pump water upon; to shower down (words) on; to bathe with water; to overwhelm with or pour ridicule on one."

47. *Cheo*, to pour, Pickering defines by "cause to flood," "to inter, to bury."

48. *Brecho*. Let it be remembered that "soak," "inundate," "drench," "overflow," "intoxicate," "overwhelm" are all constantly-recurring meanings of *baptidzo* in classic Greek. All immersionists agree to so translate it. *Brecho* is a prominent definition of *baptidzo* by all native Greek lexicons who define ancient Greek. Kouma and Gazes both give it as a prominent meaning, and the great German work of Schneider gives *brecho* as its general representative, answering to the "*benetzen*" of Pape, Rost, Palm, and Passow. Passow, Rost, and Palm all define *brecho* thus: "To wet, to moisten, to besprinkle; thence, in passive voice, to be wet, receive moisture, be wet with rain, to rain, to tipple, soaked with wine, be drunk, to pour upon, to overwhelm."*

Em-brecho, same word intensified, "to soak, to dip in."

Liddell & Scott: *Brecho*, to wet, moisten, sprinkle, rain on, mét[aphorically], shower down."

Pickering: *Brecho*, to moisten, wet, water, to bedew, besprinkle, soften, to rain, shower. Pass[ive], to be wet, soaked. Metaphorically, to be soaked with liquor, hence to be drunk or tipsy."

Stephanus: *Brecho*, to moisten, dip, soften, etc.†

Apo-brecho, to sprinkle, wet, to dip. ‡

---

* Βρέχω, benetzen, befeuchten, besprengen, dah. im. pass. sich benetzen, . . . ein mit wein ueberfülter, etc. Trukner: *Madidus*, uberschutten, überhäufen, etc. 'Εμβρέχω—einweichen, eintunken.

† Βρέχω, *madefacio, intingo, macero. Item irrigo, item bibo*, . . . *pluo*.

‡ 'Αποβρέχω, *perfundo, madefacio, intingo*, etc.

Em-brecho, "to soak, to immerse;" yet it means "To besprinkle, to sprinkle, likewise to merse."* Suidas, tenth century, defines it by "submersion."†

49. *Deuo.* Here is a word that Hesychius, fourth century, Suidas, tenth, native Greek lexicographers, give as equivalent in meaning to *bapto.* Stephanus quotes where it is used for *bapto.* It is quite important in this line.

Pickering: *Deuo,* to wet, to steep, to moisten, to soak, to dye by immersion or sprinkling, . . . to pour out, to shed, cause to flow.

Liddell & Scott: *Deuo,* wet, soak, steep, . . . make to flow, shed, . . . our [i. e. English] dew, bedew.

Groves: *Deuo,* to wet, water, moisten, bedew, sprinkle, to tinge, dye, color, to soak, soften.

Stephanus: *Deuo,* wet, moisten, imbue, stain (*tingo*), pour, besprinkle, infect, stain, *bapheus.*‡ He continues: "*Endeuo,* to bedew, moisten, irrigate," as the equivalent of *embapto,* and that as equivalent of *embrecho,* above.§

Here these great authorities place *bapto,* the root of *baptidzo,* as the equivalent of words that mean to bedew, shed down, pour, sprinkle. They sustain our laws of philology unanimously. These words that primarily apply universally to affusions, come to mean to dip, to dye, to color, to stain, to soak, intoxicate.

50. *Hugrino,* water, sprinkle, means to wet, moisten, wash.

51. *Moluno,* primarily to sprinkle (Stephanus), means to stain, to pollute, to defile.

52. Passow: *Ballo—emballo,* to cast (or strike), to be-

---

* Ἐμβρέχω, *immadefacio, immergo . . inspersa, perfundo, item mergo.*

† *Submersus,* cited by Stephanus.

‡ Βαφεύς.

§ Ἐνδέυω, that is to say, ἐμβάπτω, ἐμβρέχω. Passow gives *endeuo* as *bammati,* i. e. *bapto.*

sprinkle oneself, to pour, pour out, sprinkle, to besprinkle oneself with bath-water."* This word applies to washing where it is *louo*, to wash, take a bath. See fully under the chapter on Wash.

53. *Kludzo.*† The primary meaning of *kludzo* is bedash, sprinkle. The ancient glosses (lexicons) have "*peri-kludzo*, sprinkle, perfuse."‡ Buddæus (the lexicographer, not the later ecclesiastic writer) has it *peri-klusmati*, sprinkled.§ Galen, the native Greek lexicographer, born A.D. 130, renders it by "affusion," "infusion" constantly, and our word clyster is from it. Stephens renders it in the same way. Passow, the master critic in Greek, has "*kludzo*, wash, splash (or bedash), dabble, bedash, wet, wash, purify or cleanse," etc. Stokius: "*Kludzo*, wash, cleanse, wash (or bedew, sprinkle)."¶ Groves: "*Peri-kludzo*, to wash all round or all over, dash water, sprinkle over." Liddell & Scott: "To wash, dash, . . . to wash off, drench, to put water into the ears, and so cleanse them." So Passow. A. Campbell quotes from Aristotle, the most learned Greek and accurate in words who ever wrote, where this word is interchanged with *baptidzo*, both rendered "overflowed," the preposition *kata* being joined to *kludzo*, as often occurs, as well as *peri*, and the same *kata* is often joined to *baptidzo* in the classics. || Here is a word that primarily means to splash or bedash with water, sprinkle, inject water, that is the "equivalent for *baptidzo*." Yet this

---

* Χρόα λουτροῖς, sich mit bade-wasser bespringen.
† Κλύζω, περικλυζο.
‡ *Aspergo, perfundo.* H. Stephens's Thesaurus: *Subvoce.*
§ *Aspergine* (X, 127 Thesaurus, H. Stephens).
¶ *Eluo, abluo, lavo.*
|| Chris. Baptism, page 130: "Are not overflowed (*me baptizesthai*), but at full tide are *overflowed* (*katakluzesthai*); which word (*katakludzo*) is here used as an equivalent for *baptizesthai*." Just so exactly, and in classic Greek, too, where they contend it does *always* mean *immerse*.

word comes to mean not only to wash, cleanse, infuse, overflow, but to immerse, submerse. Stephanus renders it to "imbrue, overflow, bury, submerge." Buddæus does the same. Stokius renders also *katakludzo*, to bury, submerge.* Could a fact be more perfectly demonstrated than this, that words primarily applying to affusion come to mean wash, whelm, cover, immerse?

54. *Balal—balala.* One more example we produce from the Hebrew and Arabic—*balal*, which has the same root (*bal*) as the Hebrew word for baptize (*tabal*), and is the word that is used in the Arabic Bible to translate *bapto* and *embapto*, dip, "dip in," in Luke xvi, 24, "That he may dip" (*embapto*). John xiii, 26, "I shall have dipped." But what is the primary meaning of this word, and what other meanings develop therefrom?

(1) Freytag's Arabic lexicon defines it, "To moisten, and especially to water or soften by sprinkling or lightly pouring the water."†

(2) Castell, "To moisten and especially to water or soften by sprinkling or lightly (gently) pouring the water.‡

(3) Gesenius, "To sprinkle, water, make wet by affusion of water, sprinkle."§

(4) Schindler: *Balal*, to sprinkle, to moisten, to wet, to dip.‖

Here is a word that primarily and habitually means to sprinkle where it is a very light sprinkling of water. Yet it is the word used to translate *bapto* and *embapto*.

* *Obruo, submergo.* Stephanus: *Imbruo, inundo, obruo, submergo.*

† Freytag Arab. Lex.: *Madeficit et spec. rigavit, maceravit ve asperso aut leviter affuso humore.*

‡ Castell: Same, word for word, as Freytag.

§ Gesenius's Thesaurus: בָּלַל, *perfudit.* Arabic, *rigavit, affuso humore madefecit, conspersit,* etc.

‖ *Rigavit, madeficit, intinxit.*

PHILOLOGY, OR SCIENCE OF LANGUAGE. 195

In this list of words, as in nearly all other matters, our own humble researches alone brought out these facts, no one ever having taken up this matter, so all-important to this question. In this list of over fifty words, all the words for baptism in the Bible and older versions, such as *tabal, tzeva,* and *gasala, amad, amada, secho, bapto,* and *baptidzo,* have been left out because they are the words in question, though legitimately they, from the facts exhibited, really belong to the list.

The following facts, then, are elicited and SETTLED, viz:

1. Wash is not derived from dip or immerse.

2. A great number of words in various languages, primarily meaning to sprinkle, to pour, come to mean to wash, cleanse, purify, to overflow, overwhelm, immerse, submerse.

3. That immerse is in almost all cases, if not in all, a derived meaning, not a primary one in any case.

4. That numbers of words primarily meaning to moisten, where it is ("*affuso leveter*") with dew, drops of water, a gentle affusion, sprinkling, come to mean to wash, cleanse, overflow, overwhelm, depress, burden, immerse, submerse.

5. That words primarily meaning, and often meaning, to sprinkle, moisten, wet, where it was a very light affusion of liquid or water, come to mean to stain, to paint, color, dye, wash, cleanse, intoxicate, soak, make drunk, dip, immerse, submerse — covering perfectly the classic meanings of *bapto* and *baptidzo.*

6. That words primarily meaning to agitate or effervesce, from which often is derived violence, come to mean to sprinkle, from the violence of the fermenting or effervescing, scattering drops in all directions, staining them, hence to stain, dye, color; thence dye by dipping, to dip, immerse.

7. That words meaning to press, press down, press in, press together (the same word often has all these meanings) come to mean to sprinkle, from the juice or liquid bursting out of the juicy objects, as grapes, fruit generally, saturated materials, juicy vegetables, etc.; to pour, to color, to immerse, to submerse, from being pressed when resting on a yielding substance, as water, etc.

8. It is demonstrated to an absolute certainty that it is not merely the natural law, but the only law or habit of language, that when a word has such meanings as intoxicate, wash, overflow, overwhelm, not to say sprinkle, pour, and dip, immerse, it begins with sprinkle or its equivalent, and proceeds to develop till it comes to mean immerse, never reversing that rule in any instance in all the Semitic and Aryan tongues. Hence—

9. Not only is the boasted law of immersionists utterly destroyed, the great philological principles on which they boasted their readiness or ability to rest every thing on it, but sprinkling is established as the primary meaning of *bapto* and *baptidzo* beyond the possibility of a doubt, and by the same rule, of *tabal, amad,* and the rest.

We see also the peculiarity of word-making and derivation. A word may mean to break open, to rupture, that thence comes to mean pour, sprinkle, overflow, wash, immerse. Thus, to rupture a vessel, effect a break in it, water may gush out, pour, or be sprinkled, as the rupture is large or small. A blood-vessel may be ruptured, and sprinkle and stain, soil objects. A dam or great body of water break the levee or bank and overflow, overwhelm completely and wash off all before it, drown the living.

To press an object may cause its liquid or water or the juices in it to gush or burst out, sprinkle objects around. Thence increased, a stream pours forth, as wine from the press. Hence sprinkle, stain, and pour come from press. But pressing an object sinks (immerses) it in a yielding element, as mud, water, etc. Hence press often comes to mean to immerse.

To thrust down, cast down water, blood, etc., sprinkles. Hence words meaning to thrust, cast down, often apply to rain, showers of rain. To thrust down heavy objects into yielding elements, as water, results in immersing it.

These are examples of the developing of meanings to words. In the face of these facts how infinitely vain and utterly destitute of science are all those rules so much relied on by immersionists!

Two words may have primarily the same meaning, yet apply to different objects, consequently take on entirely opposite meanings. This occurs constantly.

The old philologists relied on arbitrary rules, took dogmatic views, and bent philology to those views; and hence the abyss of darkness and world of confusion in which they left this subject. They would assume a word to be the same with another in a kindred dialect; as *amad*, to stand, in Hebrew, and *amad*, to wash, sprinkle, in Syriac, Arabic, because spelt alike, though wholly unlike in meaning. Nay, Gesenius runs stark mad, and finds as much support or more in the remotest Aryan branches if a word be spelt with not a radical in common if they sound remotely alike! His carelessness may be seen, as well as A. Clarke and others too numerous to note, in assuming the Arabic *naza*, to leap, etc., to be the root of the Hebrew *nazah*, to sprinkle. Whereas the Arabic is *nazach*, sprinkle; and still stronger in Æthiopic *natzach*, to sprinkle. The philologist has to keep in view constantly the fact that in Semitic oftener far than Indo-European tongues ז (z) interchanges with צ (tz), both interchange with ט (*t*), ס (*s*), שׁ (*sh*), then with ת (*th*), while ב (*b*), פ (*ph*), interchange, as well as other letters. He can not trace root-meanings without observing these and many other facts. There may be a word having one or more meanings fixed and settled. The corresponding word in Arabic, Æthiopic, or Syriac may be changed in spelling by these rules, and take on many meanings not found in the Hebrew word, yet the same or kindred meaning will crop out, showing the root identity. Hence the science of philology is at once one of the most interesting, improving, and useful studies to man.

CHAPTER XVI.

BAPTIDZO—WASH.

While all admit that *baptidzo* generally occurs in the New Testament and Apocrypha in the sense of wash, cleanse, it never so occurs in the classics. Dr. Conant, out of some two thousand years of literature, could not find a place where it meant wash. On the contrary, as Schleusner says, though stating that the word in Greek writers means "immerse, merse in water," "yet in this sense it never occurs in the New Testament." So does Stokius, who urges that it applied to washing, cleansing where it was effected "by sprinkling the water," "hence transferred to the solemn rite of baptism."*

Another point. Emersion, rising out of the water, is never implied in *baptidzo*. Immersion does not involve or imply emersion. To the extent that *baptidzo*, in later Greek, where at times it occurs for a total immersion, at times for a partial sinking, immersed objects, so far as the force of the word goes, it leaves them immersed. Wherever it sinks, completely immerses, a living being, it perishes. In every instance in Dr. Conant's long list of Greek citations, and he erroneously professes to exhaust the use of the word, in not an instance does the word fail to leave the object immersed, or submersed, in or under the element into or under which the object was mersed. How could wash, cleanse, or purify, philologically come from such a

---

* See chapter on Lexicons, where these lexicons are cited.

use? On the contrary, every entire immersion in water in all cases given resulted in death. Hence *baptidzo* in the classics often means to drown. If the objects immersed by *baptidzo* were dead—inanimate—decay, ruin, or destruction ensued. No washing resulted or purification. Not only does this rule the classics out of the question, therefore, but it amazes us that men of learning should have failed to examine into the world of facts which languages present here; and even Dr. Dale, so voluminous on this subject, while professing to find new light, bases his structure as to philology upon the groundless position that wash is derived from immerse! He and those he follows have immerse to get wash, wash to get purify, purify to get sprinkle, sprinkle to get baptism; yet if the universe depended on it he could not find a word that primarily and properly meant to immerse that ever came to mean to wash, to purify, to cleanse. On the contrary, as shown in all languages, a cloud of witnesses arise to show that words primarily meaning to sprinkle, to pour, to moisten, bedew, etc. come to mean to wash, wet, soak, whelm, overwhelm, dip, immerse. The truth is completely vindicated—its principles absolutely perfect. To pour or sprinkle the liquid is to wet, moisten. If a coloring element, it stains, colors. Pouring water on objects tends to wash, cleanse. In many places sprinkling water cleanses, washes. Being purified, things are appropriated to new and better purposes. We may wash, dipping the object in water and rubbing it; but a mere dip, unlike the friction of pouring, does not wash. The dust-covered herbs, houses, trees, fences, are all washed by the sprinkling and pouring rain. Pouring may soak, saturate, drench, overwhelm, submerse. The philology is perfect and we dismiss this point.

That the Jews washed by pouring and sprinkling mostly

is seen in the use of the great laver (Chapter VII), and in 2 Kings iii, 11, "This is Elisha, that poured water on the hands of Elijah," as well as from John ii, 6, where surely they did not wash *in* the vessel, as, first, it was physically impossible as to dipping the body, and second, it would have ceremonially defiled the water (Num. xix, 21, 22; Lev. x, 34; xv, 34-36; Lightfoot, Horæ Heb. et Tal., ii, 417); third, much less would our Savior have turned water defiled by washing hands in it into wine to be used as a drink. But we have the Jews' estimate of the amount of water necessary for washing the hands, for it is urged by some that Mark vii, 3, 4, demands us to understand that the hands simply were plunged in water where the Greek is baptized. On washing hands among the Jews we have the following in Jadaim (cap. 1, hol. 1): "They allot a fourth part of a log for the washing of one person's hands, it may be of two; half a log for three or four; a whole log for five or ten; nay, to a hundred; with this provision, saith Rabbi Jose, that the last that washeth hath no less than a fourth part of a log for himself." Lightfoot, Horæ Heb. et Tal., ii, 254. Now a log is five sixths of a pint ($\frac{5}{6}$); a fourth of five sixths is five twenty-fourths or nearly one fifth ($\frac{1}{5}$) of a pint. Who could immerse or submerge his two hands in one fifth of a pint of water? Hence in Erubhin, folio 21, 2: "It is stated of Rabbi Akibah that he was bound in prison, and Rabbi Joshua ministered unto him as his reader. He daily brought him water by measure [to drink]. One day the keeper of the prison met him, and said to him, 'Thou hast too much water today.' He poured out half and gave him half. When he came to Rabbi Akibah he told him the whole matter. Rabbi Akibah saith unto him, 'Give me some water to wash my hands.' The other saith unto him, 'There is not enough for thee to drink, and how, then, shouldst thou have any to wash thy hands?' To whom he said, 'It is better that I should die [that is, by thirst] than that I should transgress the mind of my colleagues.'" That they did at times partially dip the hands or one of them, no one would question. It depended on the water, the vessel, and circumstances. This shows absolutely that they never depended on dip or immerse for washing. See also John xiii, where the Savior washed the disciples' feet, and Luke vii, 38, 44, where the woman washed Christ's feet with her tears. The learned Pococke renders the passage "put into the water," sprinkle the hands with water.* Leigh, Lightfoot, Castell, Buxtorf, etc. show the same to be true.

* *Manus aquâ perfudit* (Nat. Miscellan., chap. ix, p. 388; Gale's Reflec., Let. iv, Wall, ii, p. 96).

CHAPTER XVII.

BAPTIDZO IN THE HOUSE OF ITS FRIENDS—THE CONCORD OF THIS DISCORD.

It is certainly interesting to see how the learned immersionists conflict with each other when stating so emphatically their fundamental principles and the results of their critical researches; and still more so to notice their self-conflicting statements and infinite departures from the true laws and science of language.

Mr. Ingham (Hand-book of Baptism, p. 26) says, "The Greek verb *baptidzo* signifies to immerse, and ought to be so rendered in our translation," etc. "By immersion we mean [what! has immersion now to be defined also?] an entire covering or a complete surrounding with some element." Here the latest distinguished author, with Carson, Conant, Campbell, Fraser all before him—Cox and Morell before him—refutes Carson, rejects Gale, and ruins all former canons of immersion. Halley differs. Ingham next refutes Carson on "putting into" the element as being implied in *baptidzo;* while such men as Fuller, Mell of Georgia, and others go down before the broad sweep of his tremendous battle-ax. He quotes Dr. Halley to prove that "baptize is to make one thing to be in another by dipping, by immersing, by burying, by covering [what modes!!] by superfusion, or by whatever mode effected," etc. (page 27).

Here the strongest writer by odds that has appeared in Europe on the side of immersion as late as 1866 declares, first, that dipping, immersing, burying, covering, pouring are all so many and different modes of baptism—so it results in "complete surrounding," "entire covering"; second, that baptism may be accomplished by superfusion—pouring upon; nay, by "whatever mode effected"; third, is there any dip, or sink, or plunge in superfusion? Surely dipping is not pouring upon. Yet says the great Dr. Gale (London, 1711, p. 9), "We can not believe that it is so doubtful in Scripture, as many pretend, whether dipping only be baptism. . . . I'll begin with the words $\beta\acute{a}\pi\tau\iota\zeta\omega$ and $\beta\acute{a}\pi\tau\omega$ [*baptidzo* and *bapto*], for they are synonymous" (Reflections on Wall, ii, p. 60, Letter iii, ed. 1862). Here Dr. Gale urges that only dipping is baptism. Burying is not dipping. Covering a thing is not dipping. If pouring water on an object is dipping it, we did not know it. A thing may be dipped and not covered or buried. This Dr. Gale freely admits. He says, "The word does not always necessarily imply a *total immersion* or *dipping* [italics his] the whole thing spoken of all over, which I readily allow; but, then, sir, we should remember it is not from any thing limiting the sense of $\beta\acute{a}\pi\tau\iota\zeta\omega$ [*baptidzo*], but from something limiting the extent of the action in the subject" (Reflections on Wall, Letter iv, p. 9, vol. 2, etc., by Dr. Gale).

This is racy—is brilliant. First, *baptidzo*, he admits, does not "necessarily imply a total immersion." It does not imply "dipping the whole thing spoken of all over." That is, if a man is baptized, it does not "necessarily imply" that he is immersed totally or "dipped all over." If but a part, nay, a small part of him, were dipped or immersed, the whole man is baptized. This surrenders the whole question. It becomes rich when he adds that "it is not from any thing limiting the sense of *baptidzo*, but from something limiting the extent of the action on the subject." Exactly so. Hence when the "action on the subject" is limited to a sprinkling, a "superfusion," it is not because the word does not at times apply to "total immersion," but because something "limits the extent of the action" from being an immersion or dipping at all, and Greek applies baptize to such cases of limited action.

The plain English of the statement of Dr. Gale is this: When the administrator simply sprinkles or pours water on the subject *baptidzo* applies to it clearly enough, but it is not because of any thing "limiting the sense of *baptidzo*, but from something limiting [the administrator] the extent of the action on the subject." We subscribe to this without reservation. And because *baptidzo* is and was so limited in its action, hence it does not necessarily imply dipping or immersion.

Dr. Gale innocently prattles on, saying that though a thing be "not dipped all over," etc., yet it does not "follow that the word in that place does not signify to dip;" and "I believe Mr. Wall will allow his pen is dipped in the ink, though it is not daubed all over or totally immersed. . . . What is true of any one part may be said of the whole complexly, though not of every part of the whole separately."* Then when we pour water on a candidate for baptism, that part is covered with water. When he is sprinkled the water covers the parts on which it falls. If only the forehead is dipped, what is said or "is true of any one part may be said of the whole complexly"—so the man is dipped. Only a part is covered when water is poured; but what is true of a part may be said of the

* Reflections on Wall, vol. ii, pp. 90, 91, Let iv.

whole complexly—so the man is covered. According to this most learned of all the old immersion writers, every one who is sprinkled or has water poured on him is baptized, and it was not an immersion or total dipping, for the "extent of the action" was limited to that partial dip— i. e. only a part was covered. Nor does it differ as to the mode of covering, for you can do this as well "by superfusion" or "by pouring," Drs. Morell and Cox tell us. And to cover a part is to baptize the whole man. This is Baptist logic and argument.

Dr. R. Fuller, a Baptist,* says, "It (*baptidzo*) signifies to immerse, and has no other meaning." Yet in the same book he translates *baptidzo* by "sink" twelve times out of twenty-two instances, twice by plunge, once "dip," once "bury," once "drowned" (p. 48), three times by submerge, three times only by immerse. In less than a page (pp. 47, 48) he renders it "sink" seven times consecutively. In another place (p. 17) he renders it "sink" five times in less than half a small page. Here—

(1) He gives us an average of eleven against one against immerse.

(2) He contradicts Gale, Cox, Ingham, Halley.

(3) He contradicts himself; for to sink is not to dip. Is sink the same as plunge? Is dip equivalent to drown? Is drown or sink the same as the plunge he administers to a subject in baptizing him?

Against Ingham, Halley, and Fuller, Cox lets us know that "The idea of dipping is in every instance conveyed, and no less so by all the current uses of the terms" *bapto* and *baptidzo*. Verily, there is trouble in the camp, if Dr. Conant,† who devoted more pains and expended more

* Third ed., Charleston, S. C., 1854, p. 25, 33-37.
† Conant's book on classic use has *baptidzo* only from pages 1 to 72.

labor on this subject than all immersionists together for the last hundred years, out of sixty-three consecutive cases could render it immerse only ten times, but "whelm" and "overwhelm" fifty-three times; while A. Campbell in but two lines over half a page of a small volume renders it "overwhelm" ten times, twice in same space "overflowed," and out of thirty-four cases to prove its proper meaning only renders it immerse three times—i. e. over ten against one. Yet another defender of the faith tells us, "The idea of dipping is in every instance"! Is dip the same as whelm? Is it the same as overflow? Is it the same as sink? They are just the reverse. Yet Cox tucks about and admits a man may be immersed, covered by "superfusion," which contradicts all he has said in favor of his theory.

To make it worse Dr. Morell* says that usually it means "dip." "But it appears quite evident that the word has the sense of covering by superfusion [i. e. by pouring upon]. This is admitted by Dr. Cox. Thus far we surrender the question of immersion with Dr. Cox." Drs. Morell and Cox sustain Ingham and destroy Drs. Fuller, Gale, Mell, and A. Campbell. All this perfectly sustains the position that primarily affusion was the import of baptize, even were Cox and Morell correct in detail.

After that it is always compounded with strengthening prepositions; therefore it does not apply at all, but is rather strong proof of its not being as he represents in many cases. But in the cases between 1 to 72 it occurs about one hundred and forty-one times. In these he renders it *dip* seven times—i. e. seven against one hundred and thirty-four, i e. his own texts have one hundred and thirty-four against seven of *his* practice! It is only thirty-five times *immerse* against one hundred and six against. That is, *he* puts it one hundred and six against thirty-five for his rendering. *Could an enemy more perfectly* destroy their position than this?

* Edinburgh, 1848, p. 167.

But against all these Baptist doctors Dr. Booth* swoops down like an eagle from an unpropitious sky, or like a furious wind that threatened to unmoor all the vessels that ply on the watery grave and sweep them far up on dry land as unworthy of a place on the "deep." † He says, "The verb baptize, in this dispute, denotes an action required by divine law. . . . What is that action? Is it immersion, or pouring, or sprinkling?" "A single specific enacting term." "Baptize is a specific term." "The English expression dip is a specific term." But alas for this "specific action." It is "whelmed" by Cox, Conant, and Morell; "overwhelmed" by its advocate A. Campbell; Ingham, Conant, etc., "submerged," "sunk," "drowned;" its advocates "superfused," "soaked;" its highest points "overflowed;" its best advocates "drenched," "soaked," in their fruitless endeavors to save it. Desperation seizing them, they are now "intoxicated," "made drunk" with draughts of Quixotic remedies; "soused," "put under," "engulfed" in the house of its friends. While "undergoing" all these trials A. Campbell, George Campbell, and Conant make it "undergo" a contradiction of all this, and "endure" still another weight in the New Testament, until criticism is exhausted, consistency is wrecked, the immersion theory "perishes," and is ready to be "administered" ‡ upon forever.

* London, 1799, pp. 265, 280, 286. A. Campbell takes the same position in his debate with Dr. Rice, and in his book on Christian Baptism, that it is *specific* as to action—dip.

† Immersionists often urge that the word is allied with "deep."

‡ All these words in quotation-marks are actual renderings of this "specific," "simple" word by immersion authors of highest note, and almost every one of them given it by A. Campbell and Conant in their various works, versions, etc. We omit the "wash" in A. Campbell's revision, because he tells us it was an oversight.

Prof. Mell, of Georgia, insists that "no passage in any Greek writings up to and immediately after the time of Christ can be found containing these words—*baptidzo, baptisma, baptismos*—where they must be translated by any other English word than *dip* or *immerse*" (Baptism, pp. 16, 17). "They express the action of immersion, *and nothing else*" (p. 16). They "mean immersion, *and nothing else*" (p. 15). Italics his. Fortunately for Prof. Mell he, unlike the rest, appends here no proof-texts from classic Greek, else unmistakably we should find in his text-illustrations, as we did in all the rest of their writers, the clear, immediate, and overwhelming refutations of his bold assertion in his own proofs. Certain as fate would have followed such renderings of *baptidzo* as "sink," "whelm," "soak," "overwhelm," "plunge," "drown," "submerge," etc., and perhaps even baptism by "superfusion."*

Dr. Carson, the most popular author the Baptists have had of late years, and professedly learned, says—for each one seems determined and bent on "my position"—"My position is that it always signifies to dip; never expressing any thing but mode. Now as I have all the lexicographers and commentators against me in this opinion, it will be

---

* Since examining the book in later chapters, lo! we find he is worse than we predicted! In *three* pages of his small book (38, 39, 40) Mell translates *baptidzo* by 1. "*To lay,*" "*laid* under water"; 2. "Sink" (sunk) *five* times out of *ten* texts"; 3. "*Ruined*"; 4. "Dip"; 5. "Immerse"; 6. "*Steeped* or *soaked* in wine"; 7. "Imbued"; 8. "*Pressed down.*" He gives the English of immerse as sink here very correctly several times, and renders the *same word in one sentence* by two and *three* words, thus, "Who was *sunk*, or *immersed*, or *pressed down* by the weight of debts heaped upon him." Page 28 he says, "In Hebrews ix, 10, the translators render the word *baptismos* correctly *washing*—'which stood only in . . . *divers washings.*'" Here we have *nine* different renderings out of *eleven* texts!! We have lay, ruin, press down, soak. Apply these definitions to baptism in the New Testament—I indeed "lay" you; he shall "*ruin*" you with the Holy Ghost, etc.

14

necessary to say a word or two with regard to the authority of lexicons. . . . The meaning of a word must be determined by the actual inspection of the passages in which it occurs, as often as any one chooses to dispute the judgment of the lexicographers."

It always signifies "to dip," then, says Dr. C. If so, then it never means to immerse, sink, nor to whelm, drown, intoxicate, etc., nor "cover by superfusion." But his learned brother, Dr. Cox, says, "A person may indeed be immersed by pouring [i. e. sink, plunge by pouring!!], but immersion is the being plunged into water or (the being) overwhelmed by it. Were the water to ascend from the earth it would still be baptism were the person wholly covered by it" (p. 46).

Where is the "never expressing any thing but mode" here? Where is the dip? Where is the plunge? Where is the sink, i. e. immerse? To "dip" is to put an object either partly or wholly into an element, so that it touches it at least, and at once withdraw it. Plunge does not imply withdrawal at all, never provides for it, and implies more or less force and rapidity in execution. Immerse implies not withdrawal at all. Dip does in all these authors, as they do not use it in derived and remoter senses, as ships, boats, dipping water, etc.

BAPTISTS IN HARMONY.

Now with "all the commentators and lexicographers against" "his position," Carson insists that *baptidzo* means to "put into." Conant says it is to "put into—under." Ingham says it means to "put into." In Leviticus it (*bapto*) is rendered "put into" (pp. 31-32). He renders it "put into" ten times (pp. 27-29). Nay, indorses the idea of "coming into the condition of being under water." Now, first, to "put into," which Conant, Ingham, Carson, A. Campbell, and others say is the exact import or force of *baptidzo*, is not necessarily "to dip," "plunge," or "immerse." You can "put into" without either of these actions. Nay, second, the word pour in Greek as well as in Latin both means to "put into" and "to mix" often. "Put water into a basin"="pour" it into it. This word, that means to "put into," is translated by Passow, Wahl, and others by to "sprinkle," "besprinkle" over and again. Ed. Robinson's Greek Lexicon renders *ballo* "put or pour" several times. How ruinous to immersionists are their favorite words. No word exactly suits them. They give us immerse. They have to turn round and tell us what that means, define it in detail and by most opposite words. To "surround completely;" that won't do. The same writer in the same line tells us it is an "entire covering." Yea, it is to "put into"—it is to dip. But each of these words or expressions are widely different. In Exodus xxx, 18, I read, "Put (ἐχεεῖς, *ekcheeis*—pour) water therein." Dr. Gale says twice that "*baptidzo*" signifies only to dip or put into" (pp. 69, 74). As Christ and Moses use a word for "put into" that often means to sprinkle, to pour (*cheo* and *ballo*), and if "put into" is the meaning of *bapto* and *baptidzo*, it is crushing to immersion and very satisfactory to us. Conant says (Baptizein, p. 89), "It means simply to put into or under water (or other substance)," etc. A. Campbell (Debate with Rice, p. 126), "Put himself under the water." Dr. Gale says *baptidzo* signifies nothing "but to dip or put under or into." "Dip or put into" (Reflections on Wall, 2, chap. iii, pp. 64, 96).

A TOUCH, A FEW DROPS WILL DO.

Luke v, 38: "New wine must be put into new bottles." There is the precious word that defines immersion, that defines *baptidzo* in immersion writers. Yet this same word is rendered (Matt. xxvi, 12), "She hath poured this ointment," etc. See also Matthew ix, 17, where it occurs also. This is one of the words Hinton, the Baptist, puts for pour. It seems to us that Dr. Gale is as hard pressed as was my friend Dr. W. T. Brents, of Tennessee, at Franklin, in debate, 1873, when, being pressed on dip as used in the version of James, he said, "Could I wield the power I could dip an elephant in a spoonful of blood." Hear the learned doctor: "For if the word (*baptidzo*) does but signify to dip I ask no more. Let it relate to the whole body or a part of it only; either way I gain my point" (ii, 110). He quotes Matthew xxvi, 23, on *bapto*, "he that dippeth," "And all the use he (Wall) makes of it is only to observe the word does not here mean the dipping of the whole hand. But this is nothing to the purpose; for the question is not about the whole or a part of the subject, but whether the Greek word signifies only to dip, or any thing else" (p. 112, *ibid.*). In a word, Dr. Gale admits the word does not necessarily imply envelopment, covering, burial, but if only the subject be applied to the element, the most partial entrance by the smallest part, end of the finger, end or point of the pen, the whole is dipped! He was too good a Hebrew scholar as well as Greek not to know that at least from his own standpoint every dip in the Bible, save one or two at most, failed to be what immersionists require—they were not complete immersions.

CHAPTER XVIII.

Ancient Criticisms—Errors.

If immersionists have been in utter confusion to find adequate words to express their conception of baptism, which surely should close their mouths against other parties about translating the word, they are no less confounded as to the original or primary meaning of *baptidzo*. Not only they, but those who have assumed immerse as the primary meaning have occupied a position alike untrue and uncandid, while the more candid have been driven about without sail or rudder.

1. Beza, a favorite author with all immersionists because not understood (for, as will in due time appear, he taught that even John the Baptist poured the water on the people in baptism—*effundo*), says, " Βαπτίζω (*baptidzo*) differs from δύναι (*dunai*), in that *dunai* means to sink deeply (*submergere*)" (Annot. Matt. iii).

2. Casaubon, a name much paraded indeed, says, "This was the rite of baptizing, that persons were plunged into the water; which the very word *baptizein* (baptize) sufficiently declares [it declares nothing of the kind, and Conant and others admit it implies no particular element, applies to any material]; which, as it does not signify *dunein* (that is, a specific word for immerse), to sink to the bottom and perish, so doubtless it is not *epipolazein*, to swim on the surface. For these three words are of different significations" (Annot. on Matt. iii, Ingham, 90).

3. Terretinus, Vossius, Witsius, and Suicer all follow this almost verbatim, and the rest of the old school follow them. Pasor and other old authors follow with the same assertion about *dunai*. See Pasor's Lexicon on *baptidzo*.

Now, first, these authors use the very Greek word that they themselves render by *mergere* in every case, "sub" added, and *dunai*, one of the words for immerse; and its force is destroyed by putting it into actual English, sink, and retaining a Latin word, immerse, for *baptidzo*. Second, *dunai* (*endunai* and *katadunai*) is the very word used by the Greeks, used by the Greek fathers in nearly every case when they wish to say immerse. When they defined that the canon meant immerse for baptism, this is the word they used both in its verbal and substantive form.* Conant gives this case, "Three immersions in one baptism," as it is in the Greek.† He does all he can to conceal the force of it by rendering immerse "sink" every time, and baptism by immerse. That is, he renders the real word for immerse (*kataduo*) by sink, the true English word, and baptism by the Latin of sink. Conant quotes, "Then when we emerge (*ana-dunai*)," etc. "For that the child (*kata-dusai*) sinks down (is immersed) thrice in the font and comes up again (*ana-dusai*)," is emerged, properly. How could the child come up again?‡ Where

---

* The apostolic canons, sixth century A.D, say, "If a bishop or presbyter shall not perform *three immersions* (*baptismata*) for one initiation, but *one baptism*," etc. This is *the only* place in all their literature where *baptisma* stands for immersion, and it is plural—*baptismata*. But Zonaras, the Greek, explained this canon thus: "The canon *here* calls the three baptisms *three immersions*—*kataduseis*"—κατα and δύναι, to sink, be immersed.

† Τὰς τρεῖς καταδύσεις . . . ἐν ἑνὶ βαπτίσματι—*tas treis kataduseis . . . en heni baptismati.* Conant's Baptizein, pages 106, 108, 110, 117, 119, 133, full of examples of δύναι, *dunai, endunai, katadunai* used for *baptism*, *anadunai* for *emergence*. ‡ *Baptizein* (p. 108).

the Greek reads "the threefold immersion and emersion," Conant has it "the threefold sinking down and coming up."* In most of the cases the parties were infants under a year old. How came they up?

Heliodorus, about A.D. 390: "And being already baptized [i. e. overwhelmed by the waves, as the ship was in a storm], and wanting little of being immersed—*katadunai*—some of the pirates at first attempted to leave and get aboard of their own bark." † Notice here, in this quotation cited by Conant and *baptidzomenōn,* rendered by him "becoming immerged and wanting little of sinking, some of the pirates attempted to leave," etc., first, the ship was baptized by the storm dashing the waves upon it. It was "baptized" but not "immersed;" second, if "already immerged" how could the pirates be calculating, some whether to desert it or not and others not even yet resolved to desert it? third, notice that baptize here is contrasted with immersion. See also Dr. Gale on *dunein* (Wall, vol. 2).

How now can *dunai* mean to perish, necessarily, when not only it, but when strengthened by *kata* to give it additional force, still so far from implying such an immersion as necessarily takes to the bottom or causes to perish, it is the very word used to express the mode of the baptism which we call immersion and trine-immersion? One more case out of Conant, p. 106, "For to be baptized, even immersed (*kataduesthai*), ‡ then to emerge," etc. Again, "For as he who is immersed in the waters (*endunon*), and baptized," etc. §

---

* *Tœtrissœ katadusai kai anadusai.* Here is *dunai* with *kata* and *ana*—to express *immersion* and *emersion.*

† 'Ήδη δὲ βαπτιζομένων καὶ καταδῦναι, etc. (See Conant, page 18).

‡ *Yet Dr. Graves repeats this blunder* (Debate, p. 289).

§ *Baptizein*, 104. Ἐνδύνων ἐν τοῖσι ὕδασι καὶ βαπτιζόμενος—here we have *en dunai,* to be mersed in—immersed.

A. Campbell quotes Basil, A. D. 360: "By three immersions the great mystery of baptism is accomplished."* He adds several more where both *endunai* and *katadunai* express his idea of an immersion. Conant therefore says of *baptidzo* (p. 89), "It means simply to put into or under water (or other substance), without determining whether the object immersed sinks to the bottom or floats in the liquid, or is immediately taken out." He adds on same page that the word *baptidzo* is also used where a living being is put under water for the purpose of drowning, and of course is left to perish in the immersing element." No one will dispute this. Ingham, Carson, Cox, and A. Campbell give many illustrations of it, and A. Campbell therefore renders it to "drown." Here, then, we see—

4. That these writers demonstrate to us that *baptidzo* is used in classic Greek frequently in the very sense which they attach to *dunai*—sink that they may perish, while *dunai* is used to express the force of *baptidzo* when it is used for an immersion where the party does not perish.

5. Hence this old theory, being crushed by Conant and his associates, and utterly exploded and abandoned by them, it follows that the criticisms, views, and arguments that Pasor, Terretinus, Casaubon, Sucier, Beza, Vossius, Witsius, and others built upon such crudities, must fall so far as their support goes. On this false conceit, and the assumption denied by all immersionists that Jewish proselyte baptism was before Christ and followed by the apostles, the old immersionists of the fifteenth, sixteenth, and seventeenth centuries built all their arguments for immersion. The other was the assumption of the oneness of classic and Biblical Greek, though they, despite their theory, were forced to see *baptidzo* was an exception.

* *En trisi tais katadusesi* (Chris Baptism. p. 182).

They differ equally in selecting the word to express the primary meaning of *bapto* and *baptidzo*. Pasor, a favorite with immersionists, gives *bapto* as "derived from *bao*, Hebrew, *ba*," "whence is *bapto*" equivalent, he says, to the Latin *mitto*. Schleusner, in his Septuagint Lexicon, derives it from Hebrew *bo*, in Hiphil, *heba*.* He then gets thrust, lead to, pour together, moisten or bedew. But all this all critics, and all immersionists especially, will utterly repudiate. Gazes derives it from *ballo*, which not only implies to throw but to sprinkle and pour. Still less unscientific is the present disposition of immersionists to discover the primary meaning of words, especially of this word. Their plan is to find what is in a given age or period, a most common or prevailing use of a word, or meaning attached, and then accept that as proof absolute of its primary meaning. Yet there is not a Baptist scholar that does not know such a rule to be utterly false and unscientific. On the contrary, ninety-nine words out of every hundred in all Indo-European and Semitic languages are used most constantly in figurative senses and not in the primary sense at all. This is so true that no one will deny it, and is sufficiently explained in all scientific works on the subject of philology. The truth is, there are less than five hundred root-words in our language of one hundred thousand words. But where, in what literature, and in what department of life will words most perfectly hold or retain their primary meanings?

BAPTIDZO IN THE CLASSICS.

In medicine and theology words will most perfectly retain their primitive meaning for reasons plain to every

* Pasor: Βαπτω, . . . *derivatur à βάω pro quo βαίνω et Heb.* בָּא *unde est* βαπτω, *etc.* "Schleusner—LXX Lex: βαπτω, . . . בֹּא, in Hiph. הֵבִיא *adducor Lev.* xi, 32, *immittatur, machats, confundo, pago, madeo*"

mind. In law they will stand the next best chance. It is in the religious use of the word we may most naturally seek for its primitive meaning. In medical Greek works we may find the most proper aids to a correct understanding of it. But right here we find that we are left almost exclusively to religious use; for we have no medical work coming down from remote times in Greek, Hippocrates and Galen being the oldest, and the works of the former interpolated.

That we may see how little help can be obtained from classic Greek, let us note the following facts, which will exclude it from any place in the investigation of the Bible or New Testament use of this word:

Ingham, the Baptist, quotes Swarzius thus: "'To baptize, to immerse, to overwhelm, to dip.' To authenticate this as the primary meaning of the term (*baptidzo*), he (Swarzius) adduces the following authorities: Polybius, iii, 72, etc., Dio, Porphyrius de Styrze, Diodorus Siculus, Strabo, Josephus." Now this is a fair specimen of all arguments to discover the primary meaning of *baptidzo*. Stephanus, 1572, of whom Scapula, Pasor, Hedericus, Schrevellius, Donnegan, etc. are mere abridgments, omitting his authorities or proof-texts, gives Plutarch first, who died one hundred and forty years after the birth of Christ, and brings in Plato about last; while Aristophanes, B.C. 450, and Pindar, B.C. 522, Aristotle, etc. are not quoted. Schleusner gives Diodorus the Sicilian, sixty to thirty years before Christ, first, "of the overflowing (*exundante*) of the Nile; next Strabo, who died about A.D. 25. Wahl, who sought to improve lexicography with Schleusner, cites Josephus first, who died A.D. 93; next Polybius, who died about one hundred and twenty-five years before Christ. Passow quotes Plutarch first (see above), and Plato, the first prose-writer who uses the word, last, omitting, with all the rest, Aristophanes and Pindar, the first Greeks who are known to have used the word!! Liddell & Scott follow suit, and Ed. Robinson cites Polybius first, Diodorus Siculus, etc., and does not improve the matter an iota. Conant cites Polybius first, Plutarch next. When our immersionist friends get angry at the lexicographers and "appeal to the ultimate authority"—the writers themselves—Drs. Conant, Carson, Gale, Pendleton, Ingham, A. Campbell, *et alii,* and say every definition must be sustained by a cited text, forgetting all that though in Hebrew and Syriac, taking Gesenius's immerse and dip under, צבע, when there is no such Hebrew word at all, hence no text cited, but only the Chaldee *tzeva;* when they so constantly appeal from the lexicons to the classics, we demand, then, proof-texts for the primary meaning. To quote a writer who was born long after the commission was given to baptize, supposing classic Greek legitimate evidence, is an infinite absurdity. To suppose that the above lexicographers were discussing primitives and derivatives, yet never classifying the relative claims of writers to accuracy of style, nor their ages, no, nor their centuries, jumbling all together—hotchpotching—is to accuse them of a stupidity most disgraceful. They have not tried to trace the difference in the meanings of this word or its root, *bapto,* as they occur in different ages. They give to both of them very different and seemingly opposite meanings, as has been seen, yet no scientific reason whatever. "Dip" is not "immerse" or "sink." "Plunge" is not "overflow." "Dip" is not "whelm" nor "overwhelm." "Sink" is not "inundate." "Wash" is not "intoxicate" nor "make drunk." "Sprinkle" and "pour" are not "drown." Freund and all Latin lexicographers and all the philologists of the age demand that we trace the word to its earliest occurrence, find its meaning or meanings; then descend, tracing every shade of meaning it took on, and why, how; and thus by the "comparative philology" or scientific processes we arrive at the perfect truth. We have never seen a Greek lexicon that cited Pindar or Aristophanes on *baptidzo;* no, not even Aristotle, Alcibiades, or Demosthenes. They have done far more justice to the root βάπτω, especially Stephanus. Pindar was born B.C. 522. Between his birth and that of the average authors cited by the standard lexicons on *baptidzo* five hundred years intervene! Is this looking after the primary meaning? Between Aristophanes, B.C. 450, and the ages of the authorities cited, over four hundred years pour their powerful and all-changing tide. Not only do words change wonderfully in such periods of time, but nations rise and totter to their fall, empires come upon the vast plains of history, flash their meteoric splendors across the darkness of ages, are torn, rent, decay, and fall. Cities are founded, rise to renown, and proclaim themselves eternal; but decay eats away their vitals and change after change ensues, till only a miserable and degenerate rabble is left to tell the tale of their departed greatness, or a fisherman's net and hut alone are left as a sad memorial of the work of time. While thus empires, nations, kingdoms, states, cities, and their languages have all been changed and modified by time, yet this one word *baptidzo* is assumed by immersionists to have been a diamond of such essence, a pearl of such water, as to resist the powers that wrought change upon every thing on earth and made deep engravings on the brow of old earth itself, yet left this word unaffected. Sublime conceit! Masterly and irresistible faith!

IS THE FOOT THE HEAD?

To see how unscientific has been the methods of the old philologists we have only to name the fact that Aratus, seven hundred years later than Homer, is the first authority cited by Stephanus on *bapto*. He is four hundred years later than Æschylus, two hundred years later than Aristophanes, who uses the word unusually often for one not writing on nature or art. But of all works the most astonishing here is the distinguished Dr. Dale's. He professes to adopt a most careful system of investigating.

DR. DALE'S METHOD.

While he deserves the greatest credit—as far as we have seen his works, two first volumes—for research, his rule or canon of interpretation is so destitute of all science that it is simply preposterous. Seeking the primary meaning of the words in dispute, he never classifies authors, disregards time, the early or late date of authors; but all are thrown together without order or method, and the most arbitrary principles adopted. In classic Greek here is his order.

1. *Baptidzo.* Accidentally Aristotle is put first. But in the same table, exerting more influence though, Archias, ninety years before Christ, comes next, and as of equal influence Julian, A. D. fourth century, comes next! Lucian A. D. 120 follows. Orpheus, apocryphal and of unknown late date, comes next. Plutarch A. D. 90, the next! In his next chapter, p. 254, it is thus: Achilles Tatius, at the close of the fifth or dawn of the sixth century after Christ, quoted three times consecutively; next an apocryphal Æsop, writer and date unknown; next Alex.

Aphrod., about A.D. 200, three citations! In the next chapter he begins with Achilles Tatius, five hundred years after Christ, giving four citations, p. 283. Next, on specific influence, p. 317, he begins with Achilles Tatius again! The next cited was born about two hundred and thirty years after Christ, while for secondary use he cites Plato who lived in the fifth century before Christ. Though Plato uses the word in a metaphorical sense that is based on a literal sense, and philological science owes it to science to use the fossil remains of antiquity to resurrect the living forms of the literal language.

On *bapto* he begins with Theocritus, eight hundred years later than Homer. His fourth author is in the third century after Christ; his next in the fourth; his next in the ninth century after Christ!! That is to say, Dr. Dale, with Carson, Gale, and the rest, quote a word used eighteen hundred years later than its first occurrences to find its primary meaning. If that is philology or science then Livingstone could have discovered the head of the Nile without going up stream, but to the mouth of the river, and Jefferson should have sent Lewis and Clarke to the region of the jetties, instead of the mountains and Indian-covered hills of the northwest, to discover the primal source of the Mississippi.

We think Dr. Dale altogether wrong in his assuming—

(1) That "permanent influence" was dreamed of by those who used *baptidzo*.

(2) If "*interposition*" implied such an idea, so did *pontidzo, buthidzo, dunai, katapontidzo, kataduo*. Homer, Herodotus, Thucydides, and the best as well as oldest Greek literature we have, use the last word where later Iron-age Greek—the only kind Dr. Dale cites or can cite for his immerse—uses *baptidzo* of vessels sinking, etc.

(3) A thousand words may imply in their effect permanent influence, including kill, murder, sin; as, to cut off a chicken's head is permanent influence. In all this it is simply assuming what no Greek ever dreamed of in the use of that or any other word of mere action or mode, however varied that action.

(4) But really the earliest use we have of the word did not contemplate permanent any thing, nor particular or specified duration. It is used for abuse, aspersion, as *katantleo* is in Greek. It is used for becoming drunk, for confusing with questions, and for overflowing land with tide-water, and these are its earliest recorded uses. In not one of these is permanent or unlimited influence thought of by the writer.

(5) His treatment rests on the supposition, really, that words originate with learned, deeply-metaphysical scholars, with these abstruse and remote meanings implied. Nothing is further from the facts. Word-building is a vastly different process.

2. Pindar, the Greek poet, is the first writer in the world yet found who uses it, and he but once, and in a metaphorical sense, pointing to the use of the word for a great while before his day. Describing "the impotent malice" and abuse of his enemies who aspersed his fair fame he said, "For, as when the rest of the net is toiling deep in the sea, I am as a cork above the net, unbaptized by [the waves] of the sea"—ἀβάπτιστός εἰμι . . . ἅλμας. Scholiast, "*salis undis.*" That is, I am as sere unharmed by your raging malice and abusive epithets as the cork is above the stormy and foaming billows. The waves of malice—i. e. your abusive epithets—fall harmlessly upon me, do not overwhelm me. The Greeks, the Latins, and other nations constantly use the word sprinkle

and pour for this very idea, but they never use immerse. So we in English say, "aspersion," "asperse" one's character, "foul aspersion," for slander, abuse. Shakspeare uses "bespatter" often for the same, as well as Bunyan, "bespatter a man,"* complaining of their abuses and defamations. Taylor, Baptist historian, says, "To vindicate them from those aspersions."† Shakspeare, "I was never so bethumped with words," etc. "These haughty words bespatter me like roaring cannon-shot." Often in Arabic a word meaning eloquent means to pour, sprinkle. The first occurrence, then, is no case of immersion nor dipping, but the application of the baptizing element to the subject coming upon him, and he as unharmed by it as the cork on the waves of the sea; every effort of the wave to fall upon, drench, or overwhelm him fails.

3. Aristophanes, the poet, 450 years before Christ, uses it once. He uses it in a metaphorical sense thus, "For he is praised," says he, "because he baptized (ἐβάπτισεν, *ebaptisen*) the stewards," etc. It is here used in the sense of bespatter with epithets or words, abuse, traduce, especially ridicule. There is no immersion or dipping here. To sprinkle any one with epithets or with praise was a common expression. The Greeks had this as a common saying, "To sprinkle any one with song," "sprinkle any one with eulogies."‡ In the above cases the stronger form is used—pour ridicule upon, overwhelm with words.

4. Plato, the great philosopher, born B. C. 429, is the first prose-writer that uses the word. It occurs three times in his writings, rendered "overwhelm" every time by Conant, A. Campbell, Gale, and all other parties we

---

* Bunyan's Differences about Baptism, complete works, page 842.
† Hist. Baptists, page 330, by Benedict.
‡ Ῥαίνειν, τινὰ ὑμνῳ—ῥαίνειν ἐυλογίας τινὰ (Pindar, viii, 81, etc.).

suppose. It is metaphorically used each time. "Speaking of young Cleinias, confounded with the sophistical questions and subtilties of the professional disputants, he says, 'And I, perceiving that the youth was overwhelmed —baptized—wishing to give him a respite.'" Questions asked confusing the boy is not putting the boy into the questions, but the questions to him. The boy is not poured on the questions, but the questions are poured on to him so fast that he is confused, overwhelmed by them. By the way, whence that word confuse?* Alexander was "overwhelmed—baptized—with wine."

Plato again says, "For I myself am one of those who yesterday were overwhelmed—baptized," alluding to the drinking of wine.† Conant says, "In this use the Greek word corresponds to the English drench" (p. 70). No dip, no immerse; yet—

5. Alcibiades, B.C. 400, who comes next, was a poet, and uses it metaphorically, as have all who as yet used it. In an epigram on the comic poet Eupolis, occasioned by the offensive allusions in a play by him called *Baptæ*—those who stained, colored—metaphorically, those who bespattered with billingsgate—"You besprinkled (βάπτες, *baptes*) me in your plays [i. e. with words of abuse]; but I will destroy thee with streams more bitter, baptizing thee with waves of the sea."‡ I will pour upon you a torrent of invective; I will pour bitterest streams of abuse upon you; as with the waves of a sea I will overwhelm you. Later by centuries Plutarch speaks of one "baptized by [excessive labors] falling upon him—ὑπερβαλλουσι, *huperballousi*." He drew the comparison from "a moderate

---

* Enthydermus, chap. vii; Conant, p. 65.
† Conant, pp. 69, 70.
‡ See the Greek, Conant, p. 29.

15

226 BAPTISM.

amount of water," nourishing plants; but too much choked. There is no dip, no immerse yet; but invariably the application of the baptizing element to the subject.

BAPTIDZO—PRIMARY MEANING.

A striking instance of the twofold fact that a word may primarily mean to sprinkle or pour and then to overwhelm, flood, inundate, and also be used to express a torrent of words poured upon one, aspersion, abuse, is found in Athæneus: "You seem to me, O guests, to be strangely flooded—κατηντλῆσθαι, *kataentlaesthai,* overwhelmed with vehement words, while also waiting to be overwhelmed—βεβαπτισθαι, *bebaptisthai,* baptized—with undiluted wine."

Here the parties are "overwhelmed" with vehement words, overwhelmed with wine. The two words are used in the same sense. Dr. Conant renders *kataentlaesthai* here "flooded"—a strong phrase for overwhelm. But this word used in the same sense as *baptidzo* here primarily applies to affusion, means generally to sprinkle, to pour. Passow, Pape, Rost, Palm, Stephens all render it generally by sprinkle and pour.* Dunbar renders it "To pour upon, to bathe with water, . . . to soothe with eloquence, to overwhelm with or pour out ridicule upon one." Liddell & Scott: "To pour upon or over; hence, metaphorically, to pour a flood of words over one, to bathe, to steep, foment."

Here is a word that primarily applies to affusion by agreement of all authorities that is used by the Greeks in the same sense with *baptidzo*—just as it is often used. In Aristophanes, Demosthenes, and in Plutarch in its noun

* Pape: Darübergiessen=schütten, etc. Passow: Same, and darubcrausgiessen, uberschutten, überhaufen

form, *pluno,* to rain, pour, sprinkle, then to wash, means "to abuse, revile, reproach."*

6. Demosthenes, born B.C. 385, next uses it once, if he be the author of the speech attributed to him. He uses it greatly strengthened by the preposition διa, *dia,* thus: "Not the speakers—public declaimers—for they knew how to baptize with him—Philip"—διαβαπτίζεσθαι—*diabaptidzesthai*—τούτω, with this man. Here it "is used metaphorically, and the sense is, for these know how to match him in foul language," says Dr. Conant, p. 77; but when he makes it "souse" it is ridiculous. That figure so common to the Greek language, as well as the English, of bespattering, aspersing with foul words, and when gifted in speech, "pour out a torrent of words;" common to the Latin, very, and to the Arabic, alone makes sense and is true. In a past chapter the reader found many cases of this in the foot-notes, where words for sprinkle and pour coming to mean overwhelm, etc. were given. Consult Graves-Ditzler Debate, pp. 397-8, *et seq.*

7. Aristotle, born B.C. 384, uses it once only in all his writings. He is the first writer known to use it literally. All as yet used it metaphorically; he uses it "in the literal, physical sense," as Conant would say. Being the most learned and scientific and accurate Greek who ever lived, having the most complete and accurate scholarship of all Greeks and careful in his use of terms, and the first we have that uses it literally, we must notice closely his use of it, and thereby get all the light we can. He says, "They say that the Phœnicians who inhabit the so-called Gadera, sailing four days outside of the Pillars of Hercules with an east wind, come to certain places full of rushes and sea-weed, which, when it is ebb-tide, are not

* See Pickering's Revised Greek Lexicon, 1846, etc.

overflowed—μη βαπτίζεσθαι, *mae baptidzesthai*, but at full tide are overflowed—κατακλύζεσθαι, *katakludzesthai*."* Notice—

1. The element comes upon the baptized object. The land is not dipped—it does not penetrate into the water, nor sink into it, is not immersed, but overflowed by the rushing water.

2. It is equivalent to the word κατακλύζω, *katakludzo*. Aristotle, instead of using either word twice so closely for the same fact, uses *baptidzo* for it first, then *katakludzo*. *Katakludzo* is compounded of the preposition *kata*, to strengthen the verb, and *kludzo*. See Chapter XIII, p. 138. Its primary meaning is to bedash, sprinkle, infuse water. The word clyster is the noun of the verb, often occurring in Greek. The ancient lexicographers have *peri-kludzo* for sprinkle, besprinkle, bedash with water. Yet it comes to apply to a more copious use of it, but always with the water, the active agent, not passive—not penetrated by the object, but falling upon the object. It often means to wash also. Hence the greatest of Greek scholars in the golden age of Grecian intellect, using *baptidzo* interchangeably with such a word, crushes the immersion theory to atoms, and shows that a word primarily meaning to sprinkle or bedash with water is the equivalent of *baptidzo*. It was centuries after this that Theophylact, the Greek, used the same word, *katakludzo*, to express the baptism of the Holy Spirit. See Conant, Ex. 199, p. 113.

3. *Baptidzo* does mean, often means, "to overflow." A. Campbell, Prof. Ripley (Baptist), Swartz, M. Stuart render it overflow. Conant renders its equivalent "overflow" in the same line, but falsely renders *baptidzo*.

---

* Aristotle, *De Mirabil. Auscultat*, 136; Conant, 3. Dr. Conant shamefully translates *the one immerse*, the *other*, for exactly the same thing, overflow. A. Campbell was more candid.

ANCIENT CRITICISMS—ERRORS. 229

Yet (p. 88), summing up, he renders it "overflows," alluding to this case. But no word either primarily meaning immerse—if such a word exists—or that properly means immerse, with no other primary meaning implying affusion, can be found that means to "overflow." The three Hebrew words for immerse, *tabha, kaphas, shakha;* the six or eight Arabic words elsewhere given; Persic, Syriac, Æthiopic; *mergo, im-, de-,* and *sub-mergo,* in Latin; the Greek *buthidzo, kataduo, pontidzo, dupto* (dip), *katapontidzo,* immerse, never mean to overflow; neither the German *sinken, tauchen, ein,* and *undertauchen.* As "overflow" can not come from dip or immerse, yet does come to be a derived meaning and a LITERAL meaning of *baptidzo,* immerse or dip can not be the primary meaning of *baptidzo.*

We have now traced every occurrence of *baptidzo* from its appearance in literature by Pindar, five hundred and twenty-two years before Christ, to Aristotle—covering one hundred and thirty-eight years—dating the birth of each. We are giving the facts first; the philology is yet to appear more fully. Note—

(1) For one hundred and thirty-eight years it occurs only in a metaphorical sense.

(2) During all these years it always implied affusion, application of the baptizing element, never implying the application or sinking of the object into the element.

(3) The first time in which it occurs in a literal sense it is the application of the water to the object baptized, by the greatest of all Greek scholars.

(4) It is used by him as equivalent to a word that primarily means to bedash or sprinkle with water, as when it is sprinkled suddenly or forcibly in the face or on any part of the body. That is its most common use.

230   BAPTISM.

4. The next occurrence is in Eubulus, a Greek comic writer, about B.C. 380. It is difficult to determine in what sense he uses it: "Who now the fourth day is baptized, leading the famished life of a wretched mullet," a notedly hungry, always empty fish, according to fable. Whether the person was for the fourth day clinging to some part of the wrecked vessel, starving for three days, baptized often by the waves dashing upon him, we can not say unless we had more of "the fragment." It points that way as far as it goes. There is but the one occurrence.

The quotation "falsely attributed to Heraclides Ponticus" in this century belongs to a much later date. See Conant, p. 34.

5. Evenus of Paros* is the next, B.C. 250, Epigram: "If [Bacchus] breathe strongly, it hinders love—i. e. if a man is completely intoxicated, love's amours are defeated; for he [Bacchus] baptizes with a sleep near to death."† "Here is the metaphorical sense of the word," says Stuart, who renders it "overwhelms." From Pindar to this poet two hundred and seventy-two years intervene, yet *baptidzo* never yet occurs meaning to dip or immerse. Polybius, born B.C. 203 or 205, comes next—a prose-writer. From the times of Pindar to those of Polybius sum up three hundred and seventeen to three hundred and nineteen years. During all these stormy and changy times *baptidzo* never had been used for dip, for plunge, for immerse, but always points infallibly to affusion.

Baptidzo may have been in use hundreds of years

---

* Evenus, xv, in Jacob's Anthol., p. 99; M. Stuart, p. 61; Conant, p. 58.

† Βαπτίζει δ' ὕπνῳ—not, as nearly five hundred years later Clem. Alex. has it, εἰς ὕπνον, into sleep.

before we meet with it in the literature that has survived the waste of ages, but in its earliest use as known to us we have enough to show its primary meaning aside from the facts brought out on *bapto*. Among its prevailing classic meanings are intoxicate, overwhelm, overflow, pour over or upon, of words, then the effects of wine, questions, water. We know that none of these meanings can be derived from dip or immerse. That has been perfectly tested. They are constantly in all languages derived from words primarily meaning to sprinkle, to pour, to moisten, bedew, etc. All the facts connected with *bapto* point out the same results.

CHAPTER XIX.

Classical Usage—Summary of Facts.

Immersionists hold that the prevailing meaning of a word is its primary meaning, regarding not earlier occurrences at all, ignoring all the laws of science and word-building, development of language. But is immerse—English, sink—or dip the prevailing meaning of *baptidzo* even in the classics? We will test the matter by themselves.

1. T. J. Conant, D.D., renders *baptidzo* out of sixty-three consecutive occurrences—

(1) "Whelm" forty-five times; "overwhelm" eight times=fifty-three times; while in those sixty-three consecutive occurrences he does not render it dip, the thing they do in baptism, once even, and "immerse" only ten times!

(2) After p. 73, *baptidzo* is compounded with prepositions and does not apply properly. All the cases of *baptidzo* simply, then, are one hundred and forty-one, of which only seven times does he render it dip; i. e. one hundred and thirty-four against seven in his favor.

(3) These seven cases are not correctly rendered.

(4) Out of the one hundred and forty-one times, it is rendered by him immerse only thirty-five times, making one hundred and six against thirty-five for immerse.

(5) These are partly false renderings, as Aristotle on the "overflowing" of the land, etc.

CLASSICAL USAGE—SUMMARY OF FACTS.

(6) Not one of them has the meaning; in not one of the one hundred and forty-one cases does *baptidzo* describe or apply to the action that constitutes their baptism.

(7) Conant renders *baptidzo* by fourteen different words, giving it fourteen definitions! Yet they say "there is absolutely no word in the Greek language of more univocal sense than the word baptize" (Address by Dr. Eaton, bound up in Conant's work). Surely this was meant for a huge joke.

(8) He only finds thirty occurrences of the word before the birth of Christ that he can date, allowing a margin for that number. These he renders—

(9) One "dip" out of the thirty; i. e. twenty-nine against one for "dip."

(10) Only thirteen "immersions;" that is, seventeen against thirteen.

(11) Several of these, as Aristotle's, are wrong, leaving dip clear out, and immerse maimed forever.

2. Dr. Gale, the great Baptist of a former century, thus renders it: "Dipped in" once; "dip," three times; "laid under," once; "over head and ears," once—a peculiar verb, no doubt, very "univocal"; "drowned," one time; "drowns and overwhelms," once; "sink," ten times; "immerse," three; i. e. eighteen against three for immerse; eighteen against three for "dip," or twenty-one versus one "dip in."

3. M. Stuart, when summing up for immerse, a Congregationalist writing by request of Baptists, of forty-one cases it is—

(1) One "dip," six "plunge," seven "sink," one "immerge," three "immerse," one "overflow," twenty-two "overwhelm." That is—

(2) Forty against one "dip," or,

(3) Thirty-eight against three immerse!

(4) Twenty-three cases "overflow" and "overwhelm," of application of the baptizing element to the object, against one "dip," the word expressive of the baptism of our opponents. What is the prevailing meaning? Is it the primitive?

4. Prof. J. M. Pendleton, D.D,* out of twenty-two occurrences renders it—

(1) Plunge, eight times; dip, one; sink, five; overflow, one; immerse, two; overwhelm, five; i. e.

(2) Twenty against two for immerse—ten to one against immerse!

(3) Twenty-one against one for dip!!

(4) "Overflow" and "overwhelm," six times, pointing to affusion, against one for "dip." Does the prevailing meaning indicate the primary?

5. A. Campbell shall be heard from. In Christian Baptism, his greatest work, he renders *baptidzo:*

(1) Sink, ten times; immerse, three; overflow, one; dip, not at all; "overwhelm," ten times; i. e.

(2) Twenty-one against three for immerse.

(3) Twenty-four against not one for "dip!"

(4) "Overflow" and "overwhelm" eleven times against no dip—all pointing to affusion.

(5) He gives through his renderings, version, and quotations introduced, leaving out the parts he does not like, twenty different renderings to *baptidzo.*

Surely it is a simple word—"UNIVOCAL."

CLASSICS—SUMMARY OF FACTS.

6. Ingham, later than Conant, in his large work, Hand-book on Baptism, London, though he had A. Camp-

---

* "Why I am a Baptist," from pages 97 to 100.

bell, Carson, Gale, Conant, Booth, etc. before him, gives us this result: Omitting the Bible and Apocrypha cases, as being the ones in dispute to be determined—"submerge," one; "play the immersing match," one; i. e. "dip," one. He renders it "overwhelm" fifty times out of one hundred and sixty-nine cases. Here we have it meaning "overwhelm" fifty times to dip once, and one hundred and sixty-eight to one dip! "Immerse" is his favorite rendering. "It always means to dip"—means "nothing else"—yet means to dip only one time in all its occurrences through fifteen hundred years!

7. Dr. Carson renders it "immerse" three times; "sink," seven times; "plunge," two times; "dip," three times; "baptize," fourteen times; "put into," one time; "drown," one time—in all thirty-one proof-texts. Here we have twenty-eight against three for "immerse." We have twenty-eight against three for dip; twenty-nine against two for plunge. Yet it "always means to dip"!

If I have counted accurately, the sum of all is four hundred and fifty-seven against eighteen for dip! By the unanimous renderings of the great masters themselves we have *baptidzo* meaning something else over twenty-five times to every one time it means dip—over twenty-five against one!

With the facts from the classics and these renderings, we are prepared to test the matter by the laws of language. These renderings are far more valuable than the renderings of lexicons, because, first, these men, though far less learned in Greek than the lexicographers, were far more learned in the literature of this word. A lexicographer can not afford to devote but a few moments to the study of each word, all being equally important to him. But these men devoted years to this one word; second, they are its special friends. They have a theory to support, and many of them a very restricted, and, as some think, an intolerant, proscriptive theory, that unchurches millions of the most pious of God's people, and they start out with the assumption that *baptidzo* in the classics describes the exact action of their rite—that it always means to dip.

Dip always implies withdrawal to the extent of penetration. Immerse is sink, sink in, with no withdrawal implied.

1. We have seen that all the earliest uses of *baptidzo* were in support of affusion. Yet in Pindar, Aristophanes, Alcibiades, Evenus, poets all, it is applied to aspersing people with abusive epithets, as well as in Demosthenes. But nothing is more common to Greeks, Latins, Hebrews,* Arabs, Germans, Americans, and English than this habit; and words meaning to pour, to sprinkle especially, are most common, while immerse is not so used at all. Hence these facts establish sprinkle as the primary meaning of *baptidzo*.

2. The Hebrew words for immerse, the Greek (often repeated by us), *kataduo*, etc., the Latin *mergo*, *im-*, *de-*, and *sub-mergo*, never mean, are never employed for to abuse or sprinkle, bespatter one with epithets or words; hence *baptidzo* could not have primarily meant immerse, merse, or dip, since the above meanings can not be derived therefrom.

3. *Baptidzo* means, in the oldest of all prose-writers known to employ it, Plato, to "overwhelm," so rendered by all immersion authors and by the lexicons, being used metaphorically by Plato, born B. C. 429. But "over-

---

* See also Deuteronomy xxxii, 2: "My doctrine shall drop as the rain, my *speech* shall distill as the dew, as the small rain upon the tender herb, and as the showers upon the grass."

whelm" can not be derived from dip, as a proper word, or immerse, sink. Philologically it is absurd. *Baptidzo* does come to mean "to overwhelm," often. Overwhelm can not come from dip; hence dip could not have been the primary meaning of *baptidzo;* nor from immerse; hence it could not have been the primary meaning of the word. We never apply "dip" to a case effected by overwhelming.

4. Dr. Conant renders *baptidzo* "whelm" forty-five times between pages 43 and 72. But "whelm" can not be a meaning derived from dip, neither from immerse; hence neither of those words expresses the original meaning of *baptidzo.*

5. The earliest occurrence of *baptidzo* in a literal sense is in Aristotle, and means literally "to overflow." But "overflow" never is derived from a word that primarily or properly means to dip, nor from immerse. Neither dip nor immerse was the primary meaning of *baptidzo.*

6. *Baptidzo* often means to "intoxicate," "make drunk." Dip and immerse do not mean to intoxicate, it is never derived from such primaries; therefore they never could have been primary meanings of *baptidzo.* Neither immerse—in Hebrew, Arabic, Persic, Æthiopic, Syriac, Greek, Latin, German, nor English, neither in tongues Aryan nor Semitic—nor dip ever comes to mean to make drunk. *Mergo* rarely applies to the effect of wine, to sink under its effects.

7. Dip is urged by all immersionists as a leading meaning of *baptidzo.* But dip never can be derived from immerse; they as wholes imply opposites in action. Hence, if dip be a meaning, the word never could have primarily meant immerse.

8. Immersionists, such as Drs. Gale, Ingham, Cox,

Mell, Halley (and Conant gives many proofs), acknowledge that *baptidzo* and *baptisma* are used by Greeks where the baptism is effected by "superfusion"—i. e. pouring upon. But "dipping" can not be so accomplished, nor can "superfusion" be derived from dip, much less from immerse. Hence dip and immerse never were primary meanings of *baptidzo*.

9. *Baptidzo* means "to wash." All are agreed here.* The immersionists all make it the effect of dipping in water—that it is a figurative or derived meaning. But—

(1) Immerse never means to wash in any language on earth. It is never a meaning by figure or by fact, if the proper words for immerse in Greek, Latin, Hebrew, or English. *Mergo, immergo, demergo, submergo,* the words themselves, never mean wash. Neither of the six or eight Arabic words given that properly and strictly mean to immerse, means to wash. The same is true of the Greek *pontidzo, dunai, buthidzo, kata-pontidzo, kataduo,* all meaning definitely to immerse, to sink, sink in. The English sink, the German *sinken, eintauchen, undertauchen,* do not mean to wash, nor cleanse, no more than dip, *tunken, tauchen,* and the Greek *dupto,* dip, *kolumbao,* dip, dive, stand in the same list.

(2) Neither has immerse any necessary or philological relation or necessary connection with wash, as things are most generally washed in nature by the water coming in contact with them, and by infinite odds mostly by sprinkling and pouring. Every leaf, herb, tree, spear of grass, rock, hill, house, fence, all things in nature are constantly washed, cleansed from soiling, defiling elements by the rain.

(3) Indeed immerse as often applies to things that de-

---

* See proofs under Chapter VII on the Laver, and see Index—*Wash.*

file, corrupt, soil, as to purifying elements. Things are immersed in filth, mud, hog-styes, filthy pools, stenchy vats, sinks of all kinds.

(4). Nay, merely dipping or immersing in clear water does not necessarily wash or cleanse, does not at all. Merely dip a dirty garment in clear water and you will make poor headway in washing it, especially by one single dip.

10. Again, *baptidzo* meant wash two hundred and eighty-three years before Christ, as 2 Kings v, 10, 14, shows. It was interchanged with *louo* and its noun *lutron*, washing, cleansing, in the Apocrypha two hundred and thirty-five years before Christ, we know, and most likely much earlier. It was interchanged with *kludzo*, wash, besprinkle, etc., in the Apocrypha likewise. But *baptidzo* never took on the meaning of immerse till the middle of the second century before Christ—about one hundred and fifty years before Christ—in Polybius, who was born two hundred and three to two hundred and five years before Christ. That was a rare meaning, though, and continued as a minority meaning, as the immersionist renderings show. No lexicon gives immerse as a meaning of *baptidzo* supported by an authority earlier than Polybius. Most of them cite Plutarch, long after the birth of Christ, as the first, some Diodorus Siculus, later than Polybius. We have seen that Polybius, Plutarch, and Diodorus Siculus wrote after the great breakdown and change in the Greek language also.

Wash, therefore, antedates immerse as a meaning of *baptidzo* from at least one hundred and twenty-five to one hundred and fifty years, if not fully three hundred years. Hence it is impossible that wash or cleanse should be derived from immerse as a meaning of *baptidzo*.

11. Again, *baptidzo* means to "overflow" in Aristotle, which was one hundred and seventy-nine years before it came to mean "immerse." Hence immerse can not be an early, not to say primary, meaning of *baptidzo*.

12. Of all the words properly meaning to immerse in Hebrew, *tabha, kaphash, shapo;* eight in Arabic extensively used, *gamara, gamasa, atta,* etc.; in Persic, *ghuta;* Æthiopic, *maab, maba;* in Greek, *buthidzo, kataduo,* etc., etc.; *dupto,* dip, *immergo,* etc. in Latin, none of these proper words for immerse ever mean to abuse, slander, defame, simply because asperse, pour upon, are not in their primaries nor in them any where.

13. While these facts infallibly prove that neither dip nor immerse nor plunge was the primitive meaning of *baptidzo,* they all point out sprinkling as that meaning. In addition to these facts another great truth settles the question:

All the meanings belonging or claimed to belong to *baptidzo* in classic or New Testament and apocryphal Greek do constantly belong to a great number of words in Greek, Latin, Hebrew, Arabic, etc. that do by agreement of all authorities belong to words that primarily mean to sprinkle, to others that primarily mean to moisten where it is effected by sprinkling, to bedew, to wet, to rain. On the contrary, in no instance does a word in these languages that properly means to immerse or primarily to sink, plunge, or dip have the meanings that belong either in the classics or New Testament and apocryphal Greek to *baptidzo.*

14. In Chapters XII and XIII we have seen over fifty words that illustrate this—words not used for baptism in the Bible. They are in Latin, such as *tingo,* from Greek *tengo* (or *tenggo,* τεγγω), *madeo, madefacio, perfundo, as-*

CLASSICAL USAGE—SUMMARY OF FACTS. 241

pergo, taking on more or less the meanings of *bapto* and leading ones of *baptidzo;* Greek *deuo, brecho, kludzo, katantleo;* a host of Semitic words, many beginning with sprinkle, mean to wet, cleanse, pour, wash, saturate, intoxicate, dip, immerse. In no instance is the law reversed. From sprinkle to immerse we saw the way was natural, historic, constant. Words meaning to bedew, moisten take on stronger meanings and come to mean soak, intoxicate, saturate, dye, dip, immerse. Others primarily meaning sprinkle come to mean to pour, applied to water, to rain, which falling washes the millions of trees, shrubs, all vegetable growths, fences, houses, of accumulated dust, soot, excrescences that can be thus removed; hence to wash. Pouring rains "overflow," cause to "overflow," "inundate," "overwhelm." Overwhelming objects may and often does cause them to sink—be immersed; hence the next meaning is immerse, submerse. This we found illustrated often. Overwhelming some objects causes them "to dip," as a vessel often does; hence naturally comes that meaning.

Under *bapto* we saw that from sprinkle comes stain. We saw it abundantly in Chapter XIII. Thence we saw that it comes to apply to coloring, dyeing in any way; hence, in the easiest and best way, by dipping into the fluid the thing to be dyed. From dipping for color they learned to let it remain in for some time, i. e. immerse. Hence, sprinkle is demonstrated to be the primary meaning of both words.

15. We saw that *baptidzo* in its earliest known occurrences applies to bespattering people with abusive epithets—pouring a torrent of invectives. We know nothing is more common than for people to say such a person "poured a torrent of abuse upon me;" such a slander or

report "is a foul aspersion." We never saw it foul dipping, foul immersion. Hence the primary use of the word was for aspersion. Constantly, then—

16. Words meaning to sprinkle primarily, in great numbers, cover all meanings of *baptidzo;* words for immersion never do; hence it is absolutely certain that sprinkle was the primary meaning of *baptidzo*.

17. Let it be remembered now how seldom *baptidzo* represents "dip" in the house of its friends; how seldom immerse! That only in the later Greek it came to mean immerse at all. That these authors—the two or three who use it for immerse—lived from the middle of the second century before Christ down in remote centuries from those in which the apostles were educated; that it so occurs in a foreign secular literature unknown to their education, their early instruction; that in their own literature it always meant wash, cleanse, used religiously. And had they followed classic usage, the prevailing and earliest use of it was in the sense of affusion, and the most renowned and learned Greeks never used it for either dip or immerse, as seen by immersionists themselves, but in the sense of affusion.

18. In accordance with these facts, gathered from the chosen fields of our opponents, we turn to still another illustration, never noted by any writer any more than were the preceding facts, viz: In the period B.C. 570, *tzeva* (baptize in Syriac, Chaldee, and Arabic) occurs for the first time in history or literature (Dan. iv, 12, 20, 22, 30; v. 21). Nebuchadnezzar's body was baptized with the dew from (*apo*) heaven, rendered (*conspergatur*) sprinkled by Jerome as well as wet. See details under Versions. Later by centuries this word, to sprinkle, means to wash in the Targums. It nowhere occurs in Hebrew, notwith-

CLASSICAL USAGE—SUMMARY OF FACTS. 243

standing Gesenius assumes meanings for it for immerse when there never was such a word in Hebrew so far as literature goes!! Later still it came to apply to a partial dip, and still kept up its meanings, wash and sprinkle, as the Targums in Psalm vi, 7; the Syriac Luke vii, 38, 44; Ezekiel xxii, demonstrated. Yet immersionists contend it means nothing but immerse in the seventh century after Christ, in the Arabic version.*

19. *Shataph* (שָׁטַף), already noticed, "a pouring rain," "overflowing rain;" first means "to gush, pour out;" second, in Leviticus, fifteen hundred years before Christ, it means to wash every time it occurs, applied to what the New Testament writers call baptism; third, later in the Prophets, it is to wash, overflow, overwhelm, but never immerse; fourth, later still, in the sense of overwhelm, almost altogether; fifth, then later still, in the third century after Christ, it means mainly to immerse, submerse. See the latter use, Castelli Heptaglotton, sub. v. שָׁטַף=מָטַר in Æthiopic.

IS DIP IMMERSE?

Immersionists insist that dip is exactly synonymous with immerse. Dr. Graves, late as 1876, rewriting his speeches, Debate, 527, says, "All lexicons give dip and to immerse *as synonymous terms.*" Italics his. In reply we say:

1. All English standards giving the real meaning and early usage of the two words make a clear and perfect distinction between them.*

---

* In Carrollton Debate, as written by Dr. Graves, he says *tseva* is baptize in Syriac—dip. (See the full quotation on Versions.)

* Webster, 1878, "Dip. 1. The action of dipping or plunging *for a moment* into a fluid." Again, he defines it "to put for a moment into

2. All lexicons clearly bring out a marked difference by

(1) Defining words that have various meanings, as moisten, wet, dip, immerse, by various Latin words—*intingo* for dip, *immergo* for immerse.

(2) Words that mean strictly and always to immerse, demerse, they always define by *mergo, immergo, de-* and *submergo*, never by *intingo*, dip, much less by *tingo*. See many examples already given. Where *tabha*, immerse, e. g. is defined, Gesenius, Castell, Schindler, Hottinger, Stokius, Leigh, all use *immergo, immersit*, not one gives *tingo* or *intingo*. No lexicon gives *tingo* or *intingo* for *kaphash*, immerse, or for Arabic *atta, ghuta, amasa*, immerse, though they repeat the *mersit, de-*, and *immersit* over and again, sometimes fifteen and twenty times, giving examples. So of *buthidzo, katapontidzo, kataduo*, immerse. Nor do Kouma and Gazes, native Greek lexicographers, in defining these words use *dupto* or *bapto*, dip.

3. Neither do Kouma and Gazes use *dupto, bapto*, in Greek to define *baptidzo*, though they use *buthidzo*, immerse, sink.

4. Nor will this bold and popular assumption by immersionists bear comparing with the words for immersion in the Bible. A. Campbell, Conant, Wilkes, Graves, Gale, Carson, etc. all render immerse into English by sink. In Psalm lxix, 2, in the Hebrew, it reads, "I immerse—sink—in deep mire." Was he dipped in it? Psalm ix, 15, reads in Hebrew and Greek, "The heathen are immersed

---

any liquid." Webster, 1871, gives the true meaning of dip, as used in James's version, and those times—"to insert in a fluid, and withdraw again" (Lev. iv, 6). He thus gives the meaning of immerse—"Immerse [Lat. *immersus*, etc.], immersed; buried, hid, sunk [obs.]. 'Things immerse in matter'" (Bacon). Here is the true, literal force of immerse—it had no other force till the loose style of Baptists introduced its present uses which, of course, dictionaries have to follow.

—sunk down in the pit that they made." Were they simply dipped in it? Exodus xv, 5, in Hebrew and Greek, reads, "They immersed—sank—into the bottom as a stone." Did they simply dip into the bottom, "withdrawing" immediately? In verse 10 the same reads, "They immersed—sank as lead in the mighty waters." Were they merely dipped? In Matthew xviii, 6, the Greek reads, "It were better for him that a millstone were hanged about his neck, and that he were immersed in the depth of the sea." Would dip do there?

5. Let us put it dip where Dr. Graves and others render it immerse, sink. Example 39 in Conant, "And already becoming immerged (baptized) and wanting little of sinking"—of a ship. Render it now, "And already becoming dipped and wanting little of dipping," etc. Example 22, Debate, p. 237, of ships and the crew—"And were submerged (baptized) along with their vessels." Were the vessels that submerged merely dipped? Example 4, Debate, p. 207, "Certain desert places . . . which, when it is ebb-tide, are not *baptizesthai*—immersed, baptized, but when it is flood-tide are overflowed." Were the "desert places" dipped? Scores of examples could be added. Let these serve as samples.

6. All ancient and all more modern versions act by the same rule. They never render *bapto*, e. g. by immerse, etc. or submerse, but by *tingo, intingo, aspergo* in Latin, and by corresponding words in all other versions. As *mergo, immergo* are words so common in Latin, why in all the Bible in so many versions did they not use them if *tingo, intingo* were the same as *mergo*, etc.?

Let us now examine the Semitic words that definitely and strictly mean to immerse in current use, and notice their original import as well.

1. *Gamasa** in Hebrew means to burden; in Arabic to hide, conceal, perplex, obscure, evade, hide; then, from burden, to immerse, and currently has that meaning.

2. *Gamara*,† Arabic, to press, compress, yet constantly it means to immerse, demerse, submerse.

3. *Amatha*,‡ Arabic, to be heavy; then commonly to demerse.

4. *Dul, dala*,§ Arabic, to depress; then commonly to immerse.

5. *Gara* ¶ (Hebrew, *gur*), to descend, depress, immerse.

6. *Atta*, ‖ to oppress, press down; then, common, to immerse, demerse.

7. *Kaphash*,** to press down, immerse.

8. *Shakah*,†† *shaqa*, to depress, compress; then immerse, submerse, especially.

9. [טָבַע], *tabha*, Hebrew, Syriac, Arabic, all give "to impress." Syriac, "primarily to impress." Buxtorf gives "to press, impress or fix in, be immersed, demersed," etc. From impress comes the meaning to cut or coin money. Webster's Dictionary runs wild here after Gesenius's crude method, but were his position regarded as sound it, too, would add strength to our facts here; but we regard his views here as unsound as to tap, *tupto*, strike, etc.

1. Notice, not one of these words gives dip, *intingo*, or *tingo*, or wash, etc. as a meaning.

2. They show the true idea of immerse—sinking under a pressure, not involving, like dip, immediate withdrawal.

TINGO.

As *tingo* figures in these discussions, we prefer to present the leading facts in this connection that all may de-

* עָמַס † עָמַר ‡ עָמַת § רָאל ¶ עוּר ‖ עָטַ ** כָּפַשׁ †† שָׁקַע

termine for themselves. While immersionists have made a most forced use of this word generally, Dr. Graves, in his last three speeches on Mode, outHerods Herod in the perverseness of his statements, though not a word of all there said was said in the debate, but written down deliberately in his room in Memphis, with my manuscript speeches violently usurped, and most dishonestly held in violation of all the agreements of the parties publishing—all being Baptists, in the same house with Dr. Graves. Out of hundreds of cases of his daring assertions—they refusing to send to me a single proof-sheet of it, all rewritten with quite all he did say thrown out, all the speeches being new matter unseen by me, hence could not be anticipated—we present one sample case before we take him upon *tingo*. After citing Maimonides on washing several times, on page 493 he cites him again, and Dr. Alting thus: "Whence the Jews observe that whenever a command occurs for washing the clothes, the washing of the whole body is either added or understood." Now Dr. Graves immediately adds of me, "He [Ditzler] declares to you that 'no rabbi on earth says so.' Was not Maimonides a rabbi?" Now turn to page 460, whence he copies my words, and see the willful perversion. There I state that "Dr. G. says the 'most learned rabbins tell us that invariably in the Hebrew purifications where *rachats*, 'to wash,' is spoken of, either of the clothes or of the person, the whole body must be immersed in water.' They do no such thing. No rabbi on earth says so." Here I assert that no rabbi on earth says in all these cases the person "immersed in water." Dr. Graves now changes it to "wash the whole body," and makes my words apply to denying that!! On the same page we gave the facts and words of Rabbi M., showing they meant wash, as

Alting, his own authority, renders him, but which Drs. G., Wilkes, and all immersionists most unjustly render "dip" and "immerse."

Continuing to rewrite his speeches, knowing I would not be allowed to see and refute the glaring and reckless assertions (p. 429 of the Carrollton Debate), he says, as to lexicons defining by *tingo*, that I "was rendering those meanings which those old lexicographers indicate in Latin by *tingo* by 'to sprinkle!' In this respect Elder Ditzler has ignorantly, if not intentionally, misrepresented every lexicon he has quoted." On page 432 he pretends that my "sprinkle" in Tertullian is from "*tingo*." Dr. G. had my speeches before him, and in the lexicons he had them before him in print—clear type. Hence he knew that every word he uttered above was untrue, and most flagrantly so.

He knew that not in a single lexicon cited in all the debate, had I rendered *tingo* sprinkle, but moisten, wet, stain, as the author meant, as pages 197, 438, 88, 378, 27-30, abundantly show, and on Tertullian (pp. 244, 245, 197).

On page 482 he says, "Faustianus [misprint for Ferstianus], whom Dr. Beecher quotes as undoubtedly using *tingere* in the sense of 'to dip,' my opponent makes him say 'to sprinkle.'"

Here are two glaring statements which Dr. G. could not help knowing to be flagrantly untrue.

1. Beecher quotes and translates *tingo* in Fürst by wash, and "to moisten"* in other places, as I have done. I render it "dip" also.

* Beecher on Baptism, p. 69: "Fuerstius, in the learned lexicon, defines *tabhal, rigare, tingere, perfundere*, and last of all *immergere*. To wet, to wash, to perfuse, to immerse." On page 16 B. quotes Facciolatus and Forcellinus and Leverett, who "give it the sense [of] to moisten, to wet." Thus is this bold and false statement exposed.

2. Dr. G. says I render it "sprinkle." He knew better. It was the German "*begiessen,*" in the Latin of Fürst "*perfundere,*" that I rendered sprinkle, just as Rabbi Wise, immersionist, and S. Davidson, one of the most learned scholars of this century do. Dr. G. renders the same word, "*perfundere,*" "besprinkle." Beecher, in the same sentence referred to by Dr. G., renders it "perfuse," i. e. besprinkle.

On page 473 he says again, "Whenever Elder Ditzler, therefore, translates it (*tingo*) by 'to sprinkle,' when lexicographers give *tingo, intingo, mergo, immergo,* as the primary definition of the Hebrew *taval,* or of the Greek verbs *bapto, baptidzo,* or the Syriac *amad,* he most grossly perverts those authors, and he does it ignorantly or intentionally, nor can he escape the alternative." Dr. G. here—

1. States what he knew to be without a shadow of truth from beginning to end, as my speeches (pp. 27-30, 88, 197, 438-9, 405, 551) so abundantly show; and they were then all under his eye—in his hands.

2. He displays an ignorance that is as incurable as it is unendurable by saying that lexicographers define *baptidzo* and the Syriac *amad* by *tingo,* when not a single lexicon extant does so. Sophocles puts the patristic use of *tingo* in his lexicon without translating it. Schaaf's Syriac lexicon gives *tingo* as a meaning of the Arabic word *amada,* not of the Syriac *amad;* nor does any Syriac lexicon we have ever seen define *amad* by *tingo.* Page 313, Dr. G. quotes Scapula as defining *baptidzo* by "*item tingo.*" Page 363 I corrected him as well as on his rendering, page 338, yet after this, page 432, he says, "Prof. Toy" says "the lexicons frequently give *tingere* for *baptizein.* As to this, it is agreed that Tertullian and other Latin writers use

tingere always in the sense of to immerse." We are not surprised at any statement Dr. G. should make, unless he should for just once tell the truth as to any of these matters, but we had a right to expect better things of Prof. Toy.

TINGO—DR. GRAVES AND TOY ON.

1. Prof. Toy says, "The lexicons frequently give *tingere* for *baptizein*." Let him produce one that does so. He can not do it, save the one single work of S., just named, who does not give *tingo* as a definition, but sums up the Latin patristic use of it, not translating his words even. We point out these facts, not that it is against us, for *tingo* helps us far more than them, but we do it to expose the want of care and truth in these parties. Stephanus shows that the Latin fathers use *tingo* for baptize, but he does not define it by *tingo* for good reasons. *Tingo* oftener means to stain, tincture, color, dye than any thing else really, though moisten be its primary Latin meaning, and hence no standard lexicon would stultify itself as Drs. Toy and G. do.

2. Prof. T. says, "It is agreed among scholars that T., etc. use *tingere* always in the sense of immerse." This is utterly untrue, as we will show in due time.

Page 527 Dr. G. says, "All lexicons give to dip and to immerse as synonymous terms, as the Germans give *mergo*, *immergo*, and *tingo* as synonymous of *baptidzo*."

1. If they give *tingo* as synonymous with *baptidzo* all the better for us.

2. No German lexicon in existence gives *tingo* as a meaning of *baptidzo* in any case.

3. No German lexicon gives dip, or *tingo*, as synony-

mous with immerse, sink, for the reason that they have learning, sense, and honesty.

TINGO—DR. GRAVES ON—JEROME ON.

Dr. Graves (Debate, p. 433) says, "Jerome in the Latin Vulgate, as in all his writings, invariably uses *tingo* as the Latin synonym of the Greek verb *bapto*, to dip."

1. If this was truthfully said of Jerome it would of itself show how absurd and untrue are all the above assertions about *tingo* being the synonym of *baptidzo*; for where in the New Testament or any where is *bapto* used for baptism or as the synonym of *baptidzo?*

2. The statement is utterly untrue in all respects—utterly untrue. *Bapto* occurs in the common Greek text of the New Testament only three times, viz. Luke xvi, 24; John xiii, 26; Revelation xix, 13. *Embapto* occurs in Matthew xxvi, 23; Mark xiv, 20. Some copies have it *embapto* in John xiii, 26—Tischendorf, Lachmann, etc. Now Jerome renders the above three occurrences as follows:

Luke xvi, 24, *intingat;* John xiii, 26, *intinctum, intinxisset* (and *embapto* he renders *intingo* every time); while the third occurrence of *bapto*, Revelation xix, 13, he renders thus: *Et vestibus erat veste aspersa sanguine*—and he was clothed with a vesture sprinkled with blood. In other words, *bapto* occurs only three times in the Greek New Testament, and Jerome renders it sprinkle in one third of its occurrences, but never renders it in all the Bible by *tingo*.

3. If *tingo* be the synonym of *baptidzo*, why does not the Itala, Jerome, Beza, and the dozen other Latin versions I have by me render *baptidzo* by *tingo* at least once

in all the Bible? for not one of them does so, neither by *intingo*. Such is Dr. Graves's reliability!

LEXICONS ON TINGO.

Let us now cite the standard lexicons in order on this much-abused word. As it is derived from the Greek *tengo*, as Carson justly tells us and all scholars know, we begin with the lexicons on the original. And as Drs. Graves, Wilkes, Campbell, etc. so parade the primary meaning and assume that the first meaning presented is the primary, we may hope they will not fly from their own positions.

1. Groves: "*Tengo* (τεγγω), to moisten, wet, water, sprinkle, bedew."

2. Liddell & Scott: "*Tengo*, to wet, moisten, to bedew with, especially with tears; weep, to shed tears, a shower fell, . . . III. To dye, stain; Latin, *tingere*," etc.

3. Stephanus: "*Tengo*, to moisten, to make wet," with tears, dew, rain.

4. Pape: "*Tengo*, moisten, wet, shed tears."*

5. Passow: "*Tengo*, moisten, wet, shed tears."

6. Rost and Palm: "*Tengo*, to moisten, to wet, to shed tears," etc.

Let us now have the Latin lexicons on this word, as spelled in Latin, translated immerse and dip always by Drs. Conant, Graves, Wilkes, etc.:

1. Andrews: "*Tingo*, to wet, to moisten, (B) to soak or color, to dye, color, tinge."

2. Freund: "*Tingo*, to wet, moisten, *tengo*, *brecho*, *hugraino*, [moisten, shed tears, rain, sprinkle, water, sprinkle], to moisten, to bedew, to bathe, wash, dip in, plunge, immerse; color, stain, tinge, tint."

* Benetzen, anfeuchten, Thränen *vergiessen*.

CLASSICAL USAGE—SUMMARY OF FACTS. 253

3. Ainsworth: "*Tingo*, first, to dye, color, stain; second, to sprinkle, to imbrue; third, to wash; fourth, to paint."

4. Anthon: "*Tingo*, moisten, wet," etc.

5. White: "*Tingo*, moisten, wet," etc.

This is making poor headway to show that *tingo* is synonymous with immerse.

6. Ovid: "*Tingere*, wet the body with sprinkled water."*

7. "And seems to sprinkle with briny dew the surrounding clouds."†

Here in both cases *tingo* is defined in its effect by sprinkle—by a Latin who lived in the apostolic age.

8. "By chance his hounds, led by the blood-stained track."‡

Was the ground immersed or dipped in the blood of the wounded stag?

9. Calvin: "It is of no importance whether all who are baptized [*tingati*] are immersed [*mergantur*], and that thrice or once, or water is only poured on them." §

Here Calvin, as all the fathers writing in Latin, uses, as Cyprian, Tertullian, etc. did, *tingo* for baptize, just as Germans do *taufen*, we baptize; and when he expresses the different modes in which we could be baptized—*tingo* —he gives immerse and pour water on them. One more father.

10. Archbishop Sebastian, of Metz: "Then let the priest take the child in his left arm, and holding him over the font let him with his right hand three several times

---

* Ovid, Met. vii, 599: *Tingere corpus aqua aspersa.*

† Ovid, Met. xi, 498: *Et inductus aspergine tingere nubes videtur.*

‡ *Sanguine tincta suo* (Ovid, x, 713). See Louisville Debate, page 430, where many such texts are given, the fruit of much research.

§ Institutes, lib. iv, chap. xv, sec. 19.

take water out of the font and pour it on the child's head so that the water (*aqua tingat*) wets his head and shoulder."*

Notice here the mode is given; the water is "poured on the child so that it (*tingat*) wets his head and shoulders." *Tingo* is the effect of the pour.

11. Ovid: "Let us wash (*tingo* is the word) our naked bodies with water poured upon them."†

(1) Here the mode in which *tingo* is effected is again given—the water is poured upon the naked bodies.

(2) It shows the manner of ancient baths.

(3) Drs. Graves, Toy, etc., as well as Carson, say that *tingo* is equivalent to *baptidzo* in the lexicons and the Latin fathers, Tertullian, Cyprian, Jerome, etc. Conant renders it immerse constantly also as well as Wilkes.

(4) All these are as literal uses as language can offer. They are real persons, washed with real water, literally poured upon them.

12. Horace: "And wet (*tinguet*) the pavement with wine." What was the mode of *tingo* here where wine was let fall on the pavement?

13. Ovid: ‡ "He beat the ground, stained (*tinctam*) with guilty blood."

14. Calpuronius: "To wet (*tingere*) the pastures with dew." Here the dew falls on the pastures and (*tingo*) wets them. What was the mode?

Aside from hosts of like citations, Fürst uses *tingo* in his Latin lexicon to define the word that in his German lexicon is defined by *benetzen*—wet. Schindler, Castell,

---

* Wall, i, 577: *Aqua tingat caput et scapulas.*

† *Nuda superfusis tingamus corpora lymphis.*

‡ Hamum: *Scelerato sanguine tinctam.* I reread Ovid to select from him, because he was *contemporary* with the apostolic period.

CLASSICAL USAGE—SUMMARY OF FACTS. 255

etc. use *tingo* constantly where it is with tears, dew, rain. We have always frankly stated, also, that in some cases *tingo* means dip, plunge. And Dr. Graves cites such cases as if it were a contradiction! Have we not given cases where hosts of words mean to wet, moisten, nay, to sprinkle and pour, that also mean to dip, etc.? What do such partisans hope for, or what excuse can they render for such conduct?

CHAPTER XX.

BAPTIDZO, SINK, IMMERSE, SPRINKLE—WHY DO NOT WE TRANSLATE?—WHY DO NOT THEY TRANSLATE?

As scholars all agree, it is rare, if ever, that one word exactly represents or is the exact equivalent of another. But where one word, as wash, purify, cleanse, for baptize, occurs, it does necessarily represent all the meaning, and no more of the word than the last limiting word contains. It limits the other word altogether to what is necessarily contained in that word. This becomes the more decisive when the words occur a great many times by the same school of writers, yet is invariably thus used. Thus *baptidzo* is wash, cleanse, or purify wherever its ritualistic import or design is referred to in the Bible. Eph. v, 26; Titus iii, 5; Heb. x, 22; Acts xxii, 16; John iii, 22-25; Ps. li, 2-9, etc. See above. The entire force or meaning *baptidzo* was intended to have in the New Testament is contained in the words cleanse, wash, or purify. Inspired men in the above texts thus limit its force. It is in this view that *baptidzo* as referring to the Christian rite can not be represented by any modal word—immerse, dip, sprinkle, pour—because in the Christian use no one of those words represents necessarily the wash, the cleanse, the purify of *baptidzo*. Sprinkle could and did represent the mere daily baptisms of Mark vii, 4, being mere traditional sprinklings.

But it is said we will not translate *baptidzo* by sprinkle

in the New Testament. Why not translate it by a plain English word, sprinkle, and not transfer, merely Anglicizing the Greek word *baptidzo?* Answer—

1. Wherever the solemn rite of Christian baptism occurs in the New Testament all ancient versions that were in languages kindred to the Greek—all that allowed of it—transferred the word in all such cases. This was the universal practice from the old Itala, the Coptic, the Vulgate, on through the centuries till the days of King James, including the Italian, Spanish, French, Lusitanian, Wycliffe, from the Vulgate, Tyndale, 1526, and the four or five English versions, with James's as the last.

2. In every place in the New Testament where the rite of baptism with water is mentioned, not Christian, but Jewish baptism, it can be rendered sprinkle, and is the correct rendering (Mark vii, 4; Luke xi, 38).

3. Hence the two best and most ancient copies of the Bible known, copied nearly sixteen hundred years ago, with a number of later manuscript copies, render it "sprinkle themselves" in Mark vii, 4. See Versions, for all the facts here.

4. There is that in the solemn rite of Christian baptism, as just shown, that no mere modal word can represent. *Baptidzo* obtained a significance that no mere word of action could represent in Christian baptism.

WHY NOT TRANSLATE INTO ENGLISH?

5. No immersionist does render *baptidzo* by a plain English word throughout the New Testament. They have never done it and never will do it, putting it in the text as a rendering. They carefully put it in an Anglicized Latin word—immerse, the English of which is to "sink in,"

"sink." In the Louisville Debate, p. 566, we elaborate this fact, saying, "Now, immerse, simply and literally and always, means to sink, sink in. This is the English." Elder Wilkes replies, p. 574, " He tries very hard to prove that *mergo, immergo*, . . . mean to sink. I believe him. I will save him trouble on that subject by telling him that I know that these words mean to sink." Again, p. 599, he brings it up again and says, " We have Anglicized immerse from *mergo, immergo*. It is not necessary for us to give a definition of this word [immerse] now. We know what it means; we are agreed about that." . A. Campbell renders *baptidzo* sink over and again. See where the renderings are detailed.

Dr. J. R. Graves, Carrollton Debate, p. 520, "All the Latin fathers, . . . one and all, understood *baptidzo* to signify *mergo, immergo, tingo, intingo*, to sink in," etc. Page 389 he has it "sinking in," and often so.

Now apply that rendering throughout the New Testament. "Came John, the sinker-in." "I sank in none of you but Crispus," etc. "Go, disciple all nations, sinking them in in the name," etc.

Hence, ancient copyists render it by sprinkle for baptize.

When it appears, as has been shown, that long before *baptidzo* came to mean to immerse it was taken by the Jews to mean to wash, purify, and thus limited in religious use (Eccles. xxiv, 25; Judith xii, 7), this of itself settles that question. When *bapto* came to mean stain, color, though in earliest usage it was always by affusion (see it fully demonstrated in Chapters XI–XIII), yet when it came to mean stain, color, it soon came to apply to coloring where the art of dipping in the fluid was practiced. It applies where the fluid is sprinkled on, drops on the garments, and where the garments are dipped. Hence, when *bapto* is used for stain, it does not imply any particular mode, but only implies the force or necessary limitations of stain in whatever way it may be effected.

CHAPTER XXI.

BAPTIDZO IN ARISTOTLE, ETC.

1. We have traced *baptidzo* from its first appearance in literature among the Greeks, so far as that literature has survived, down to Aristotle, B.C. 384, covering a period of one hundred and thirty-eight years.

2. In all this period it occurs only in a metaphorical sense, pointing to an earlier literal use.

3. In all cases the usage demonstrates that it was as yet never used for dip, never for immerse.

4. It demonstrates that it primarily meant to sprinkle, thence to pour, thence to wash, to saturate, to drench as the effect of pouring water. Thence it came to mean to soak, intoxicate, make drunk. From pour came overflow, overwhelm. From overwhelm came sink, as a later meaning still. From sink came drown, as its effect.

Let it be remembered that no lexicon in existence gives to *baptidzo* the meanings dip or immerse till Polybius, Diodorus Sicilus, Strabo, and Plutarch.

ARISTOTLE, B.C. 384.

Aristotle uses *baptidzo* only once in all his writings, so far as found.

"Certain places full of rushes and sea-weed, which when it is ebb-tide are not overflowed (*mae baptidzesthai*), but at full-tide are overflowed" (*katakludzesthai*).

1. Let this case be very carefully examined, for it is the first time in Greek literature in which we come upon the word used literally.

2. It is used by the most accurate and careful and learned of all Greeks.

3. It is interchanged with another word, used in exactly the same sense, both rendered by "overflow," as Stuart, A. Campbell, etc. render it.

4. There is no dip here; no one will venture to render it by dipped.

5. It is not immerse. "The places," lands subject to overflow, did not sink, did not merse or immerse; but—

6. The literal water came upon the land. The baptizing element came upon the object, baptizing it. Whether every part of the land was overflowed by the water we can not know. All the reasonable probabilities are that, like all other average districts of country of like kind, parts were overflowed, parts, higher spaces, were not. Yet the whole is baptized.

7. The most valuable point, though, is the light this literal text throws on the philology of the word. Overflow is a literal meaning of *baptidzo* in Aristotle's day. Overflow can not be derived from dip as a primary meaning. Hence dip never was a primary, nay, never was a meaning of *baptidzo* at all.

8. Further, *baptidzo* is interchanged with *perikludzo*. *Perikludzo* is rendered sprinkle by Stephanus and others.* Passow gives wash, bedash, wet, for *kludzo*. Groves gives for *perikludzo*, "Wash all round or all over, dash water, sprinkle all over."

Liddell & Scott: *Kludzo.* See on former page.
Glosses: To sprinkle.†

* Buddæus and Stephanus have περικλύσματι, *periklusmati, aspergine.*
† *Aspergo, perfundo.*

Here is a word—*kludzo*—that primarily applies to such aspersions and inspersions as sprinkling water over the body, dashing it on the face, washing out the ears, and from which our noun clyster is derived, coming to mean overflow and to inundate and *baptidzo*, used in exactly the same sense by the most learned of all Greeks.

7. Eubulus, B.C. 380, comes next. He uses the word once, its sense altogether uncertain, and hence we omit it.

8. Evenus, B.C. 250, uses it once, "Wine baptizes with stupor or sleep" (ὑπνῶ, *hupnō*). This is a metaphorical use again and has no dip in it.*

9. Polybius now appears, born about B.C. 205. He wrote about B.C. 150 or 160, say. He is the first Greek who uses *baptidzo* for immerse, the earliest cited by any lexicon for such a meaning. Next, about B.C. 66 to 33, Diodorus Siculus; then, later, Strabo, and A.D. 90 Plutarch uses it at times for overwhelm, at times for immerse, i. e. sink; then still also for intoxicate, etc.

These writers do not write in the ancient, classic style, but are the introducers of a coarse, greatly-modified style of Greek, as Liddell & Scott in the introduction to their lexicon tell us. But long years and centuries before this *baptidzo* was used for the religious washing of the Jews, and its religious import and action settled before the word came to mean immerse. It never does mean to dip, as we saw.

* If any one urge that, at least we may say, one sinks in sleep, so may we say, "Pour delicious slumber o'er mine eyes." Poets often use pour for such an idea. And there is no *dip*.

CHAPTER XXII.

Baptidzo in Later Greek—Conant.

In addition to the facts adduced, we will copy a few later cases adduced by Dr. Conant as the strongest cases in favor of his immersion theory. In his *"Baptizein"* we select—

1. Page 10: "And those of the submerged (baptized) who raised their heads, either a missile reached or a vessel overtook"—"their heads being raised."*

Not one of these parties was totally under the water. Conant translates it "submerged." He tries to make them rear their heads after being "submerged." No such thought or fact is in the Greek. "But the elevated heads of those baptized either a missile reached or a vessel captured." Though these parties were partly immersed the heads, with of course a part of the shoulders, were above the water. In that condition some were shot with their missiles, others were captured. There was no complete envelopment.

2. Plutarch (Conant, p. 11): "A bladder, thou mayest be immersed (baptized); but it is not possible to thee to sink." † The Greek reads, "A bladder, thou mayest be baptized, but it is not fated to thee to be immersed." Drs. Conant, Campbell, Carson, Gale, Graves, all use the

---

* Τῶν δὲ βαπτισθέντων τοὺς ἀνανεύοντας ἢ βέλος ἔφθανεν, ἢ σχεδία κατελάμβανε.

† Ἀσκὸς βαπτίζῃ· Δῦναι δέ τοι οὐ θέμος ἐστίν.

English sink for the Latin immerse in its Anglicized form, and Conant conceals the truth constantly by a play upon those words. Why render *baptidzo* there by immerse, and *dunai*, which always means immerse, by the English word sink? The bladder was baptized, but would not go under. We know they will not go under of themselves. This is just the kind of classic baptism as the other preceding it in Josephus, save that the man mersed deeper in the sea-water than the bladder. Neither was enveloped, covered.

3. Conant, 11, 12, Ex. 25: "The soldiers . . . dipping (baptizing) with cups, and horns, and goblets, from great wine-jars and mixing-bowls." Who believes the cups, goblets, and horns were entirely submerged in the wine? But there are some strange points here. Where was ever *baptidzo* used for "dipping horns" or any thing else? We have seen, all admit, that *baptidzo* is used often, commonly, for becoming drunk, intoxicated, etc. Hence it reads, "The soldiers becoming drunk — intoxicated — out (*ek*) of great wine-jars,"* etc., "with cups and horns, and goblets," "along the whole way were drinking to one another." The *ek*, "out of," forbids dip as the meaning here.

4. *Ibid.* 18: "And already becoming immerged (baptized) and wanting little of sinking, some of the pirates at first attempted to leave (the vessel) and get aboard their own bark."

(1) Here to conceal the facts so patent the doctor renders *baptidzo* by "becoming immerged," and immerse, in Greek, he renders again by sink, the English of immerse. And this in face of his just admission and statement that *baptidzo* implies as complete sinking where the parties

* Οἱ στρατιῶται βαπτίζοντες ἐκ πίθων μεγάλων.

perish, as *dunai*, contrary to Suicer, Pasor, Beza, whom A. Campbell follows.

(2) The Greek reads, "And already being baptized and wanting little of being immersed* (*katadunai*), some of the pirates at first attempted to leave (the vessel) and get aboard of their own bark."

(3) If the *baptidzo* immersed the vessel—completely enveloped it—i. e. if it put it entirely under the water—why did it not go to the bottom at once, as all vessels do—ships—whenever they by such calamities go clean under?

(4) Why does the writer say that although the vessel was "already baptized," yet it was not yet "immersed," yet "wanting little of being immersed." Dr. C. will not deny that immerse is the literal meaning of *katadunai*.

(5) Though the vessel was "already baptized," yet the parties are consulting, talking together, about leaving the ship. How could this occur among a part of the pirates if the vessel had "already been immersed"—wholly enveloped under water?

5. Conant, p. 20, Ex. 42: "'The whole sword was warmed with blood' (Homer) . . . as if the sword were so imbathed (baptized) as to be heated." This is a later Greek writer commenting on the ancient Homer's words, the former using the words "warmed with blood," the latter baptized with blood.

(1) Baptize here is not immersion.

(2) It was by effusion—the blood gushing out on the sword.

(3) Conant then commits the unpardonable literary sin of rendering Homer's stronger word, "*hupethermanthœ*," by "warmed," and the tamer critics less intense word *thermanthœnai* by "heated"! The Greek is, "As if the

* Ἤδη δὲ βαπτιζομένων καὶ καταδῦναι μικρὸν ἀπολειπόντων.

sword were so baptized [with blood—*haimati*] as to be warmed."* Surely the blood that flowed from the pierced head of Echelus† did not immerse "the whole sword." It is a clear case of effusion of blood on the sword.

6. Conant's 69th Example, p. 33, is his strongest for "dip." "Casting a little of the ashes [of the burnt heifer] into a fountain and dipping (baptizing) a hyssop branch," etc. In this case—

(1) Dr. Conant changes the ordinary reading of the Greek text, which can not be allowed.

(2) Conant admits that the copyist of the Greek text has been guilty of "an error in copying." He thinks "the common reading" of the Greek ‡ shows the same thing. But he renders it differently, "immerse," not dip, by indorsing the Latin scholiast. Unquestionably the Greek he and Bekker make is wrong, as it violates the whole tenor of Greek usage. His own Greek, given in the note, which is "the common reading," is, "and baptizing some of the ashes into the fountain;" pouring or immersing them into the fountain, whichever rendering you prefer, it equally suits my present object. It is not dip. The hyssop is not the object of *baptidzo* by this "common reading." And were it so, it would be clear evidence that the error of the copyist was in putting it *baptidzo* for *bapto*.

7. *Ibid.* 22: "He did not plunge in (baptize) the sword, nor sever that hostile head!" The Greek is, "not even to sever that hostile head." Clearly the word here is not

---

* Πᾶν δ' ὑπεθερμάνθη ξίφος αἵματι . . . ὡς τε θερμανθῆναι.

† Homer's Il. xxii, line 476, on which the unknown writer comments, using *baptidzo*. Homer never uses it.

‡ Which begins thus: Βαπτίσαντές τε καὶ τῆς τέφας ταύτης εἰς πηγὴν — which an old author he indorses renders—*ejusdemque cineris oliquantulum in aquam immergentes*. But this is infinitely different from *dipping*.

"plunge in," as if point foremost, but edge foremost, to "sever the head" from the body. In cutting off the head no one plunges in a sword point foremost. We know how a sword is used in cutting off a man's head. *Baptidzo* here expresses (Chrysostom) this act. Immersion, envelopment is out of the question.

8. *Ibid.* 23: "And that the immerged (baptized) ship beyond all hope is saved, is of the providence of God;" "in the sudden coming as of storm or tempest." Clearly this "immerged ship" is not "immerged." If the *baptidzo* put it clear under, it never was saved or could be. It is baptized by the waves dashing upon it, but not immersed. That the baptized ship "contrary (or against hope) is saved"—παρ ἐλπίδα. Yet C. puts it, "beyond all hope." It is not there. Where is the "all" in the Greek?

9. Conant, p. 32: "And dipping (baptizing) his hand into the blood, he set up a trophy, inscribing it," etc.

(1) Suppose we were to accept this rendering, it does not prove their theory of immersion; for there is no evidence from their rendering that complete envelopment of the hand in the human blood took place.

(2) There is every reason to suppose it did not take place, for who would immerse their entire hand in blood merely to have blood on a finger with which to write an inscription on a trophy?

(3) It is long after Christ, and therefore belongs to the later, corrupted Greek.

10. *Ibid.* His 50th Example, pp. 23, 24, is more than doubtful as to a total immersion.

11. (Josephus 33): "He plunged (baptized) the whole sword into his own neck."

No immergence, no total envelopment here.

12. *Ibid.* 34: "Immerse (baptize) it (the pessary) into breast-milk and Egyptian ointment." The ancient Egyptian pessary or "blister-plaster" was wholly different from the pessary of modern science and wholly different in application. It was compounded of "honey, turpentine, butter, oil of lily or of rose, and saffron, each one part, with sometimes a small quantity of verdigris"* and used as a blister. It was baptized with, or wetted partially in the "milk of a woman"—that is the Greek. † Immersion was not necessary nor possible.

13. *Ibid.* 34. His 71st Example is rendered, like many others, to conceal the facts. "The mass of iron drawn red-hot" was "by the smiths" (plural), and is "baptized with water" to "quench its fiery glow." Such a large mass of iron, red-hot, is not plunged into water to be cooled. It is against plunge. Such "a mass of red-hot iron" plunged into water would throw quite all the water out and all over the smiths, baptizing them.

14. "Plunge (baptize) the sword into the enemy's breast." No total envelopment here (p. 37, *ibid.*).

15. *Ibid.* 38: "Plunge (baptize) his right hand in his father's neck." The hand or weapon in it was not likely to be enveloped, completely submerged in his father's neck.

Conant, p. 2, Example 2: "But most of them (ships of the Romans), when the prow was let fall from on high, being submerged (baptized) became filled with sea-water and confusion."

If "submerged" how could the people become confused and the vessel fill up with sea-water? The ships evidently became partially overwhelmed, sea-water ran in

---
* Ἐς γάλα γυναικὸς.
† Dunglison's Med. Dictionary, p. 37.

in great quantities, and the Romans became confused thereby. But how could men fighting on a vessel, as they did in that day, remain on deck in a state of confusion or nonconfusion after the vessel was sunk clear under water, " being submerged "?

Now, the above texts are all copied from the literal use of *baptidzo* presented by Conant (though one or two at least, if not three or four are not literal cases), clearly showing that even in classic, yet Iron-age Greek after *baptidzo* came to mean to immerse, it still, in that age, did not generally or often apply to complete immersions; and that to express complete immersion they generally supplied, as seen, *dunai*, *katadunai* to express that idea.

Another point is clear, that wherever *baptidzo* does completely immerse a living object it perishes.

That "whelm," "overwhelm," and such uses of *baptidzo* point to affusion—the element descending, falling on the object—may be seen further by the very words used, clearly pointing out this fact. Take from Dr. Conant the following examples:

Page 79, Example 162: "Achilles Tatius: For that which, of a sudden, comes all at once and unexpected, shocks the soul, falling on it unawares, and whelms (baptizes)."* Here, first, the word *baptidzo* is much strengthened with a preposition far stronger than merely the word uncompounded; second, the mode is defined—the element that baptizes (*katebaptize*) does so by "falling on it." Where is the dip, where the plunge, where the sink here?

Page 66, Example 136, Dr. Conant quotes Philo: "As though reason were whelmed (baptized) by the things overlying it."† Here the things that rest or fall upon

---

* Ἄφνω προσπεσόν καὶ κατεβάπτισε.
† Τοῖς ἐπιοῦσι, the things upon it.

(*epi*) the reason, "food and drink," baptize it, "resting upon it."

Tatius (Conant, p. 26, Example 56) : "The blood . . . boiling up through intense vigor, often overflows the veins, and flooding (*perikludzo*) the head within, whelms (baptizes) the passage of reason." Here is affusion, not dipping.

CHAPTER XXIII.

Baptidzo in Patristic Greek.

We introduce baptism among the fathers by citing Clemens Alexandrinus, A.D. 190.

"But purity is to think purely. And indeed the image* of the baptism [of the Bible] was handed down from Moses to the poets thus—

"'Having besprinkled herself with water, having on her body clean garments, Penelope comes to prayer.'†
'But Telemachus, . . . having washed his hands at the hoary sea, prays to Athene' (Minerva). This custom (*ethos*) of the Jews, as they also often baptize themselves upon a couch, is well expressed also in this verse, 'Be pure, not by washing, but by thinking.'"‡ Here—

1. Sprinkling the water on herself before prayer was an image (*eikōn*), likeness, of the baptism taught in the Bible.

2. "Sprinkled herself with water." The word is com-

---

* Εἰκὼν, *image*, not σύμβολον, symbol, but image.

† Odyssey iv, 759, is where he cites Homer.

‡ Ἁγνεία δὲ ἐστι φρονεῖν ὅσια καὶ δὴ καὶ ἡ εἰκὼν τοῦ βαπτίσματος εἴη ἂν καὶ ἡ ἐκ Μωΰσεως παραδεδομένη τοῖς ποιηταῖς ὧδέ πως.

Ἡ δ' ὑδρηναμένη καθαρὰ χροΐ εἵματ' ἔχουσα. Odys. iv, 759.
Ἡ Πενελόπη τὴν εὐχὴν ἔρχεται.
Τηλέμαχος δὲ . .
Χεῖρας νιψάμενος πολιῆς ἁλός, εὔχετ' Ἀθήνῃ. Odys. ii, 261.
Ἔθος τοῦτο Ἰουδαίων, ὡς καὶ τὸ πολλάκις ἐπὶ κοίτῃ βαπτίζεσθαι.
Εὖ γοῦν κἀκεῖνο εἴρηται·
Ἴσθι μή λουτρῷ, ἀλλὰ νόῳ καθαρός. Clemens Alex. i, 1352.

pounded of *huder*, water, and *raino*, to sprinkle. Liddell & Scott's Lexicon renders the word "to pour water over one's body."*

3. Washing the hands at the sea was an image of baptism. Where was the immersion in these cases?

4. It was the custom of the Jews to "baptize often upon a couch"—not after the couch, not (*apo koitaes*) from a couch, but (*epi koitae*) "upon a couch." The suggestion of some that it refers to purification after pollution upon a couch is far-fetched and against the grammatical force of the words.

5. Clemens precedes the sentence with these words: "In like manner they say it becomes those who have washed themselves (*leloumenous*) to go forth to sacrifices and prayer pure and bright." The suggestion of Carson, followed by Elder Wilkes, makes (*epi koitae*) "upon a couch" refer to sexual relations. But both Penelope and Telemachus were preparing for prayers, not baptizing because of or from sexual defilement, neither having been thus polluted. Indeed the poets knew nothing of that rite. The custom Clemens refers to was one taught not merely by Moses, but by the poets, and he tells us what it was as practiced in the poets—they sprinkled themselves with water. And here he uses *raino*, *nipto*, *louo*, and *baptidzo* all for the same thing—baptism. We have seen in the laver argument what the washing of the Jews was.†

---

*Λουτρὰ ὑδράνασθαι χροΐ (Eur. El. 157), to water, to sprinkle with water, to pour out *libations; mid.*, to bathe, wash oneself (L. & S. on same).

†Hervetus, a Greek, who translated Clemens, and was his commentator, knowing all the facts, says, "The Jews washed themselves, not only at sacrifices but also at feasts, and this is the reason why Clement says that they purified or washed upon a couch; that is, a dining-couch or triclinium. To this Mark refers, chap. vii, and Matthew, chap. xv.

BAPTISM OF THE ALTAR.

In Origen, on John i, 25, we read, "How came you to think that Elias, when he should come, would baptize, who did not baptize the wood upon the altar in the days (times) of Ahab, although it needed purification [or cleansing—*loutron*] in order that it might be burned when the Lord should be revealed by fire; for this [baptizing the wood upon the altar] was ordered to be done by the priests."*

Now let us cite the facts referred to by the learned Origen, born only some eighty-three to eighty-five years after John the Apostle died, found in 1 Kings xviii, 31-35, 38: "And Elijah took twelve stones, according to the number of the tribes of the sons of Jacob, unto whom the word of the Lord came, saying, Israel shall be thy

Tertullian refers to it when he says, "*Judaius Israel quotidie lavat*—daily washes."

The only argument relied on for such far-fetched assumption as that of Carson is, Clemens had page 1184, nearly two hundred pages apart—ἀπὸ τῆς κατὰ συζυγίαν κοίτης . . . βαπτίζεσθαι—to baptize from the couch on account of sexual intercourse. This is as different from the other as day is from night. Ἀπὸ is not ἐπὶ, as Carson assumes. Κοίτη is not κοίτης, much less is κατα συζυγίαν, which latter is the word for sexual intercourse. "Baptize ἀπὸ from a dead body," ἀπὸ "from the market" (Mark vii, 4); "sprinkle ἀπὸ from an evil conscience"; "Baptize yourselves ἀπό from anger, malice, covetousness," etc. (Chrysostom). That is Greek. But were it ἐπὶ, it would be infinitely different. Sexual intercourse is not expressed by ἐπὶ κοίτῃ any where in the world. In Origen's rendering of Genesis, Jacob sat upon his couch—ἐπὶ τὴν κοίτην. Opera Omnia, vol. 2, p. 145, ed. 1862.

*Origen: Πόθεν δὲ ὑμῖν πεπίστευται Ἡλίαν βαπτίσειν τὸν ἐλευσόμενον, οὐδὲ τὰ ἐπὶ τὰ τοῦ θυσιαστηρίου ξύλα, κατὰ τοὺς τοῦ Ἀχαὰβ χρόνους, δεόμενα λουτροῦ, ἵνα εκκανθῇ, ἐπιφανέντος ἐν πυρὶ τοῦ Κυρίου, βαπτίσαντος; ἐπικελεύεται γὰρ τοῖς ἱερεῦσι τοῦτο ποιῆσαι, ου μόνον ἅπαξ, λέγει γάρ, etc. . . . ὁ τοίνυν μὴ αὐτὸς βαπτίσας τότε, κ. τ. λ. πῶς κατὰ τὰ ὑπὸ τὸν Μαλαχίου λεγόμενα επιδημήσας βαπτίζειν ἔμελλε (*Origenis Opera Omnia, Tomus Quartus,* vol. 4, p. 231, 1862).

name: And with the stones he built an altar in the name of the Lord; and he made a trench about the altar, as great as would contain two measures of seed. And he put the wood in order, and cut the bullock in pieces, and laid *him* on the wood, and said, Fill four barrels with water, and pour *it* on the burnt sacrifice, and on the wood. And he said, Do *it* the second time. And they did *it* the second time. And he said, Do *it* the third time. And they did *it* the third time. And the water ran round about the altar; and he filled the trench also with water. . . . Then the fire of the Lord fell, and consumed the burnt sacrifice, and the wood, and the stones, and the dust, and licked up the water that *was* in the trench."

Basil, A.D. 310, says of this event, " Elias showed the power of baptism on the altar. . . . When the water . . . was for the third time poured on the altar, the fire began. . . . The Scriptures hereby show that through baptism," etc. Other fathers speak of it as baptism. This is enough.

Notice now—

1. It was "the wood upon the altar" that was "baptized."

2. Elijah had the priests who brought the water to "pour it on the burnt sacrifice and on the wood."

3. Origen says they "baptized the wood on the altar."

4. Basil says he showed the power of baptism on the altar, "when the water . . . was poured on the altar."

But immersion ingenuity is not wanting even in so clear a case as this. A. Campbell suggests, following the astute Carson, that twelve barrels of water "overwhelmed" the altar, submerged, "as it were," the altar. Indeed! Let us see into this.

1. It was an altar built of stones on the top of a mountain—Carmel.

2. It was during the great drouth—every thing burning up.

3. Wood was then laid upon the altar of stones, enough for an ox to be laid thereupon.

4. A slaughtered ox was placed upon the altar thus built, "on the wood." Now, how could this altar, or the wood on it, be immersed? Where is the "plunge"? Where is the immerse, sink in? Where is the "dip"? Where is the action, the specific action? Where is the mode? the "burial," cover up? But we are not done.

5. No such vessel as our barrel was known then. The word* in the Hebrew (*kad*) never means barrel. Except the place where the widow had a measure of meal hid away in a barrel, and this place, it is never rendered barrel, and in that place it means pitcher—enough meal to make a little cake only being hid. No lexicon, no ancient version ever rendered it barrel. No scholar will ever contend that it has any such meaning. The ancient Greek version has it bucket, water-pot, or pail. Gesenius, Fürst, and all others define it, "bucket, pail, both for drawing water and carrying it." Gregory Nazianzen expresses it exactly, alluding to this baptism: "Cast [the water] over it from water-pots." Four pitchers or rather buckets of water were poured on this altar and the ox three times repeated. Before the second or third bucket could be poured on, the first would run off. Where is the "overwhelm"? But—

6. The little trench dug around the altar had to be filled with extra water. "And he filled the trench also

* כַּד *kad*, כַּדִּים *kadim*, pitchers, never means barrel, and is *never* so defined in any version of antiquity, or in any lexicon we ever saw. It occurs in Genesis xxiv, 14, 15, 16, 17, 18, 20, 43, 45, 46, where Rebekah draws water out of a well with one; so Judges vii, 16, 19, 20; Ecclesiastes xii, 6, "pitcher"; 1 Kings xvii, 12, 14, 16, "barrel."

with water" (1 Kings xviii, 35). The trench held (*sabhib*) one and a half peck measure.

7. After the water had been poured on, the trench filled, still "dust" was found under and about the altar. There could have been no overwhelming with water, therefore. The fire consumed the dust, and licked up the water that was in the trench. These are the facts. Twelve buckets of water, only four at a time, or one at a time till four were poured on, then a pause, then repeated, never immersed, dipped, or plunged the altar, nor the wood on it. All together doubled, quadrupled, would not do it. They did baptize the wood, the altar. Wilkes, dodging all the above facts in the debate (p. 576), urges for "an overwhelming. That altar and that victim were as drenched, or as wet, or soaked with water" as if "immersed." Alas, how was he drenched with water? It was "poured." The wood was baptized, not "as it were" "overwhelmed." It was baptized. O, but Wilkes says, "a man comes out of the rain, and we say he is drenched." "It means an overwhelming." Not exactly. No one speaks of a man merely drenched in rain as overwhelmed. But what was the specific water, the mode of his drenching? He is baptized; you say drenched. It is a literal act, a literal drenching, a literal person and rain; no metaphor here. How was he baptized? "The water was poured," says Mr. Wilkes. Yes, and so baptized the object. Origen is commenting on John i, 25, 26, where they thought Messiah would baptize. It is of baptism practiced under Christ he is discoursing. It is literal, therefore. The water was poured out of water-pitchers on the wood that was on the altar of stones, on the dry and parched heights of Carmel. As immersionists insist so earnestly that "*baptidzo* always means to dip," "expressing nothing but mode," let them

apply "dip" here. How came you to think Elias would dip . . . who did not dip the wood upon the altar? in the face of the fact that literal water was literally poured by "literal" men, out of "literal" water-pitchers, upon the literal wood of the literal altar, baptizing it?

NOVATIAN'S BAPTISM.

No one case of baptism in all history has been so perverted by immersionists as the case of Novatian, A. D. 251. After I published the original Greek in Louisville Debate (p. 590), with a literal translation, it is pleasant to see Dr. Varden, of Kentucky, publishing to his Baptist brethren a translation, word for word as my own, telling them how incorrect were the partisan uses made by false renderings of this passage. Here is a literal rendering of the passage: "To him, indeed, the origin [or author] of his profession was Satan, who entered into and dwelt in him a long time; who, being assisted by the exorcists, while attacked with an obstinate disease, and being supposed at the point of death, received it [baptism] in the bed on which he lay, by being sprinkled—if indeed it is proper to say that such [a wicked] person received it,"* baptism.

1. Not a single doubt is thrown on the mode of this baptism. "He received it"—*elaben*.
2. It was by sprinkling.
3. When he recovered he never was rebaptized, never

---

*·Ω γε ἀφορμὴ τοῦ πιστεῦσαι γέγονεν ὁ σατανᾶς, φοιτήσας εἰς αὐτον καὶ οἰκήσας ἐν αὐτῷ χρόνον ἰκανόν, ὃς βοηθούμενος ὑπὸ ἐπορκιστῶν, νόσῳ περιπεσὼν χατεπῇ, καὶ ἀποσανεῖσθαι ὅσον οὐδέπω νομιζόμενος, ἐν αὐτῃ τῇ κλίνῃ ᾗ ἔκειτο, περιχυθεὶς ἰλαβεν εἰ γε χρὴ λέγειν τὸν εἰληφέναι. Eusebius, Eccles. Hist., b. vi, chap. xliii, p. 401, sec. 15; *Recensuit Edwardus Burton, Oxonii,* etc., 1838, vol. 1.

was asked to do so, nor complained of by any one for not doing so. Had any doubt existed as to the mode of his baptism they could readily have baptized him.

4. If baptism is immersion, how could they say, "He received immersion by being sprinkled!"

Scott (immersionist) copies it from Baptist sources thus, "He received baptism, being sprinkled with water on the bed where he lay, if that can be called baptism!" No such phrase as the last occurs in the Greek. The *ton toiouton* is masculine, and refers to the wicked person, not to baptism, as the merest tyro in Greek can see.

As immersionists have so perversely quoted the action of a council on this—Neo Cæsarea, Canon 12th—we quote the favorite immersionist historian, Neander (vol. 1, p. 338, revised edition of Torrey, 1872): "Its object [the ecclesiastical law] was simply to exclude from the spiritual order those who had been induced to receive baptism without true repentance, conviction, and knowledge, in the momentary agitation excited by the fear of death. In Novatian's case every apprehension of this kind was removed by his subsequent life." Again, as to the law (Canon 12th, A.D. 314) it says, "After it had been here declared that a person baptized in sickness could not be consecrated as a presbyter, it was assigned as a reason, 'that such faith did not spring from free conviction, but was forced.'" And "an exception was made, viz. unless it might be permitted on account of his subsequent zeal and faith."

We now give the Canon 12th of Neo Cæsarea: "If any one be enlightened [i. e. baptized] during sickness (νοσῶν), he can not be advanced to the priesthood, for his faith is not of a settled purpose, but of necessity, unless indeed perhaps this defect is overlooked on account of his subsequent diligence and faith, and through the scarcity of men."

Ambrose: "He who wished to be purified with a typical baptism (*typico baptismati*) was sprinkled* with the blood of a lamb, by means of a bunch of hyssop."

Cyrill, of Alexandria, on Isaiah iv, 4: "We have been baptized not with mere water, nor yet with the ashes of a heifer [in the water of sprinkling], but with the Holy Spirit," etc. Here the sprinkling of Numbers xix, 13, 18, 22; Hebrews ix, 13, quoted also, are baptisms.

Jerome, A.D. 385, on Ezekiel xxxvi, 25: "'Then will I sprinkle clean water upon you.' So that upon those who believe and are converted from error I might pour out the clean water of baptism."

PATRISTIC BAPTISM.

Here this most accurate and wise of the fathers, and most learned of all the Latin fathers, held Ezekiel xxxvi, 25, to be water baptism, just as Cyprian, A.D. 251, did.

Cyrill, again, 426: "He will make the early and the latter rain to come down upon you as of old. . . . (Joel ii, 23, 25). There has been given to us, as in rain, the living water of holy baptism."

Sulpicius Severus, A.D. 403: "Remember that thou hast, under the hallowed dew of the font and the laver, been sealed with the chrism."

The Centuriator's (quoting Socrates) Hist. Eccles., vii, 17, tells of a font "out of which the water is poured upon those baptized." †

**Adspergebatur.*

†*Baptizato aqua superfusa . . . Aquam in imo alveo fiut . . . effluxere existimaret, alveo baptisterii, etc. . . . aqua rursus penitus evanuit* (Soc. vii, 17).

Constantine the Great was baptized by sprinkling.

Cladovius, A.D. 499, king of the Franks, was sprinkled in his baptism.

Germadius, of Marseilles, A.D. 490, said, "The person baptized was either sprinkled (*aspergitur*) or dipped (*intingitur*)."

Lactantius, A.D. 325: "So likewise he might save the gentiles by baptism; that is, by sprinkling the purifying water."*

Cyrill treated both Isaiah i, 16 and Leviticus viii, 6, 7, both wash and sprinkle water, as baptism.

Ambrose baptized Theodosius the Great by sprinkling.

Hilarius said, "There are not wanting daily sick persons who are to be baptized."

The Præter Ariontheus was baptized by sprinkling.

Tertullian: "These two baptisms he poured forth from the wound of his pierced side." †

Ambrose: "Whence is baptism unless from the cross of Christ?" ‡

John of Damascus: "The baptism of blood and martyrdom by which Christ suffered himself to be baptized for us." §

Origen and Athanasius held to the same.

Origen on Luke xii, 50: "For Christ shed his blood," etc. "For it is the baptism of blood alone that renders us more pure than the baptism of water. 'I have a baptism, etc.' You see, therefore, that he called the shedding of his blood baptism."

All the fathers of these centuries refer the baptism

*Sic etiam gentes baptismo, id est, purifici roris perfusione salvaret.
†*Duo baptismus.* Paris ed. 1634, pp 35-37.
‡*Unce sit baptisma nisi de cruce Christi?* I, 356.
§ Τὸ βάπτισμα δ' αἵματος καὶ μαρτυρίου ὃ καὶ ὁ χρίστος ὑπερ ἡμῶν ἐβαπτίσατο.

just named to his crucifixion, to the shedding of his blood and the water from his side, and not, as immersionists and some modern lexicons, to his sufferings, e. g. in the garden, etc.

Ruth's Reliquis Sacræ, iii, 489: "So that he, expecting to die, asked to receive the water . . . baptism. And he baptized him by sprinkling in the couch where he lay." * This is in almost the same words of the learned Eusebius. Note, "He baptized him." It was by sprinkling the water on him. Notice, it do n't say he sprinkled him—"he baptized him by sprinkling him."

Tertullian is emphasized a great deal by immersionists, and indeed he is the first man in all the world who names dipping or immersion for baptism. But it was by three immersions, the parties naked. But he supports affusion as well. His facts show that they stood them in water to be baptized very often, the baptism being by affusion, but in water to "imbibe" the "mighty grace of water." He says, "Not † that I deny that the divine benefit . . . is, in every way, sure to such as are on the point of entering the water; but what we have to labor for is that it may be granted to us to attain that blessing; for who will grant to you, a man of so faithless repentance, one single sprinkling of the water whatever?" ‡

Again, on the question of whether the twelve apostles were baptized or not, he urges, "Others make the suggestion—forced enough to be sure—'that the apostles then served the term of baptism when, in their little ship, they were sprinkled [*adspersi*] and covered with the waves; that Peter also was mersed enough [*satis mersum*] when he

---

* Ἐν αὐτῃ τῇ κλίοῃ ἡ εκεῖτο περιχύθεντα δήθεν ἐβάπτιζεν.

† Tertullian, Repentance, vi, 267.

‡ De Pœniten, chap vi.

walked on the sea.' It is, however, as I think, one thing to be sprinkled [*adspergi*—as were the eleven], or intercepted by the violence of the sea [as was Peter]; another thing to be baptized in obedience to the discipline of religion." "Now, whether they were baptized in any manner whatever, or whether they continued unwashed (*illoti*)," etc.

1. Here, though some parties "enter the [baptismal] waters," they do it from superstitious ideas of its virtue, but are baptized by sprinkling.

2. Had the eleven received the sprinkling water voluntarily, in obedience to the discipline of religion, it would have served for baptism, in his estimation.

3. Tertullian uses *adspergo*, *lavo*, *tingo*, *perfundo*, as well as *mergo*, for baptism, repeating *adspergo*, sprinkle, a number of times.

BAPTISM WITH TEARS—WITH BLOOD.

4. The water and blood shed from Christ's side were "baptisms." Surely the water that was shed from the side of Christ was not a dipping. The blood that he shed did not dip him. Yet Origen, Tertullian, Ambrose, Athanasius, John of Damascus, all held them to be baptisms. So did the Syrian fathers.

Eusebius's Eccles. Hist., A.D. 324, b. iii, ch. 23, records that a backslider was overtaken by the aged John the Evangelist and was reclaimed thus: "Then trembling, he lamented bitterly, and embracing the old man [John] as he came up, attempted to plead for himself with his lamentations, as much as he was able, as if baptized a second time with his own tears."*

* So also the old Latin version of Eusebius, *lachrymis denuo baptizatus est*.

John of Damascus reckons seven baptisms, the last "seventh, that which is by blood and martyrdom, with which Christ himself for us was baptized."

Hilary, speaking of baptism, says, "That which by suffering of martyrdom will wash away [sin] with faithful and devoted blood."

Athanasius, fourth century, says, "For it is proper to know that, in like manner, the fountain of tears by baptism cleanses man." Again, "Three baptisms, cleansing away all sin whatsoever God has bestowed on the nature of man. I speak of that of water; and again, that by the witness of one's own blood; and, thirdly, that by tears, with which, also, the harlot was cleansed." Chrysostom holds the same.

PATRISTIC BAPTISM.

Will our immersion friends tell us how a man is dipped in his own blood? Will they explain how a man is dipped in his own tears? Will they resort to the metaphorical, and say "they were as it were" overwhelmed with grief or suffering? That will not serve for an explanation.

1. They are not metaphorical, but real baptism.
2. They were held to be sufficient baptisms by those most learned of all the fathers.
3. Even if we were to assume the absurd position that they were metaphorical baptisms, all metaphors are based on realities, and the one must correspond in the main points to the other. If only dipping is baptism, shedding tears, shedding one's blood on himself, can not change literal dip into metaphorical pour or sprinkle.

But samples from the fathers are enough, and these are

given. We do not regard the views of the fathers, especially after superstitions came in like a flood, as of much importance. Their testimony as to facts are more valuable by an infinite degree. We have given these mainly to offset the assertions of immersionists as to the views of the fathers.

FACTS ON THE HISTORY OF BAPTISM.

1. While water baptism originated in the universal symbolism of water, with innocence, purity as the way to innocency, immersion originated in supersitious views of the efficacy of the baptismal waters. This is seen in the virtue attributed to lustrations or washings by all ancient nations.* Ovid says, "Our old men believe that all wickedness and all manner of evil may be removed by purification." Again, the Latins held, "All disorder of the soul is washed away by purification of this kind."† Tertullian, *De Batismo*, says, "At the sacred rites of Isis, or Mithra, they are initiated by a washing (*lavacro*); they expiate villas, houses, temples, and whole cities, by sprinkling with water carried around. Certainly they are baptized (*tinguntur*) in the Apollinarian and Eleusonian rites, and they say they do this to obtain regeneration, and to escape the punishment of their perjuries. Also among the ancients, whoever had stained himself with murder expiated himself with purifying water." Hence, T. tells us of the "medical virtues" water "imbibed" under the consecration of the priest in his day. "How mighty is the

---

* See Demosthenes on the Crown; Diogenes Lær. 222; Plutarch on Diogenes; Ovid's Met., lib. xiv, 950; iv, 478; Jer. xi, 23; Porphyry of the Egyptians: Τρὶς τῆς ἡμέρας αἐλουσοντο φυχρῳ.

†*Omnis ejusmodi peturbatio animi placatione abluatur.*

grace of water!" "All waters, therefore, . . . do, after invocation of God, attain the sacramental power of sanctification. . . . They imbibe at the same time the power of sanctifying."*

ORIGIN OF IMMERSION.

Theophylact says of those immersed, "For as he who is immersed in the waters and baptized is surrounded on all sides by the waters," etc.† Such party—"bathing the whole body, while he who simply receives water [by affusion] is not wholly wetted on all places." ‡

Here you see that by the third and fourth centuries the virtue of baptismal water was established, as Neander shows abundantly in his history, aside from our facts from different sources mainly.

Dr. Gale quotes Reland to prove that the Mohammedan custom was that "the water must 'touch every hair of the body, and the whole skin all over' . . . This manner of washing the whole body is necessary in order to purification" in specified cases (Wall ii, 97).

1. Up to these times mode never entered into the controversy of baptism. It was the motive, the question of sincerity or insincerity alone that was involved, as in Novatian. But now in Cyprian's day, middle of the third century, the quantity of water, the touching of all parts by the water, began to attract attention. If any part was untouched, sin might lurk there. Hence—

3. Whenever the cleansing efficacy of the water was

* De Bap., chap. v, 286, vol. 1.

† Conant, *Baptizein*, pp. 22-3.

‡ Conant, 104, for the Greek, ὅλον τὸ σῶμα βρέχων, wetting the whole body, while he who merely receives the water—ὑγραινομένον, *hugrainomenon*—water sprinkled, sprinkled with water.

established copious affusions of water in baptism followed. Then the insertion of the party "deep in the water"—up to the arms and neck sometimes followed—that the sanctifying grace might be "imbibed," while water was copiously poured on the head as the baptismal rite.

4. As yet mode never entered into the essentialness or validity of baptism. The point was to have every part touched by the water. In the extract from Maimonides this superstition is seen among Jews as well as among the fathers. Had the candidate been dipped repeatedly—immersed completely a hundred times—they would have held it invalid for baptism had the subject been so enrobed as to prevent the water from reaching his person. Even as a true symbolism this would be correct, showing not mode or action, but contact of the pure water constitutes the baptism.

Tertullian shows where parties were mersed in water thus; then the baptism follows: "A man is mersed (*mersus*) in water, and amid the utterance of some few words is baptized (*tingatur*), and then rises again," etc.

Augustine, next to Jerome the most learned of Latin fathers, is thus cited by Archbishop Kendrick on Baptism: "Unless wheat be ground and sprinkled with water, it can not come to that form which is called bread. So you, also, were first ground, as it were, by mystic exorcisms. [See the superstitions now.] Then was added baptism: Ye were as it were sprinkled, that ye might come to the form of bread."* On this the Archbishop says, "St. Augustine remarks [quoting the above—'sprinkled with water'] . . . This being addressed generally to the faithful, most of whom were solemnly baptized, leads us to infer that even in solemn baptism aspersion

* Sermon ccxxviii, *ad Inf. de Sacram.* 1417.

was often used, water being sprinkled on the candidate while he stood deeply immersed" (Kendrick on Bap., p. 156, ed. 1852).

We quote the above the more because the Catholics have been so misquoted on this question, Bossuet's Jesuitical statements being relied on as if worthy of regard.

Hence Robinson, the great Baptist hero of history, says, "A Greek baptism, where, beside, trine-immersion, superfusion is practiced, or a baptism where the laver was too small, and where the body was immersed in the laver, and the head was immersed by superfusion" in the days of St. Lawrence and Strabo. Hist. Bapt., p. 108. "Immersed by superfusion"!! How absurd! He cites St. Lawrence on those who immersed, yet baptized by pouring—"superfusion"; e. g. the party "was immersed in the waters" while the priest copiously "poured the water upon his head";* and this often occurred. In cases often the laver was too small where they immersed to submerge the whole man, and in such cases where "the head could not be mersed," "the water was administered by pouring, the rest of the body by immersion,† so that no part of the man should be without the sacred washing." In other cases "they simply poured the water on the heads of those to be baptized."‡

5. The first time mersion appears or immersion as a religious rite is in these superstitious days. Tertullian is the first and only man of his day in North Africa who

* *Utpote qui aquis immersus erat, benedicit, sinistra urceum aqua planum super ejusdem caput effundit. Urceus iste ex ære etiam nunc ibidem in sacrario, etc.*

† *Ergo quia caput mergi non poterat, superfusio aquæ adhibebatur, immersio ad reliquem corpus, ut nulla pars hominis expers esset sacri lavacri. Ibid.*

‡ Robinson cites also where in trine-immersion in other cases "*aquam capitibus baptizandorum superfundunt,*" etc.

names it, and the first time he names it trine-immersion was the rite. Superstitious practices are united with it of a most revolting kind, showing it was all born of superstition.

6. The first time we find baptism practiced as a single immersion, as now practiced, is in the History of Sozomen, in the middle of the fourth century. He treats it as an innovation never known before.* No immersionist has given or can give a case where baptism was practiced in all the records and literature of the church till the fourth century after Christ.

7. Hence no Latin father, in all their voluminous works, is found that during the first two and a half centuries of the church, renders *baptidzo* by *immergo*, nor a Greek that renders it by *kataduo*, immerse. But after the third century they soon introduce these terms, and they become common.

8. Where Tertullian uses *mergo, mergito*, it is not in defining *baptidzo*. Indeed, when he uses *mergo* he immediately uses *tingo* (baptize) as expressive of a different idea. Hence, to constitute " one baptism " they used " three immersions "—*kataduseis*.

9. In all these periods baptism was by affusion also. Hence—

10. Not a single father, Latin, Greek, Syriac, or Arabic, for the first three centuries ever refers to Romans vi, 4; Colossians ii, 12, " Buried by baptism into death," as water baptism, a fact utterly incompatible with the supposition that mode was regarded as essential or that it was water baptism.

---

*Sozomen's Eccles. Hist., chap. xxvi, pp. 282-284. He urges that Eunomius "devised another heresy"—a single immersion, instead of "trine-immersion." It was "an innovation," he a heretic in doing so. See the full quotation in Louisville Debate, pp. 593-4.

11. In all their disputes over the efficacy of immersion as a sanctifying means, in the third and later centuries, as if a mere sprinkle of water failed to convey as much grace, not once do they question the mode when performed by sprinkling, never that of pouring, nor appealed to the meaning of the word, as if among them it necessarily implied immersion. They do agree that "more benefit is imparted" where the water, regardless of mode, whether by "mersion" or by "superfusion," comes in contact with "all parts of the body."

12. All the most ancient baptisteries (none earlier than the third century); all ancient and earlier allusions to it; all picture representations of it in earlier times, sustain affusion. But after all, of what value are the testimonies of the fathers on this subject, after the third century at least or even the second, when the Bible and philology so overwhelmingly demonstrate the truths we hold?

CHAPTER XXIV.

Tabal, Hebrew for Baptidzo.

But we have a source of light still on this subject that is as instructive in philology as it is overwhelming, in proof that our views are infallibly correct on this subject. All scholars and critics are agreed that—

1. [טָבַל] *Tabal* (pronounced *taval, tabhal*), the Hebrew word for *baptidzo*, occurs sixteen times in the Old Testament, once being in composition.

2. As Schleusner says, it corresponds to *baptidzo*, though as Suicer and Beza show, it answers more to *rachats*, as to use.

3. It is often translated *bapto* in the Greek Scriptures.

4. It is generally rendered dip in James's version, though never the equivalent of complete immersion.

5. It is translated *baptidzo* (baptize) by the Septuagint (2 Kings v, 14), the version largely used by the apostles.

6. It is translated baptize constantly by all ancient writers who treated of it, by the lexicons, and is the word most constantly used for the ancient proselyte baptism by Jews.*

7. Like the classic *baptidzo* it was not a word of religious import ordinarily till a later day. Once in the Bible it is religiously used—meaning "purified"—"Whom Jehovah hath purified—*lustravit*" (Gesenius).

* Sinceri Thesaurus, vol. 1, art. *Baptidzo* and *'ma;* Wāhl's Clavis, *ibid.;* Beza Annot. Matt. iii; Trommius's Concor. LXX, art. Bap.; Schleusner, *ibid.;* Louisville Debate, pp. 479, 416-17, etc.

8. It is frequently the translation of *rachats* (רָחַץ), the word immersionists insist always implied immergence in the ancient Jewish Targums.*

9. It is often translated by *tseva* in the Targums, and the immersionists claim this as the word of words for immerse, which M. Stuart freely gives up to them.

Let us examine the lexicons, then the occurrences of this word, then its root-meaning, in the light of science and of history. The smaller manuals, lexicons of highest repute, are those of J. Simonis, edited by Wetstein, 1757, later by Winer, Stokius, Leigh, J. Buxtorf, 1639, and Gesenius of the present century. They all define *tabal* exactly alike, same that Buxtorf has *demerset*, sink down or under as a meaning. These three then give it *tabal*, "to moisten, dip, immerse." † Gesenius once also renders it "purify." ‡

Hottinger, Hectaglotton, 1661, renders it to moisten, wet, stain, dip, to wash. § We will expose the blunders and self-contradictions of Gesenius, whom Rabbi Wise clings to, at the end of this chapter. The careless rendering of Gesenius by Robinson, and the confounding by immersionists of the partial dip, in the Pentateuch, to moisten a bunch of hyssop, etc. with a total immersion, has caused confusion here.¶ The word immerse in Hebrew—*tabha* (טָבַע)—all the lexicons define by immerse (*immergo*),

---

* It is so rendered 2 Kings v, 10.

† *Tinxit, intinxit, immersit.* Buxtorf: Also *demersit.*

‡ *Lustravit,* Thesaurus *sub voce Tebaliahu.*

§ *Etymologicum Orientale Lex. Harmonicum Hectaglotton,* Heb., Chal., Syr., Arab., Samaritanæ, Æthiopicæ, Talmudico—Robinicæ, a Jah. Henr. Hottengero, MDCLXI. The "*abluere,*" wash, refers simply to rabbinic and Chaldaic use.

¶ See Louisville Debate, pp. 436-7, 473-4, as examples, as if dip, dip in, and immerse were exactly the same. If so, *why* the three words, and why the *tinxit, intinxit, immersit*?

promptly, never by *tingo*, which shows a marked distinction. Dip is a derivative meaning of *tingo* as it is of *bapto*, *tabal*, etc. But that we may see who is correct as to the meaning intended by the lexicographers, let us appeal to the great folio works they have left us, wherein they elaborately explain the whole matter, and we will be left in no doubt.

THE GREAT STANDARD FOLIO LEXICONS.

1. We introduce the leader of this august tribunal, the illustrious Schindler, whom Dr. Leigh, indorsing other great names, calls "the greatest scholar in Christendom." His lexicon, Pentaglotton, 1612, thus deposes on "*tabal*, Chaldee, *tebal:* to moisten, dip, sink, immerse for the purpose of wetting or cleansing, sink down or under. In such wise (thus), to wash, as the thing is not made clean, but merely touches the liquid either in whole or in part, to baptize."*

2. Buxtorf, usually styled "the Prince of Hebrew scholars," so often quoted by immersionists as their champion, thus defines it in his great folio, the result of his life's labor. It is only his manual quoted in the Louisville Debate, pages 450 and 675. *Tabal*,† to moisten,

---

* Lexicons Pentaglotton, Hebraicum, Chaldaicum, Syriacum, Tal.— Rab. et Arabicum, professor ancient languages in the principal institutions of Germany, MDCXII. טָבַל, Chal. טְבַל *tebal, tinxit, intinxit, mersit, immersit, tingendi aut abluendi gratia, demersit; ita lavit, ut res non mundetur, sed tantum attingat humorem vel totam vel exparte, baptizavit.*

† *J. Buxtorfii Lexicon Chal. et Rab. opus* xxx *annorum, Basileæ* MDCXXXIX. *Tebal, tingere, intingere, dem. im, intingi, im, Rabbinis usurpatur pro Lavare se, abluere aliquid in aqua. Ablutio autem est vel Vasorum, vel hominum. Hominum ablutio fiebat immersione corporis tatius in aquas. Et hinc . . . ita ut res abluenda ab aliquid ei aducereus non tota abluatur, et ab aquá contingatur. Sedur Tatiareth, Betza,* folio,

to dip, sink down, immerse, be dipped, immersed. It is used by the rabbins for to wash oneself, to cleanse any thing in water. But the washing is of the vessels or men. The washing of men—persons—may be accomplished by immersing the whole body in water. The washing of vessels also hath its own peculiar regulations. And here the rabbins are very careful, and notice the minutest matters that pertain to the purification which they accomplish in the washing, so that the object to be cleansed from any thing adhering to it is not washed all over, but sprinkled with the water." He then quotes Ledar Taharoth, that they "cleanse (*tabal*) all things before the Sabbath."

3. Stokius is not a folio, but stands so high with Mr. A. Campbell we notice him. Defining it quite as the manuals, and as equivalent to *bapto* and *baptidzo*, he adds, "So that it touches (or is touched with) the moisture (liquid) in whole or barely in part," etc.*

4. Ed. Leigh, Critica Sacra. This great scholar defines it as the rest above, adding, "The object is not purified, but merely touched with the liquid either wholly or partly, to baptize."†

5. Castell. We come now to quote the largest and most remarkable Oriental lexicon that has ever been compiled, in which all the words in the Hebrew, Chaldee, Syriac, Samaritan, Æthiopic, Arabic, and Persic manuscripts, as well as printed books in Walton's famous Polyglott, are contained, by Edmund Castell, S.T.D., London, 1669. This immense folio in two volumes, containing forty-six hundred and twenty-two immense pages was

172. "*Contingatur*" is compounded of *con*—with, and *tango*—to touch. It is rendered besprinkle by the lexicons also.

* *Ut attingat humorem ex toto, aut saltem exparte, Clavis Heb.*, etc.

† *Res non mundetur, sed tantum attingat humore vel tota, vel parte, baptizavit.* This is not a folio, but most eminent critic.

the result of the labors of nineteen of the ablest scholars and critics in the world at the time, employed on it seventeen years, aggregating over three hundred years' labor, allowing for the death of some before finishing the work. Native Jews, rabbis, Arabs, and such men as Lightfoot, Wansleb, Murry, Beveridge, assisted in the work. Being thus assisted he excels all others in accuracy and research, up to that period, and he had before him the results of Schindler, Buxtorf, Walton, and Golius, etc. Hence it is equivalent to nineteen lexicons, made and condensed by nineteen authors so renowned.

[טָבַל] *tabhal,* "to moisten, dip, sink down, immerse, (English, dip or dabble), baptize. It differs from *rachats* (wash) because it is a washing to purify an object. Dipping, but it merely touches the object to [or with] the liquid, either in part or in whole." Rabbi David Kimchi, Gen. xxxvii, 31, etc.

"Chaldee, *tebal,* same as the Hebrew, where the rabbins use it for to wash oneself, cleanse any thing in water. But the washing is either of vessels or of men; later it was by the immersion of the whole body in water, but not always. Pocock, P. M. No. 390, etc.; Rabbi Levi, Sept., etc.; Rabbi Solomon."*

In the face of all this immersionists will say, as Elder Wilkes does,† that "it *never* means to wet or moisten, not once; it *never* means to wash, but it *always* means to *immerse.*" Italics his.

*טָבַל, *tinxit, int, dem. im.* (Angl. to dippe or dabble) *baptizavit: differt a* טָבַל *quod lotio sit ad rem mundandum: Intinctio, autem rem humidam contingat tantum, vel exparte, vel totam.* R. Dav. (Gen. xxxvii, 31, etc.).

Chal., טְבַל, *i. q. Heb. ib. Rab. Lavit se, abliut aliquid in aqua. Ablutio autem est, vel vasorum, vel hominum; posterior sit immersione corporis totius in aqua; at non semper* (Pocock, P. M. No. 390, etc.; R. Levi, Sept, Hauct. p. Tes. R. Sol). † Louisville Debate, p. 453.

6. Fürst. We now quote the latest and most scientific Hebraist that has lived for ages, Rabbi Fürst.

The greatest Hebrew lexicon ever yet produced, restricted to the Hebrew and a few Chaldee verses in the Hebrew Bible, as well as the only one yet that has any claim to a correct analysis of the root-meaning of words, is by the great Jewish rabbi, Julius Fürst, 1840, and his perfected lexicon of a much later date—last edition 1867.*

* On the fluctuations of Hebrew lexicography, the following facts presented by the learned Hävernick, and fully vindicated by Delitzsch, Hupfeld, and Ewald, later by Fürst, no scholar can gainsay: "A General Historico-critical Introduction to the Old Testament, by H. A. Ch. Hävernick, late teacher of theology in the University of Konigsburg, MDCCCLII (1852)." This is held by scholars to be the best introduction to the Old Testament ever produced. Page 221, he shows the different systems espoused to develop the study of the Hebrew language. "The *formal* conception of the stems" was an important point—all important. "Both (schools) set out from the principle that the *radices* (roots) of the Hebrew are *biliteræ* (two radical letters forming the base of the word), and that the grand meaning of the biliteræ must be evolved from the meaning of the letters composing it." He shows that Danz founded the best later school. After Ch. B. Michaelis and Storr "there . . . prevailed . . . a certain *empiricism* which is to be viewed in relation to the earlier as a *retrogression* in the method of investigation, and by which penetration into the Hebrew was little furthered. *To such an empirical mode of treatment,* in opposition even to what had been before attempted, did Vater yield himself. However distinguished for careful collecting of materials and tasteful arrangements are the lexical and grammatical works of Gesenius, they are, nevertheless, *confined to this* EMPIRICAL STANDPOINT," 223-4. "' By Ewald's Kritische Grammatik' this was for the first time assaulted, and a *scientific* investigation of the language, proceeding upon the proper laws of speech, and placed upon a footing of due harmony with the historical appearance and development of the language, was entered upon. His efforts and those of Hupfeld have thus *once more* begun to create positively *an epoch* in the study of Hebrew, an advance which is also beginning, at least, to make itself apparent *in the lexical* department." " Buxtorf still remains the completest compilation of lexical and grammatical matter here, and *there is still wanting a* GENUINELY SCIENTIFIC and independent, even in the grammars of the J. D. Michaelis, Winer (He

The first is a great folio, with complete concordance. The one in German (lexicon), the other in Latin:

Fürst: *Tabal*, to moisten, to wet, to sprinkle; to immerse. The root is *bal*. Compare the words derived from the same root with kindred meanings—to flow, drop down, pour, pour water on, stream forth, sprinkle. Septuagint, *baptein, baptidzein, molunein.**

In his later lexicon, where he brings out all the results of his labors, 1867, this distinguished Jewish professor, of Leipzig, thus defines *tabal*, to baptize: "To moisten, to sprinkle, *rigare, tingere;* therefore to dip, to immerse. . . . The fundamental signification of the stem is "to moisten, to besprinkle."

Elder Wilkes, and some writers following him, in his last speech, to which I had no reply, says, page 675 † (Lou. Debate), "Is it not singular that he (Fürst) should say it means to moisten, to sprinkle, and therefore to dip or immerse?" He urges, then, that there must be some error here. It would be strange indeed; but Elder Wilkes ought to have known that it was not true, nor should he have waited till his last speech to say so, lest it might be brew older works), and others." I have had Hupfeld's work some fourteen years—the ablest yet out. Of him he says, "In more recent times they (these principles) have found, *for the first time*, a worthy critic in Hupfeld" (Note, page 222). Now, as Ewald and Hupfeld brought out the true principles of Hebrew study, and demolished the empirical system of Gesenius, Furst takes up their results and brings them out in all their force, and makes a new era again in Hebrew study. The far-fetched and utterly silly analogies of Gesenius are crushed, and the true laws for discovering the root established.

* טָבַל, *rigare, tingere, perfundere* (German edition, begiessen), *immergere. Radix est bal* בַּל . . . *compara modo verba eadem de radice orta abal, bal, zabel, shabal,* etc.

† Page 680, Mr. Wilkes says again, "I know it does not make any sense to say that the word *taval* means 'to sprinkle or pour,' and therefore to immerse, 'to dip.' That is not good sense." *Who says* it? . . . Not Furst, as *his* own quotation shows.

TABHAL, HEBREW FOR BAPTIDZO.

corrected. Fürst copies his Latin definition, and the word that W. says always means dip, immerse, and from which dip is developed—*tingere,* thus: *rigare, tingere;* therefore to dip, etc.; i. e. as it means *tingere,* so it comes to mean to dip. See above where it is just as in his lexicon.

Let us sum up now.

1. All give moisten, wet, as the most common meaning.

2. All give immerse as a derivative, and not primary meaning. Not one gives it as a primary meaning.

3. All of the great masters say that if the object merely touches or is touched by the liquid or water it baptizes it.

4. That immersion was a mode by which Jews baptized sometimes, not always; and it was a later practice than by affusion or barely being touched (*ab aqua*) by the water. Buxtorf and Castell.

5. That the primary meaning of the word is to besprinkle, sustained by all words of the same root.

6. Gesenius, the great immersionist lexicographer, assumes, first, that its root is the same with *deuo* in Greek, to bedew, sprinkle, shed forth; second, that the root, meaning immerse never has such meaning in all Bible literature.* He never renders it immerse, but dip (*intingo*), as well as "to purify."

---

*Gesenius, 1833-4, Thesaurus, 1835-6, traces טָבַע, *tabha*, immerse, and טָבַל, *tabal, tabhal,* to the same root—טב (*tab*). Rabbi Wise, of Ohio, follows him in a published letter, and misquotes and utterly *tortures* Furst's language, yet admits it dips *wholly* or *partly*. Gesenius says טָבַל is the same as "Hebrew and Arabic טָבַע," and adds, " The primary syllable is טב (*tab*) . . . depth, and immersion. Compare Goth. *Duip,* Engl. *deep,* Ger. *tief*; also, Goth. *daufen,* Ger. *taufen,* Engl. *dip*; Gr. δύπτω (*dupto*), and softened δεύω (*deuo*)." Such jargon is absolutely a

7. Castell's nineteen lexicographers, Stokius, Leigh, Schindler, Buxtorf, and Fürst, equivalent to twenty-four, twenty-three of whom are the greatest ever known. Add Rabbi Kimchi, who defines it the same way, and in tenth century, whom Gesenius exalts above all, we have twenty-five with us, and Gesenius thrown in.

Dr. Barnes is often quoted by immersionists. On *tabhal* he says in his Notes on Matthew iii, 6 (vol. 1), where he takes it up from *baptidzo,* "In none of these burlesque. But if correct, it destroys the whole immersion fabric. Δεύω, which he holds is same root with *tab,* we have seen means to bedew, sprinkle, shed upon," etc. So we are sustained, and might stop. But we will not let him and his admirers off so easily. Gesenius says under טָמְאָ *tamœ,* to be or become unclean, impure, to be defiled, polluted. He renders *tabhal, tinxit, intinxit, immersit,* and "*lustravit*" under its composition form. Syriac, *tama,* to pollute . . . The primary idea is that of immersing. See in טָמַן *taman.* (a) Chiefly spoken of Levitical uncleanness, both of persons and animals (i. e. animals not to be eaten. See Lev. xi, 1-31), and also of things, as buildings, vessels, etc. Twice does Gesenius assert that "the primary idea is that of *immersing,*" etc., speaking of טב as the root. Yet he can not, and he does not, adduce a single word that has *tab* as the root that ever means to immerse, dip, or plunge. On the contrary, out of over one hundred and fifty references which he gives himself, he never renders it immerse or dip; nor dared he do so. He renders it "defile, pollute, profane, e. g. the name of God (Ez xliii, 7, 8); the sanctuary (Lev. xv, 31; Jer. vii, 30); a land by wickedness and idolatry (Num. xxxv, 34; Jer. ii, 7," etc.). The texts show that it was often done by *touching,* as a dead body (Lev. xi, 24), "toucheth the carcass," etc. (v. 26), "toucheth," etc. Here then is the root of his favorite word that means, *primarily,* "to immerse." Yet *never* means to immerse in a single place in all Hebrew literature. On the contrary, he shows that it is done in most cases by a *mere touch,* in many by *affusion,* in some by *sprinkling,* as in case of blood, or water that is unclean, etc. He is wild in his idea of *nazah,* getting it from Arabic *naza,* where it is clearly the same with the Arabic *natzach,* to sprinkle; Æthiopic, *nazach.* Lastly, Gesenius getting all his support from Indo-European languages, where in his greatest Essay on Philology he utterly repudiates that source as a reliable aid (see it also in the Bib. Repos., 1833) is utterly inconsistent. We will further test the root *tab* directly, and see the result.

fifteen cases [he misses one] can it be shown that the meaning of the word is to immerse entirely. But in nearly all the cases the notion of applying the water to a part only of the person or object, though it was by dipping, is necessarily to be supposed."

Lightfoot, next to Pocock and Fürst, of all the scholars in centuries past was the best versed in rabbinic literature. In the famous and often misstated discussions of the Assembly, 1643, it is stated in his life that one man asserted that this word, pronounced in later times *tebeilah* (baptism), "imports a dipping overhead." Lightfoot answered him "and proved the contrary, first, from a passage of Aben Ezra on Genesis xxxviii [xxxvii, 31]; second, from Rabbi Solomon Jarchi, who, in his commentary on Exodus xxiv, saith that Israel entered into covenant with sprinkling of blood and *Taybelah* [i. e. *tebal*, baptism], which the author of the Epistle to the Hebrews expoundeth by sprinkling (Hebrew ix. . . In conclusion, he proposed to that Assembly to show him in all the Old Testament any one instance where the word used *de sacris et in actu transeunte* implied any more than sprinkling."

All that Wetstein, Alting, Meyer, etc. have on this question is taken from the above masters. Who, then, best knew of the matter?

Gesenius made a futile effort to run *tab*, the word he erroneously assumes to be the root of *tabal*, through the Aryan tongues into *daub*, *dob*, *daupian*, etc., *doopar*, when in the Semitic families, so much nearer home, *dub*, *dob*, *daba* would have come far nearer giving the truth and science of his dip. דוב (*dub*) in Chaldee, to flow, flow down, to rain (bedew); Syriac, *dob*, make wet, flow; Samaritan, to flow; Arabic, moisten, make wet.* Kin-

Fluxit, defluxit, profluxit, roravit, liquefecit, the latter repeated over and again.

dred to it, same word strengthened, is *duph; dup;* Arabic, *dapa,* or *dipa,* to make wet,* macerate.

As Gesenius has been so earnestly pressed into service by Elder Wilkes, etc. we will cite what he says in his famous and very learned essay on Sources of Hebrew Philology and Lexicography, to show again his defective and contradictory statements: "3. But the most important by far of all the languages kindred to the Hebrew, and in every respect the most fertile source of Hebrew etymology and lexicography, is the Arabic, one of the richest and most cultivated, and also in its literary history one of the most important languages in the world." "The Arabic the best and surest help."† He gives "words which stand in connection with the Indian tongues," i. e. Aryan branches, as simply a few words in music and natural history. Yet on *tabal* he violates all this, and seeks all his help in Aryan languages and ignores the Arabic that was full of help on that very root. In the late Webster's Dictionary all this folly is copied, and they give for dip, " Ger. *döpen,* Sw. *döpa,* D. *doopen.*" Webster never put it there of course; they state that fact in the introduction. Ed. 1878.‡

**Humectavit, maceravit.*
† See also more in his "Arabische Sprache" and "Arabische Literatur" in Ersch and Gruben's Encyc.; Eichorn, Wachler, Bib. Repos, 1833.
‡ Why did they not then cite the Arabic *dipa,* or *dapa, dup,* etc.?

CHAPTER XXV.

Primary Meaning.

Let us now examine as to the primary meaning of the term baptize as it occurs in Semitic languages, the apostles being Hebrews.

In religious use words longest retain their primary meaning. In Genesis the word baptize first occurs, and we have seen it is in the sense of sprinkle. We now propose to apply to טָבַל *tabal* (pronounced *taval*) the rules and laws by which the true meanings, and primary meanings, of all words are now found by philological scientists. Before we do this let us hear A. Campbell on the rules applied: "Derivative words legally inherit the specific though not necessarily the figurative meaning of their natural progenitors, and never can so far alienate from themselves that peculiar significance as to indicate any action specifically different from that indicated from the parent stock. [We have seen how utterly void is this in our examples of words meaning to sprinkle, pour, dip, immerse, etc.] Indeed (continues he), all inflexions of words, with their sometimes numerous and various families of descendants, are but modifications of one and the same generic or specific idea." He then runs one word, "dip," through such inflexions and says, emphasizing every word, "Wherever the radical syllable (*bap*) is found the radical idea is in it" (Chris. Baptism, pp. 119, 120). That is, as Mr. Campbell applies this to *bapto* and *bap-*

tidzo, if we select all the words compounded or derived from the root *bapto*—its radical idea, the root being *bap* with the force of "dip"—we will find dip in every such word.

We have *bapto, baptos, baptæ, embapto, baptidzo, embaptidzo, kata-baptidzo, anabaptidzo, baptismos, baptisma, baptisis, baptistæs,* with all possible inflexions—*ebaphon, ebaphæ, bammati, bebammenon;* the letter *p* exchanged for an *m,* to be resumed again. In all these is the root *bap;* hence always the idea of dip. So reasons the immersionist. We are not now objecting to all this as a rule, but deny the dip as the primary idea. We now test baptize in Hebrew where it occurs more than one thousand years before we come up with it in the Greek any where. As we gave above thirteen or fourteen variations of *bap,* the root, let us select about an equal number of variations of the root of the Hebrew word baptize (טָבַל *tabal*). *Bal* is the root of the word. Now what is the prevailing "idea" of this root of the word in Hebrew? Fortunately in Hebrew we have great light here in kindred tongues in which the same root occurs in many words, with the same meaning, while unfortunately in the kindred tongues to the Greek, Latin, and other Indo-European tongues, no assistance has been found, no kindred root.* In the Arabic, Gesenius and all philologists agree is our greatest help to critically learn the Hebrew and understand the genius of it.

In Arabic we select the root itself—

1. בל (*bal, bala*). Freytag thus defines *bal*: "To moisten, and especially to make wet or soft by sprinkling

---

* It is to be hoped research in the Sanskrit may find the root of this word. We feel perfectly certain if it is found it will be as in the Hebrew and other languages.

or light affusion of liquid. VIII to bedew, be made wet."*

Castell: "*Bal*, to moisten, and especially to make wet or soft by sprinkling," i. e. water. Lorshbach's Syriac Thesaurus—*bal-confudit*, to pour together.

2. Arabic, *bal-a-la*, same root. Schindler: To sprinkle, make wet.† Gesenius: To moisten, to make wet by affusion of water [liquid], to sprinkle. ‡

3. *Babala* (root *bal*, Gesenius). Buxtorf, Gesenius, Castell, all, "sprinkle." §

4. בָּלַל (*bal-al*). This word in the Arabic Bible is the translation of βάπτω (*bapto*), and throws a flood of light on all this question from a philological standpoint. It bears exactly the primary relation to baptize in Hebrew that *bapto* does in Greek. Let us then give it at length as it is so directly and essentially related to baptism. Leigh in his *Critica Sacra* gives "to pour, sprinkle."¶ Castell: "To be sprinkled, to sprinkle." Schindler: "To pour, besprinkle, sprinkle." Gesenius: "To sprinkle, to moisten, make wet by affusion of water, sprinkle." But it does not stop with that meaning. It goes on and develops the following: "To sprinkle, make wet, moisten, dip, to water, make wet (Luke vii, 38, 44)," (equal to *brecho*) (Ps. vi, 7, (6); Luke xvi, 24, rendered from (βάπτω ἐμβάπτω) *bapto*, *embapto*; John xiii, 26, dip. It is repeatedly used for "dip," "dip in."

5. נָפַל *naphal*, *na-bal*, root *bal*. Targum, "pour out" (*effundo*, Castell).

Madeficit, et spec. rigavit maceravit ve asperso aut leviter affuso humore. VIII. *Maduit, rigatus fuit.*

†*Perfudit, humectavit.*

‡*Rigavit, affuso humore madeficit, conspersit.*

§ Each gives "*conspersit*.'

¶*Conspersit*; Castell, *Perfudit, conspersit*; Schindler, *Fudit, perfudit, conspersit*; Gesenius, same as No. 3 quoted. So Freytag.

6. שָׁבַל *Sha-bal*, "to flow, to pour." Fürst, Arabic, "to rain, flow down."

7. אָבַל *Abal*, "rain." (Castell, Arabic), "moist."

8. בַּל BAL, "rain."

9. בּוּל *bul* (*bal*), "to flow, stream forth copiously." Fürst, etc.

10. *Mabal* Arabic, *ma-*BAL-*a*, "to flow copiously, to moisten."

11. יָבַל *ya-*BAEL, *bal*, the root, "to flow, to stream." Fürst.

12. וָבַל *wa-bal*, Arab. to pour rain, to rain copiously and vehemently; rain.*

13. יָבַל *ya-*BAL, "to flow, to stream, to pour, drop down, moisten." Fürst.

Thus we see that affusion is in every word that has the root of the word baptize. More evidence is useless. Let us now test *tab* (טב), Gesenius's idea of the root, and see if it is immerse. We have seen that his assumptions sustain us, but we do not want to be sustained by error. His position, too, crushes the immersion theory, as it makes "bedew," etc. come from immerse.

Let us now take the words that have *tab* as their root, and see the meaning of such, Gesenius being one of the prominent judges.

1. *Ratab* (רָטַב), Gesenius defines thus: "To be wet, moisten with rain (Tob. xxiv, 8), also with sap . . . espec[ially] of the moisture of juices of plants," etc.

2. *Natab* (נָטַב), Æthiopic, same as the Hebrew *shalab*,† to distill or shed drops, as dew-water, etc.

3. *Nataph. Tab* is the root—*tab-taph*: "To drop, fall in drops, to distill. . . . In a similar manner the Arabs

---

*Imbrem effudit, copiosè et vehementer pluit . . . imber (Castell).

† Castell and Fürst, *distillavit gutta. Heptaglotton*, 2283.

PRIMARY MEANING. 305

transfer the idea of watering, irrigating" [or wet], etc. (Gesenius.)

4. *Zab, zub,* is kindred to *tab,* with kindred meanings, to flow, of water, blood, etc.

5. צוּף *Tsuph.* In this word the *ts* stand for *t*, and *tab* is the root. It means "to pour, pour out, irrigate, flow."

6. *Shataph, tab* the root, "to gush or pour out" (Gesenius). This word comes to mean to immerse in later literature. We pass the blunders of Mr. Wilkes on the accusative, as the meaning of the word determines whether we regard it as accusative or dative in all these texts.*

* Not one case where *tabhal* occurs has the noun the signs of the accusative. They are dative or accusative *as the sense may require.*

20

CHAPTER XXVI.

TABHAL.

Seeing in the last chapter that all Hebrew lexicographers sustain the position that to besprinkle or touch even the person with water, baptizes, let us examine this word in the Bible and rabbinic Hebrew. It occurs sixteen times in the Bible. In our English version, which, as the Baptists truly say, is only a revision of a former version—Tyndale, 1526-1534—made by immersionists, and when Hebrew and Greek were but poorly understood as to philological principles, it is rendered dip in all the places where it occurs as a verb. Of it Mr. Wilkes (Louisville Debate p. 453), says, "It *always means to immerse.*" Italics his. Again, "The word *taval* (*tabhal*) is used sixteen times in the Hebrew Bible,* and every time it means IMMERSION." Now, what do Mr. W. and his colaborers in immersion mean by immerse? Evidently to sink clear and completely under the element, so that every part is enveloped, covered. That is what they mean. Now, a careful examination of each, of all, its occurrences will show and demonstrate that it never means immerse nor dip in their sense of that word. A few passages excepted, say about three, as Job viii, 31, the object to be obtained by *tabhal* was not dip in any sense, while immersion is wholly

---

* It occurs sixteen times as noun and verb, thus: Leviticus x, 6, 17; ix, 9; xiv, 6, 16, 54; Numbers xix, 18; Ruth ii, 14; Exodus xii, 22; Deuteronomy xxxiii, 24; Job ix, 31; 1 Samuel xiv, 27; 2 Kings v, 14; viii, 15; Joshua iii, 15; Genesis xxxvii, 31.

out of the question in every case. The only object of the word, in about thirteen of the places where it occurs, was to wet the object slightly, moisten, saturate so as to sprinkle objects. In some of these cases a partial dip would be most natural, and was the process, but in no case was there an immersion. Let us examine a few.

1. In Exodus xii, 22, the blood is used to saturate, or moisten the bunch of hyssop. No mode is involved. The bunch of hyssop most naturally would be "touched to" the blood, moistened with it, very partially dipped.

2. In Leviticus iv, 6, 17, the priest was to moisten his finger with the blood. A "mere touch" would do this—any contact. The finger in the case could not be immersed. In Exodus xii, 22; Leviticus iv, 17, the Greek is with, *apo*, by means of the blood; Hebrew *min*—not *in*. This utterly forbids dip, as immersionists say *apo* "helps out" of the water (A. C.). Or does *apo* mean "into" and "out of" both, just as it suits? It means neither of them.

In Leviticus xiv, 6, it is impossible that "the living bird, and the cedar wood, and the scarlet, and the hyssop" should all be immersed "in the blood of the bird that was killed." It was done thus: "A stick of cedar wood was bound to a bunch of hyssop by a scarlet ribbon, and the living bird was to be attached to it; that when they dipped the branches in the water the tail of the bird might be moistened, but not the head nor the wings, that it might not be impeded in its flight when let loose."* The moistening of a part of the bird was baptizing the bird. In verse 51 he was to baptize the cedar wood, hyssop, scarlet, and living bird (*b'dom*) with the blood of the slain bird, and "with the running water" (Heb.). Only a part of the bird was made wet, yet the bird was baptized.

* Jamieson, Fausset, and Brown's Commentary on Leviticus xiv, 6.

FIRST OCCURRENCE ON RECORD OF BAPTISM.

In Genesis xxxvii, 31, is the first occurrence in the world of a baptism. As it is the oldest document in the world by a thousand years (save other Bible records), and older than any of the Bible occurrences by from four hundred to five hundred years, it is very important as showing the earlier and primary meaning of the word:

"And they took Joseph's coat, and killed a kid of the goats, and dipped the coat in the blood; and they sent the coat of many colors, and they brought it to their father" . . . (verse 33). "And he knew the coat; it is my son's coat; an evil beast hath devoured him."* The Targum of Onkelos reads as the Hebrew, *tabal*, baptized with blood.

1. The object in baptizing this *toga* or outward cloak was to impress the father that a wild beast had slain Joseph.

2. In that day men were quick to detect, reading less than we, and thrown constantly upon their instincts and self-protection. Nor was Jacob noted for stupidity by any means. What beast or animal would submerge the outer garment in one's blood in slaying him? It would be rent off first of all and receive but little of the blood comparatively. These men showed great cunning, and would not make the blunder of immersing the coat.

3. The father, just as they intended, knew the coat "of many colors." If submerged in blood how many colors would it have had?

4. The ancient versions take the same view, and are above all authorities on the meaning of the word.

*וַיִּטְבְּלוּ אֶת־הַכֻּתֹּנֶת בַּדָּם *vayyitbelu* (*tabhal*) *eth-hakuto-neth baddam* —and baptized—sprinkled—the coat with the blood.

(1) The Greek used by the apostles translate it sprinkle,* stain, i. e. by sprinkling. H. Stephanus says, "The primary meaning (of *molunein*) is to sprinkle." †

(2) The Targum of Jacob Tawus renders it "bedashed," i. e. sprinkled with blood.

(3) The Latin Vulgate (*tingo*), stained with blood.

But the old Peshito-Syriac, the oldest and purest version and most literal in the world, translates it "sprinkle." It reads ‡ (פַּלְפְלוּה) *phalpheluh* [or *palpeluh*, soft], sprinkled with blood. It is remarkable that here this old, invaluable version renders baptize by the other word we gave, *balal*, for its root is *bal*, as Gesenius and Fürst show, and is thus rendered by Buxtorf in his folio lexicon of rabbinic Hebrew and Chaldee; for the Chaldee and Syriac are the same word, same meaning.

פַּרְפֵּל (*phalphael*), *conspergere; et conspersi pulvere gloriam meam* (*phalphael*) (Job xvi, 15)—"I have sprinkled my head (*horns, glory*, is the Hebrew) with dust."

Esther iv, 1: "And sprinkled (*conspersus, phalphael*) his head with ashes." Gesenius's Thesaurus: "*Bal-al*, same as Chaldee בּוּל, פַּרְפֵּל, *phalphal, conspersit;* Syriac, *phalphal conspersit;* Chaldee and Syriac, to sprinkle."

---

* Dr. Graves (Debate, p. 530) has only this answer to all these facts, after corresponding with Drs. Varden, Conant, Toy, etc., for help to aid in writing up a reply after the debate: "In one instance [Greek translators] where (Gen. xxxvii, 31) they translated it [*tabal*] figuratively 'to dye.'" That would be so if *molunein* did not mean sprinkle. But the Syriac has no figurative rendering, they put it *sprinkle*, and leave all sensible people to apply the *effect* of sprinkling blood on a garment. Passow, Rost, Palm, and Liddell & Scott all render *molunein* "sprinkle," *besprengen.*

† *Primitiva notio est conspergere.* H. Stephanii Thesaurus Grecæ Lin., v, p. 6223. Liddell & Scott: "Μολύνω, to stain, sully, defile, sprinkle," Sprinkle is the *mode* by which μολύνω, stained primarily.

‡ (וְפַלְפְלוּה) *wephalpheluh lekietino*, sprinkled the coat—*tunic.*

Castell's Heptaglott: *Phalphal,* Syriac, "*conspersit—* sprinkle."

We will add one passage more of Hebrew now, where *abhal* occurs among the old Hebrew writers about or near Christ's day.

"There was not any like to Benaiah, the son of Jehoiada, under the second Temple. He one day struck his foot against a dead tortoise, and went down to Siloam, where, breaking all the little particles of hail, he baptized, *vetabhal,* himself. This was on the shortest day in winter, the tenth of the month Tebeth." Lightfoot's Horæ Habraicæ et Talmudicæ, vol. 3, p. 292.

It is useless to argue such a question as immersion or dipping here. Does it always mean immerse? Thus the root-meaning of the lexicons, the Bible use, and ancient Hebrew usage, and the translations, all agree that it is to sprinkle, to moisten.

CHAPTER XXVII.

ANCIENT VERSIONS ON BAPTIDZO—THE SYRIAC.

All scholars, all linguistic critics, and all lexicographers are agreed that the ancient versions of the Hebrew and Greek Scriptures are all-important to lexicographers and expounders of the Word of God. All appeal to them as the very highest authority in determining the force and current meanings of the words of Scripture. Hence some have carried this to even a dangerous extent. Of this class we may name Dr. Gale, A. Campbell, Mr. Pendleton, of Bethany—all immersionists. The latter assumes that Christ, "in speaking to 'a ruler of the Jews,' did not use the Greek language." He tells us "he spoke in Hebrew or Aramaic," i. e. Syriac, all of which is true, but he uses it very doubtfully.* Gale assumes that the Peshito-Syriac translation was made from the autographs of the apostles. That may be true, yet the assumptions based on it may not be true. A. Campbell tells us of "the original word used by the Savior in his native Syro-Chaldaic language." †

1. The Syriac, or Syro-Chaldaic, as some call it, was the vernacular, the spoken language of the Messiah and his people in his day on earth. In it he preached habitually, as did his apostles generally.

2. The translation known as the Peshito was executed,

* Millen. Harb. Nov., 1867, pp. 582-3.
† Debate with Rice, and in Chris. Baptism, 135.

beyond all reasonable doubt, in the apostolic age, and as a rule at least, gives us the very words used by Christ in his sermons and discourses. Hence all of the most learned critics in the Syriac maintain that this version was made in the first century. Of these may be named the great Walton, Kennicott, S. Davidson, Lowth, Carpzov, Leusden, Stiles, Palfrey; while Michaelis and Jahn put it at "the close of the first" or "the earlier part of the second century."*

3. The Syriac being the tongue of Christ and his apostles, and of the great body of all the first Christians, it is absurd to suppose they did not have a translation of the Bible. The kings of Syria, in Edessa, were converted to Christianity in the middle of the apostolic age. It is absurd indeed to suppose they had no translation.

4. All ancient traditions of all the Syrian churches, "Nestorian, Monophysite, Melchite, and Maronite, in all of which this version has been in public use time out of mind, and has ever been revered as coeval with the origin of those churches."

5. They all held it to have been made therefore in the

---

* Walton, Prolegomena to his Polyglot, pp. 92-95, says, "For the New Testament being written in Greek, whose vernacular language was Syriac, every where savors of Syriacisms. Hence Ludovicus (author of a Syriac lexicon, etc) affirms that the true import of the phraseology of the New Testament can scarcely be learned except from the Syriac." "They conceived in Syriac what they wrote in Greek." Pres. E. Stiles, D.D., of Yale College, says, "The greater part of the New Testament was originally written 'in Syriac,' and not merely translated, in the apostolic age." All the fathers held that Matthew, if not Mark and Hebrews, were written first in Syriac. Bolton held that "nearly all the epistles must have been first composed by the apostles in Aramæan (Syriac), their native tongue." The learned Bertholdt defends this view. "The Syriac translator has recorded the actions and speeches of Christ in the very language in which he spoke" (J. D. Michaelis). So held in almost the same words Martini, W. Francius, Palfrey, etc.

apostolic age. Hence its great purity and symplicity. Hence they say, "But the rest of the Old Testament [books] and of the New Testament were translated with great pains and accuracy by Thaddeus and the other apostles." No refutation of this can be adduced.

6. Of this version Dr. Judd, indorsed and copied by Dr. J. R. Graves in the Appendix he published to M. Stuart on Baptism, says, "The old Syriac, or Peshito, is acknowledged to be the most ancient as well as one of the most accurate versions of the New Testament extant. It was made at least as early as the beginning of the second century, in the very country where the apostles lived and wrote, and where both the Syriac and the Greek were constantly used and perfectly understood. Of course it was executed by those who understood and spoke both languages precisely as the sacred writers themselves understood and spoke them. . . All the Christian sects in Syria and the East make use of this version exclusively" (p. 245).

7. Such a version thus executed was indorsed thus by the whole body of the apostolic ages and the scholarship of the whole Syrian church. Its renderings of *baptidzo* must be of the greatest moment, therefore.

Dr. Gale (Baptist) says, "The Syriac must be thought almost as valuable and authentic as the original itself, being made from primitive copies in or very near the times of the apostles." By primitive he tells us what he means—"The autograph" of the apostles. Reflections on Wall, vol. 2, 118.

Origen, born only eighty-three to eighty-five years after John's death, cites the Peshito as a familiar version already long in use. It was cited A.D. 220 as an established standard of authority. Ephraem Syrus quotes one who wrote thus who treats it as established in his day. So valuable is it that Gotch, A. Campbell, Conant, Judd, all head their list of versions with the venerable Peshito.

The truth is, that if it were not executed till the second century, it uses the words for baptism used by Christ and the apostles any way. Of that no one would express a doubt.

AMAD IS BAPTIDZO.

The Peshito translates *baptidzo* by *amad*. It is all-important now to know the exact meaning of *amad*.

Dr. Judd (Baptist) says, "All the authorities agree in assigning to this word the primary and leading signification of immersion."* Dr. Judd copies from the real Castell, and not from Michaelis's edition, abridged, which leaves off the important word involved here.

We now quote the lexicons as they are.

Castell: This great work, embodying three hundred years of labor, by native Arabians, Jews, native Syrians, being based on two lexicons on the Syriac part, made by Syrians centuries before, and the equivalent of nineteen of the greatest scholars all Europe produced in that renowned age, the seventeenth century, defines *amad* thus:

"*Amad*,† primarily, to wash [literally to be cleansed or

---

*Appendix to Graves's M. Stuart, p. 246. Since the above was written, Dr. Graves (Debate, p. 530) says, *Amad* in Syriac, as *all standard lexicographers* testify, PRIMARILY signifies to immerse." A. Campbell (Chris. Bap., pp. 135-6) says essentially the same. Dr. G. never uttered such a sentiment during the debate. That, like nearly all else after the first few speeches, was rewritten, and so was never seen by me till the book was out. We loaned our Castell to Dr. Graves, and he knew what it said.

†*Amad, Prim. ablutus est, baptizatus est* (Matt. iii, 16; Luke xix 11, 38, etc.; Matt. iii, 7, etc.; Luke vii, 30). *Aph* [for *Aphel*, derivative] *immersit* (Num. xxxi, 24); *baptizavit* (Acts xix, 4, 16, etc.); *ablutio, baptizatio, baptizatus, lavacrum*.

washed], to baptize." Matt. iii, 16, etc.; Luke xix, 11, 38, etc.; Matt. iii, 7, etc.

"*Aphel* [i. e. derivatively], to immerse (Num. xxxi, 24). Noun from *mamudhitho*, cleansing, baptism, washing." Arabic—same word, same root—"to baptize, to make wet with rain."* Under *amak*, "The Arabians also lisp in pronouncing *amak, amath, amad, amat*—to be immersed, to bedew, sprinkle with water [or rain] (the earth, herbs, etc.), sprinkle with water [rain or dew]. A horse wet with water, also sprinkled. Morning dew, also wetting the earth, field, bedewed, sprinkled with dew [or rain] wetting, etc." †

J. Michaelis's *amad*, to wash, baptize. *Aphel* [i. e. derivatively] to immerse. ‡

PESHITO SYRIAC.

Oberleitner: "*Amad*, to cleanse [or wash], to baptize. Derivatively, *aphel*, to immerse, to baptize." §

*Arabic, *amada*; *baptizavit*; A. *madore pluviæ affecta fuit*.

†Arabic, *et balbulivit in pronunciatione* (i. e. *amath, amad, amat*), *immersus fuit, maduit, rore perfusa fuit* (*terra, terba*, etc.), *rore perfusa. Equus aqua rigætus, et perfusus. Res matutinus, et terram irrigans. . . Rore perfusus, mademus*, etc. (Heptoglotton, Ed. Castell, 280).

‡ As Michaelis is misquoted in his note to the abridgment from Castell we give it. *Mihi verisimilius, diversum plane ab literarumque aliqua permutatione ortum ex gamotha, submergere.* That is, he simply urges (1) That *amad* does not mean in Syriac *to stand*, as some thought; (2) That he thinks that there has been an exchange of letters, that it should be *gamatha* instead of *amad*—a perfect absurdity. Yet Dr. Graves boldly tells us in substance that M. says it is immerse, etc. On derivative *Aphel*, Dr. Green's Heb. Gram., p. 101, sec. 77, *a* may be consulted, where it answers in Hebrew to "*derivative* verbs," in Greek and Latin. (See Hoffman's Syr. Gram., etc. in detail.)

§ *Amad, ablutus, baptizatus est. Aphel amed immersit, baptizavit.*

4. Catafago: "*Amad*, the being wet with rain."* This is the only meaning he gives it.

5. Schaaf: "*Amad*, to cleanse [or wash] oneself, to be washed, to be dipped, to be immersed in water, to be baptized." He then supposes it to be of a word spelled like it in Hebrew; then he gives the Arabic through its conjugations; then resumes the Syriac, giving it baptize all the time. Then—

"*Aphel* [derivatively], to immerse, to baptize. To immerse (Numbers xxxi, 23). To baptize (Acts i, 5; xi, 16; xix, 4).

Mamudhitho (noun), baptism, place of baptism, washing, cleansing.†

6. Hottinger, 1661, a lexicon of Hebrew, Chaldaic, Arabic, Syriac, etc., etc.: "*Amad*, to baptize" (*baptizare*).

7. Gutbier: "*Amad*, to baptize, to be baptized." He then gives "to support" as the meaning all now reject, because it was based on the old false assumption of kindredship with the Hebrew word "to stand," followed by Gesenius.

8. Gesenius: "Among the Syriac Christians *amad* is to be baptized, because the person baptized stood in the water."‡

9. Schindler, 1612: "*Amad*, Arabic *amada*, to be baptized, to be immersed in water, to be wet, to be washed;

---

* Catafago, secretary to Soliman Pasha, 1839-40, etc., corresponding member of the Asiatic societies of Paris and Leipsig, of the Syro-Egyptian Society of London, translator of various Oriental works, living in Aleppo, in Syria, in Beirut, etc. 1858. It is an Arabic lexicon.

† "*Amad, abluit se, ablutus, intinctus, immersus in aquam, baptizatus est Aphel amed, immersit, baptizavit. Immersit* (Num. xxxi, 23); *baptizavit* (Acts i, 5, etc.). Noun—*baptismus,-'ma,-terium; lotio, ablutio.*"

‡ *Apud Syros Christianos* (*amad*) *est baptizatus est, quia baptizandus stabat in aqua.*

for they who were baptized stand up,* . . . to wash oneself," etc.

Schindler so mixes the Syriac and Arabic it is impossible to tell which meaning is meant, particularly for the Syriac and Arabic. The fact he and Gesenius state is true, but not because of kindredship in the Hebrew and Syriac word. But it was an early custom for the candidates to stand "immersed in the water" "to be baptized," noticed elsewhere.

Beza is often quoted as saying *amad* is always immerse. He says of "*baptizein*, to dye, to moisten (*madefacere*), to immerse," and argues this in the old style; then adds, "Neither is there any other meaning of the word *amad* which the Syrians use for baptize."† Beza then finds "wash, cleanse," in *baptidzo* by consequence, then pour as the mode.

I have Lorsbach's great folio work, but it is not yet completed as far as to *amad* or any word relating to baptism, being in numbers issued as fast as they can.

Now, then, we have—

1. All these Syriac lexicographers, equal to some twenty-five, giving wash (cleanse) as the primary meaning of *amad*.

2. Not one gives immerse as the primary meaning.

3. Not one gives immerse as a current meaning.

4. All give immerse both as a derived meaning and as a rare one.

5. Not one gives immerse as a New Testament meaning, and they could find but one place in the whole Old

---

* Syr., *amad*; Arabic, *amad baptizatus, in aquam immersus, tinctus, lotus fuit: Stobant enim qui baptizabantur,* . . . *sese abluisset.*

† *Tingere, cùm παρὰ τὸ βάπτειν dicatur, et cùm tingenda mergantur, madefacere, et mergere.* Then—"*Nec alia est significatio,*" etc.

Testament where *amad* meant immerse; and in that place the Hebrew and Greek have not the words for baptize.

6. Over and again it means to sprinkle, to wet with dew, wet with rain, bedew—all being cases of sprinkling.

7. I had the pleasure of finding where the Greek word *louo* (λούω), to wash, pour,* is twice translated *amad* in Susanna xii, 6; xiii, 15, in London Polyglott of Walton.

8. In John v, 2, 4, 7; ix, 7: "Go wash at [or in] the baptistery," shows that *amad* in its noun-form expressed the *nipto*, wash, which was simply application of water, not dipping.

9. The Peshito, or the translation of Revelation, made only a little later, translates *bapto* by "to sprinkle." †

10. It translates *tabhal*, Greek, *baptidzo* (2 Kings v, 14), by *secho*, wash, a word never meaning dip or immerse, but primarily "to pour." It applies—*secho* does—in the ancient Targums when Joseph "washed his face." In the New Testament it applies (*secho*) to washing a dead body, as that of Dorcas, wetting a couch with tears, etc. ‡

11. In the first case of the Hebrew word for baptize in all literature (Gen. xxxvii, 31) it is translated sprinkle by the Peshito.§ Such are the facts in this great version.

12. And it is worthy of remark, that in no case have the Hebrew words for immerse, *tabha, kaphash, shakha,* or the Greek words *budthidzo, kataduo, pontidzo, katapontidzo,* immerse, or *dupto,* dip, or *bapto,* sometimes to dip—*embapto* dip, ever been translated in Syriac or Arabic by *amad.* If *amad* was immerse, why not do this?

*See under *Wash.* No lexicon had as yet made that discovery, nor writer. See it in Carrollton Debate, p. 148.

† Revelation xix, 13, *zelach,* "sprinkled with blood."

‡ Hottinger defines the root-syllable, *sacha,* "to pour out," *effudit.* Castell, *effudit aquam, profudit.* In Arabic, "vehement rain."

§ See all the quotations and facts Chapter XXIII of this work.

13. But the old Syriac has another word for baptize, in ancient Syriac and Arabic, *tseva; tsavagh* in Arabic, or *tsavaga*. The ancient sect known as Sabeans or Tsabeans, derived their name from daily baptizing.* Baptist writers think *tseva* was the word used by Christ in the commission.† They insist *tseva* always means immerse. It is the same in Syriac, Chaldee, and Arabic.

(1) The great Oriental philologist and scholar of the present age in Hebrew and kindred languages, was Fürst, Professor of Hebrew, etc. in Leipsic, Germany. He thus defines it as late as 1867-8: "*Tseva*, to moisten, to besprinkle, to baptize; Paal (form), to water, to moisten." To besprinkle, to moisten, is its "fundamental signification."

(2) Gutbier defines it "to moisten, to wash" (*lavit*).

14. But let us test this word in the Bible. In Daniel is the only place where it occurs in Chaldee—the only place where *tseva* occurs in the Old Testament original (Daniel iv, 20), "And his body was baptized (*tseva*) with the dew of heaven." Was this dipping? O, cries the immersionist, "dews are very heavy in Chaldea, and his body was as wet as if immersed!" Indeed! But no matter how copious the dew, it does not read "as wet as if dipped or immersed." It uses no metaphor either. It is as historic and unmetaphorical as when it says "the people were baptized." It is as literal as when it says "Philip baptized him," the eunuch. "His body was bap-

---

* See the Note in Michaelis's edition of Castell: *Sœbii nomen Mendœosum*, i. e. *discipulorum Joannes, qui ita a baptizando dicti, baptistœ, seu, ut Grœci illos vocant* ἡμερο—βαπτισται. See Neander's Church Hist., also, and Gieseler.

† Dr. Graves (Debate, 390), as published, says, "In this [the Nestorian Ritual of Syria] the verb *amad* is used interchangeably with *tsevœ, which has no other meaning but to immerse*." He used not a sentence in all that published speech in the *spoken* one.

tized with the dew from heaven." It was a literal man, literal dew, a literal baptism.

15. The Vulgate of Jerome, A.D. 380-383, translates this: "And his body was sprinkled with the dew of heaven."* In the Chaldee it is repeated four times. In verse 22, the Vulgate again reads, "His body shall be sprinkled (Chaldee, baptized) with the dew of heaven."† As Jerome was the ablest Syriac scholar and Hebrew in all the church save in the Syriac branch at that time, and his version was sustained by all scholars, it certainly is conclusive on this point.

16. Psalm vi, 6 [in the Hebrew 7], "My couch have I baptized (*tseva*) with my tears." What was the mode?

SYRIAC VERSIONS.

17. Ezekiel xxii, 26: "Thou art the land that is not (*tzeva*) baptized [English, purified]; no, upon thee the rain has not fallen."‡ We know the mode of this baptizing. We need no lexicons to aid us.

18. Luke vii, 38, 44. Remember that most likely we have here word for word the very words in the language Jesus used; for it is his vernacular, as the English is yours. It occurs twice in the same sense. "Simon, into thy house I came; water upon my feet you gave me not [so runs the Syriac], but she [the woman] with her tears my feet hath baptized!" We know the mode. We need no lexicon. I would not give one such witness as this—being in the very age of the apostles, in the very language in which Christ and his apostles preached, made in such a

---
*Et rore cœli conspergatur.
†Et rore cœli infunderis.
‡Metro, necheth.

language by such men, universally received as true to the Greek when all that membership knew what apostolic preaching and practice were—I would not give one such authority for a thousand lexicons written fifteen hundred years after the death of the apostles, and after the Dark Ages with their superstitions had rolled between.

In the light of these facts, we see Castell translate *tseva* by "to moisten, imbue (Is. lxiii, 3); to immerse, to baptize (by immersion), to pour out, baptism," etc.* So Schindler: "To moisten, to dip in dye or liquid, imbue or infect, color, wash, moisten, to water, to baptize."†

Such are some of the facts on this word. Yet they tell us it always means to immerse. Even M. Stuart, with strangest inconsistency, pointed to this word as one definitely meaning to dip, immerse! when it was the very word translated *bapto* in Theodotian which in those very places he insisted were "gentle affusions." It shows the carelessness of great and good men on this subject at least.

In the Koran this word (chap. xxxiii, 20 or 21) occurs "in the sense of syrup, juice, or sap."‡

Tinxit, imbuit (Is. lxiii, 3), *immersit, baptizavit* (*per immersionem*), *effudit, baptismus.*

†Schindler: *Tinxit* (of *tseva*), *intinxit, colore vel humore, imbuit seu infecit, coloravit, lavit, madefecit, rigavit, baptizavit.* Gesenius: *Pual* and *Ith*—the only form it has in the Bible—"to wet, moisten, to be wet, moistened." While Gesenius is careful to tell us it means dip, immerse, in Hebrew, when the word never occurs a single time in all the Hebrew language, and to dye, in the Targums, is it a merit after this blunder, to fail to tell us it is one of the leading words for wash in the Targums? It not only translates *tabal*, but frequently translates *rachats*, "to wash," "pour." It is the word in the Targum in Leviticus viii, 6, where Aaron and his sons are washed "with water"—*rachats* in Hebrew, while in the Syriac and Targum of Onkelos, it is *secho*, wash. In Numbers xix, 10, 19, wash is *tzeva* in the same, as well as verses 7 and 8.

‡ Its root is defined by Fürst, to pour, trickle, drop, etc. Gesenius: "To flow, to trickle; of water, to pour."

In *Assemanni Bibliotheca Orienatlis* we read of a distinguished bishop named Simeon Bar Tsaboe, who was martyred, "and he indeed (*tzeva*) baptized his garments with the blood of his own body."*

AMAD IN SYRIAC LITERATURE.

Dr. Gotch, Elder Wilkes (Lou. Debate, p. 579), and Dr. Varden urge that the following text is in favor of immersion, viz: "And that yet, at a small river that same head of thine should be subject to be bowed down and baptized in it" (Bible Questions, p. 130, by Gotch). We observe—

1. This is in the fourth century after Christ, as they tell us. We freely admit immersion was often practiced in those later centuries, though affusion was practiced as well.

2. He was baptized, even in their version of Ephraem, not in, but "at the river"—"at a small river" (*Lenahero*). Hence it was not immersion.

3. If his whole body was immersed, why speak only of his head as bowed "at the small river," which was clearly to receive the water poured upon it? No one bows his head simply to be immersed when the whole body is put under.

4. The figure of Ephraem is, that as the waters of the sea were subjected to Christ's feet, so now his head is bowed in subjection to the waters of Jordan, poured upon it in baptism. The rendering "in it" is equally literal—"with it," the waters of the "insignificant stream."

5. All ancient pictures of Christ's baptism represent him as standing "at the river," head bowed, to receive the water poured upon it, while John stands with a little

* Tomus i, 2.

vessel pouring the water on his head. No such ancient picture represents him as immersed.

6. We relied on the old Peshito version made in the apostolic age and the greatest of lexicons to define the words when lexicons are appealed to as evidence. The forced rendering of Hebrews vi, 4, " Who once submitted to baptism "* by " descending into the baptistery,"† is sufficiently refuted by the fact that no such innovation as a baptistery was in existence in all the Christian Church till the third and fourth centuries.‡

5. Bernstein confounds *amad* with the Arabic *gahmat*, immerse, another word altogether. There is no dip in the

*Lemamudhitho nechtho, " submisit," as well as " descendit," and mamudhitho is baptism, the noun in the New Testament. See Schaaf's Syr. Lex. N. T.

† Since the above was written, Dr. Graves, who in the debate could not be induced by any process to try to meet my facts on the Syriac and the later versions, in his clandestine way of *rewriting* his speeches with mine before him, and by accident a *part* of which, repassing through Memphis, I saw and hastily answered in transit, professes to cite Bernstein's lexicon to Kirch's Chrestomathy, and renders *amad*, " he was dipped, . . . he dipped, etc. The point of the arrow *sank* into his brain," etc. We reply, 1. He fails to give us the original, and we know his utter unreliability. 2. Kirch's Chrestomathy is made up of the Syriac in its latest stage, its death-struggles in the thirteenth and later centuries, especially on Bar-Hebræus, who wrote half Arabic half Syriac dialect in the last part of the thirteenth century. This is a *little late*. 3. Bernstein's lexicon is only a partial lexicon or glossary, defining words found in this late author, *and as used by him, not as used in the Bible.* Why quote such a work? 4. Dr. G. falsely translates the lexicon all the way through, as well as Bar Ali! He renders *mersus, immersit se, dipped*, yet the same word he in the same sentence translates " *sank*," where the arrow sank, "*immersit se*"—immersed itself into the brain.

‡ Stuart on Baptism, by J. R. Graves, p. 183: "This practice of building *baptisteries* is *well known* to be an *innovation* upon the more ancient usage of the church. In the time of Justin Martyr [A.D. 166] there were no such accommodations as these." So Wall, vol. 2, p. 457-8; Hist. Inf. Bap.; and cites the great historian Bingham to prove they existed not till about fourth century.

whole glossary on this word. Bar-Hebræus cites "the great Basil" to justify his superstitious ideas of the wonderful virtue of water—"From the beginning [the Holy Spirit] infused life into the waters" (in Gen. i, 2). Hence their immersion theory to absorb the sanctifying virtues of the water!

Dr. G. actually translates Gutbier's word "*baptizavit*" on *amad* by "immerse"!! (p. 388). He copies Dr. Varden's renderings on Bar-Hebræus, thirteenth century, still, where Bar-Heb. comments on Job xli, 1, saying the leviathan "plunged in the depths of the sea." How could a leviathan, that was already in the depths of the sea, "plunge" or "dip" himself, in a Baptist sense of dip? He was already under the water. What is the meaning, then? And this is the best they can do to meet our crushing facts!

There is no record or hint of such. In the days of Justin Martyr, the middle of the second century, of Irenæus and Tertullian, no baptistery was known.

But though we rely on the Bible facts, or versions of that book, let us take up the literature of the Nestorians and Syrians generally, and see the result.

Dr. G. (p. 389) cites Numbers xxxi, 23 (24): "All that abideth not the fire ye shall plunge it (Syriac, *amad*) in water." First, this is the only place in the Bible where Castell, Schaaf, etc. could find *amad* used for, as they thought, immerse; second, it is not a case of baptism, as in the Hebrew and Greek no word is used that is ever used for baptism; third, there is no proof of immersion in the text. The Hebrew phrase so rendered is in the Vulgate rendered, "Shall be sanctified by the water of expiation."

Dr. G. tells us, then (p. 389), "'His grand old Syriac

ANCIENT VERSIONS ON BAPTIDZO.

version supports' my position that Romans vi, 4, refers to water baptism!" But he says not how; why? It reads in the Syriac exactly as in our English version, and has not a drop of water in it. "Therefore (or for) we are [present tense] buried with him by baptism into death"— *lemauntho*. The great Walton renders it in Latin, *Sepulti enim sumus cum eo per baptisma ad mortum*. Where is the support? He makes the baptism of Christ (Luke xii, 50; Mark x, 38, 39), as all modern immersionists do, refer to his "sinking in a flood of afflictions" etc! All the fathers, as shown, Syriac, Latin, Greek, refer that baptism to the blood and water on the cross baptizing him.

AMAD IN LITERATURE.

1. In a discussion among the ancient Syrian churches, on many things, they name the matters of the form of the verb they use, *amad*, and say, "When he baptizes, even with the invocation of the Trinity, and with a washing of natural water, immersion, or sprinkling, it is not true baptism," "unless the proper word is used also." *
Again, "If, when he baptizes, he uses that [form of *amad*] for the present imperative, if other things are right, especially the intention, immersion in natural water, ablution, or sprinkling, with the invocation," etc.†

2. In *Bibliotheca Orientalis*, vol. 4, page 260, we read, "When Christ the Lord was baptized in the Jordan, say Simeon the Presbyter and John Zugbi, John the Baptist filled a little vessel with the water that flowed from his sacred body, and preserved it until the day he was beheaded, when he delivered it into the custody of his dis-

---

* *Bibliotheca Orientalis, tom.* iv, CCL (250), *ablutio, immersione, vel aspersione*, in Latin.
† *Ibid., in aquam naturalem immersio, ablutio, vel aspersio*, etc.

ciple, John the Evangelist. To this same John the Evangelist, they add, when Christ instituted the eucharistic supper, and distributed a part to each of the apostles, he gave a double portion; the rest of which he took, and delivered in the same way as the other—in a little vessel of water. And, afterward, he poured into this same vessel the water which flowed from the side of Christ when hanging on the cross; and the blood that flowed from his side he mixed with the eucharistic bread. This, they say, was the leaven of the eucharist, that the leaven of baptism. For the apostles, after they had received the Holy Spirit, before they went forth, divided this water and eucharistic bread among themselves, which they were to use as an element in administering baptism." Now—

1. We cite this not as a fact, but as showing what those ancient Syrians believed as to Christ's baptism and that practiced under the apostles.

2. Christ is believed to have stood in Jordan to be baptized. The water was poured on his head, and "flowed down his sacred side."

3. The amount put in little water-vessels, caught from his side thus and from the cross, was sufficient for baptizing. Hence it was not immersion.

4. In the same great Syriac compilation (tom. iii, 357), the Syrians thus held as to baptism. There are seven kinds of baptism recorded: 1. . . . washing. 2. Legal baptism, purifications according to the law of Moses. 3. Baptism . . . of cups, brazen vessels, couches, etc. . . . 6. Baptism of blood—I have a baptism to be baptized with,"* etc. 7. Baptism of tears—*mamudhitho dheme.*

---

* Syr., *moro ve mamunutho aith li dhemad.* Yet immersionists persist in referring the baptism referred to here to "overwhelming" sufferings in the garden, and to "sinking in a *flood* of afflictions"! Heavy on *flood*.

1. These are all recorded as literal baptisms under the head—*Al mamudthitho*—baptism.

2. No one will contend that the blood shed in martyrdom, and that which was shed by Christ on his own body was immersion.

3. Baptism with tears was not a clear case of dipping. Such are the facts in the Syriac. Of course they often immersed "in the Dark Ages," and as often mersed the party waist deep or more, and baptized by affusion.

Once more, let it be remembered that the three Hebrew words that definitely mean immerse, the one that often applies to a partial dip, *tabhal*, and the numerous Greek words for dip and immerse—*buthidzo, kataduo, katapendizo*—immerse, are in no case in all the Bible translated by *amad* in either Syriac or Arabic. Why did they not do so if that word meant in that day immerse? Dip occurs repeatedly in our English versions in both Testaments, but never is the original of such places *amad* in Syriac or Arabic.

CHAPTER XXVIII.

The Arabic Version.

Dr. Gotch says, "Of native words employed by the Syriac, the Arabic, Æthiopic, Coptic, etc. all signify to immerse." Of course Drs. A. Campbell, Graves, Judd, Wilkes, Brents, etc. follow suit in this assertion as well as Ingham.

This and all Arabic versions, having the same renderings of *baptidzo*, were made when the Arabic was the language of renown, and led the intellectual world. At this time, "the Saracen Empire [Arabic] was dotted all over with colleges, . . . in Mesopotamia, Syria, Egypt, North Africa," etc. (Draper). They made translations of Plato, Aristotle, the Iliad, Hippocrates, Galen, etc. etc. from the Greek. There were seventy public libraries in one single province. One man spoke seventy-two dialects. The royal court was rather an academy of learning than of statecraft. Amid this blaze of intellectual light and knowledge of Greek the Arabic versions were made. Gesenius says, "In every respect the most perfect source of Hebrew etymology and lexicography is the Arabic," "to it [the Arabic] belongs the first place among all this class of philological auxiliaries" (Bib. Repos. 18, 33).

1. These versions render *baptidzo* by *amada*, the same as *amad* in Syriac just examined.

2. It is rendered over and again by *tsavagha*, the same as the Syriac *tseva*, which see in the last chapter.

THE ARABIC VERSION. 329

3. They translate it by *gasala* (Luke xi, 38; Mark vii, 4), and its nouns, *baptismos* and *baptisma* (Heb. vi, 2; Mark vii, 4, 8) by the noun-form of *gasala*. Of *gasala*, to baptize, wash, besprinkle—

(1) No lexicon in existence renders it by dip, or plunge, or immerse.

(2) Castell, who had native Arabians to assist him, renders it "to wash, to cleanse, etc. To be sprinkled with water, to wash diligently, to wash off the body (members), to wash oneself, etc., to moisten, to be sprinkled, . . . to besprinkle."* It occurs for washing the face (Matt. vi, 17; Ps. lxxiii, 13; Lev. viii, 6), and when the head is sprinkled with rose-water, etc.

In the face of the fact that not a lexicon—neither Golius, Freytag, Kosegarten, Catafago, nor the great Castell—gives dip, or immerse, or plunge, or sink for *gasala*, or its nouns, but define it by wash, cleanse, where it applies to washing the face, the members, dead bodies, and sprinklings, what are we to think of such assertions, not to name the facts of the first chapter, and those next to come?

Gasala repeatedly translates *nipto*, to wash the hands, that means to rain (Job xx, 23); e. g. *brecho* in Symmachus's version—rain in ours. Yet the word that translates such a word translates *baptidzo*.

CODEX VATICANUS, FOURTH CENTURY.

The great Codex Vaticanus, about A. D. 325, translates *baptidzo* by sprinkle (Mark vii, 4).† It being the Jew-

---

* Castell, *gasala, lavit, abluit*, etc., *sudore, perfusus fuit*, . . . *diligenter lavit, perluit membra, se abluit*, etc.; *maduit, perfusis f..t*, . . . *inspergit*.

† Βαπτισῶνται is rendered there ῥαντισῶνται, besprinkle.

ish baptism, unauthorized by Christ, the copyist translates it into its mode in that place.

CODEX SINAITICUS, A. D. 325.

This great copy of the Bible, with seven other ancient ones, translates *baptisontai* (Mark vii, 4) by sprinkle.*

ITALA AND VULGATE.

The *Itala*, made in the second century by converts of the apostolic age, is, next to the Peshito, the most valuable translation we have. Jerome's Vulgate and it are the same on those points:

1. They transfer *baptidzo* in every instance in the New Testament, not translating it at all.
2. They translate *tabal* (Greek, *baptidzo*) (2 Kings v, 14) by wash, *lavo* (wash, bedew, sprinkle).
3. They translate *bapto*, sprinkle (Rev. xix, 13).
4. They translate the Chaldee for baptize, same as Syriac and Arabic, *tzeva*, by "to sprinkle" twice.†
5. They never translate either *baptidzo* or *tabal* by immerse.

ÆTHIOPIC VERSION.

Of this version that zealous Baptist, Dr. Gale, says, "The Syriac and Æthiopic versions, which for their antiquity must be thought almost as valuable and authentic *as the original itself*, being made from *primitive copies, in or very near* the times of the apostles, and rendering the pas-

---

* Βαπτισῶνται is rendered ῥαντισωνται.
† Daniel iv, *conspergatur, infunderis*.

THE ARABIC VERSION.

sage (Num. xix, 13, *bapto*) by words that signify *to sprinkle*, ... very strongly argue that he (Origen) has preserved the same word which was in the autograph."*

This is more just of the Syriac, Sahidic, and Itala. The Æthiopic has a word expressing definitely to immerse, *maab*, "to overflow, submerse." It is never used for baptize, etc. Now this version renders—

1. *Bapto* by *to sprinkle*, as Dr. Gale observes.

2. It renders (*katharismos*) purification, always performed by sprinklings (see John ii, 6; Heb. ix, 13, 19, 21; Num. viii, 7; xix, 13-15) by baptism.

3. It never renders *baptize* by immerse or any word equivalent to dip.

4. It renders *baptidzo tamak*, which Castell renders, "to be baptized, to baptize." Neither he nor Hottinger renders it by dip, plunge, or immerse. It is the same as *tamash* in other Oriental versions — same word. Schindler renders it in Hiphil form (derivative meaning) by plunge, wet, dip, wash, and gives Psalm vi, 7, "baptized my couch with my tears," as his first proof-text.† It is kindred with *tamal* also, which never implies immersion, but constantly applies to affusions. It renders John v, 4; ix, 7, Siloam, where the people washed by baptistery, as the Syriac. Castell gives both plunge and moisten—*rigavit*, always affusion—as meanings of *tamash*.

5. This version renders *baptidzo* by *mo, moi*—"water." It is the same root with *moh*—"sprinkle with water, pour, rain, water, juice, fluid, water."‡ *M'ho*, moisten, pour.

---

* Reflect. on Wall's Hist. Inf. Bap., Letter V, vol. 2, 118, ed. of 1862.

† *Hiphil* of *tamash, mersit, tinxit, intinxit, lavit* (Ps. vi, 7), *liquefaciam*.

‡ Castell, *aqua, perfusus est, pluviam fudit*, ... *aqua* ... *aquam*, etc. — no immersion. Hottinger, *tinxit, baptizavit*, moisten, baptize. Æthiopic, *m'ho liquescere, liquefieri, fundi*. Castell, 2003.

332 BAPTISM.

Here is one of the words translated from *baptidzo* that simply means to water, without specifying mode, while the same word essentially, same root, means to sprinkle with water, water, pour, rain. So testifies this great author.

The Amharic, a later version, renders it as the one just noticed generally, and need not be noticed separately.

THE COPTIC.

This version of the third century, made in Egypt where learning was then in a high state of cultivation, translates—

1. *Bapto* by sprinkle (Rev. xix, 13).
2. It renders *baptidzo* by *tamaka*, same as the above in Æthiopic, a word of affusion.
3. It never renders it by immerse.

EGYPTIAN, THIRD CENTURY.

In the third century the Egyptian version was made.

1. It renders *baptidzo* by *oms*, which is of the same root as *amada, amad* in Syriac and Arabic, wash, baptize, sprinkle, make wet.

BASMURIC, THIRD CENTURY.

1. This version translates *bapto* by sprinkle in Revelation xix, 13.
2. It habitually transfers *baptidzo*.
3. It never renders *baptidzo* by immerse, dip, or plunge.

SAHIDIC, SECOND CENTURY.

1. It transfers *baptidzo*.
2. It never renders it immerse.
3. It translates *bapto* sprinkle (Rev. xix, 13).

While we only have these facts from these versions, we regret we have not copies of them personally; for then no doubt our researches would bring out valuable and startling facts as in the Syriac, Arabic, Vulgate, and ancient literature, etc. Having the Persic we are enabled to give more light on it, however.

PERSIC.

The Persic renders *baptidzo* by several words. It has a word (*autha*) meaning emphatically to immerse. See Golius in Castell, p. 408. But it never renders *baptidzo* by it or any word implying immersion. It renders *baptidzo*—

1. By *sustan, shustidan,* thus defined in Golius's lexicon: Washing, baptism; to wash (besprinkle, cleanse); washing, cleansing, baptize. [*Lavacrum, baptismus, lavare.*] Gen. xvii, 4; xix, 2; Ex. ii, 5; John iii, 25 (*lotio*), lotus; John xiii, 10, *baptizare;* Matt. iii, 6-13. Castell.

2. It renders it by *shuhar, shue,* "to give a bath or administer a washing [pour water for it]; to fall in drops of water, distill; to baptize. [*Lavandum dare, stillare, . . baptizare.*" Castell.]

3. It renders purifying (John iii, 25) by baptism.

4. *Baptidzo* is translated into the word used Exodus ii, 5, washed, *epi,* at the river; Genesis xviii, 4, where it was with "a *little* water;" in John xiii, 10, where Christ washed

their feet, unquestionably by applying the water; for he would not plunge all their feet into the same basin, in "unclean" water. It was water "upon" the feet. Luke vii, 38, 39-44.

ITALA, BEGINNING OF SECOND CENTURY.

1. This version renders *bapto* by sprinkle, *asperso*.
2. It never renders *baptidzo* by dip or immerse. This is the more remarkable if *baptidzo* was equivalent to immerse, since immerse is a Latin word, and this Latin version should have used it if *baptidzo* meant immerse. That was the very place for it.
3. It renders *tabhal* by *lavit* (2 Kings v, 14), wash, besprinkle.
4. It transfers *baptidzo* throughout.
5. It renders *baptize* in Chaldee by sprinkle, *conspergatur*.

JEROME'S VULGATE, A.D. 383.

The Vulgate, so patiently rendered by the learned Jerome, based on the Itala, but made more smooth and elegant in style, is, like the Itala, of great value.

1. It translates *bapto* by sprinkle (Rev. xix, 13).*
2. It transfers *baptidzo* habitually.
3. It never renders *baptidzo*, or any word for baptize, by immerse.
4. It translates *tabhal* (Greek, *baptidzo*) (2 Kings v, 14) by *lavit*, wash, besprinkle.
5. It translates baptize (*tseva*) (Dan. iv, 22) sprinkle.†

* Greek βεβαμμένον αἵματι. Beza: *Et amictus erat veste tinctá sanguine.* VULGATE, *Etvestitus erat veste aspersa sanguine.*

† Daniel x, 22, *et rore cœli* INFUNDERIS.

6. It translates the same word (*tseva*) in Daniel iv, 20, sprinkle.*

LUTHERAN VERSION, 1522.

The Lutheran version, 1522, renders *baptidzo* by—
1. *Taufen*, to baptize, without implying mode. But when the version was made sprinkling and pouring were the general, yea, universal practice. This all acknowledge, and A. Campbell says so, quoting Erasmus.† Luther poured the water on the infant's head when he said, "*Ich taufe euch mit wasser.*" It is downright dishonesty to pretend that by *taufen* he and the various German translators meant dip, whatever may have been its former force. With them it neither meant dip, sprinkle, nor pour, but was used as the Latins used *baptidzo* and *tingo*, for baptize.

2. In 2 Kings v, 14, *tabal—baptidzo;* Luke xi, 38; Mark vii, 4, *baptidzo* is rendered *waschen*.

3. *Bapto* is rendered in Revelation xix, 13, sprinkle (*besprengt*).

The Lusitanian version renders both words in the same places the same—*baptidzo*, wash; *bapto*, sprinkle.

The Jerusalem Targum renders *rachats* ("wash, pour") by *taval*, and *tabal* by *rachats;* the latter also by "washed

---

* Daniel x, 20, *et rore cœli* CONSPERGATUR.

† Chris. Baptisms, p. 192: "Erasmus, who spent some time in England, during the reign of Henry VIII, observes, 'With us [the Dutch], the baptized, have the water poured on them. In England they are dipped.'" And yet Judd, Ingham, Brents, Graves, all repeat the oft-refuted assumption that *taufen* was meant by the German of Luther for immerse, and so render it! So of all the kindred versions, in the face of the fact that all those nations baptize by sprinkling, as A. Campbell admits, and they all know. Those versions all use different words in their versions for the dip of our version. But we have abundantly seen how they treat lexicons of all kinds, authorities, and versions as well.

their face with tears" (Gen. xliii, 30). This shows that these words were words of affusion.

The Arabic and the Targum render Psalm vi, 6, 7, "wet my couch with my tears," *brecho*, with the word that translates *baptidzo* and *tabal*.

It is useless to multiply facts. The sum of all this is—

1. For fifteen hundred years after the Christian era not a single version made from the original Scriptures supports a case of immersion.

2. Every version made supported affusion, and with overwhelming force. We have not quoted Wycliffe and several German versions falsified by Conant as made from the Greek. They were all made from the Latin, and hence have nothing to do with *baptidzo* or *bapto*. They would support us, especially Wycliffe, who has baptize wash, and for the *aspersa* of Jerome, sprinkle. But Wycliffe never saw a Greek Testament. The same applied to the Rheims, made from the Latin.*

These versions establish the following facts:

1. That affusion is so clearly taught in the Bible as the proper mode of baptism that all the pains and prejudice of James's translators, being honest but deeply prejudiced, could not obliterate them.

2. That *bapto* continued to mean sprinkle as well as to stain, color, and dip.

3. That *baptidzo* never was synonymous with dip, plunge or immerse in any age of the world.

---

* The Danish version, 1524, has *dobe*, baptize; the Swedish, 1534, has *dopa*, baptize; the Dutch, 1560, *doopen*, baptize. These words may once have represented dip—primarily, moisten, wet, for aught we care. The point is, what did the *translators* mean by these words? *No honest man will pretend that they meant* immerse, since they all then baptized by sprinkling in *those* countries, all immersion authorities so testifying. Hence they would use those words when sprinkling the parties as we use *baptize*.

4. That baptize is translated by words meaning to wash, to cleanse, to sprinkle, besprinkle in all the best and purest versions from the apostolic to our times.

5. Finally, no version of the fifteen centuries after the Christian era renders *baptidzo*, or words for baptize, by immerse or its equivalent in any language.

CHAPTER XXIX.

WASHING, CLEANSING, BAPTISM—WASH IN THE OLD TESTAMENT, BAPTIZE IN THE NEW TESTAMENT.

The inventive genius of immersionists is only equalled by their marvelous capacity at blundering, and their boldness in trampling under foot every law of language is only surpassed by their blind persistence in reproducing and reaffirming all the old quotations that have been exposed as garbled and entirely unreliable.

They find color, dye, stain as definitions of *bapto, tingo,* etc., and all assert that color, stain, dye, come from dip! They see wash, cleanse, as meanings of *baptidzo;* they come from dip also!

FACTS ON WASH.

1. The wash [Hebrew, *rachats;* Greek, *louo, nipto, pluno, kludzo*] . . of the Pentateuch, especially in Exodus, Leviticus, and Numbers, all parties agree is the *baptidzo* with its nouns of the New Testament. However much the design and use may have varied, the wash of the one is the baptism of the other. We quoted much on this subject in the chapter on the laver baptisms.

2. All immersionists as well as affusionists generally maintain that the washing of Acts xxii, 16; Ephesians v, 26; Titus v, 5, 6; Hebrews x, 22, is a repeated reference to baptism, immersionists holding it to be baptism itself.

Dr. Carson says, "The word [*rachats*, wash] ALWAYS includes *dipping*, and *never* signifies less."*

3. All are agreed that the Greek word *baptidzo* means wash, cleanse, and most writers add purify. First. All standard lexicons, classic or biblical, render it wash, or cleanse. Second. All ancient versions without an exception, where they translate the word, at times in the New Testament, render it wash.†

4. All parties agree that for full fifteen hundred years— from the days of Moses till the close of the first century— from the origin of baptism as a sacred, heaven-ordained rite, to the commission of Christ to baptize, wash was constantly used, and for thirteen hundred years was the main word used for the rite—was the word employed at its first performance by Moses (Lev. viii, 6); hence the propriety of looking into this word in the various languages with more pains than has been the custom.

On Hebrews x, 22, Dr. Graves cites and comments on it thus: "'Our bodies washed with pure water.' I have *no doubt* that this passage refers to Christian baptism."‡

THE WASH OF THE OLD TESTAMENT THE BAPTISM OF THE NEW.

Wash, *rachats* in the Hebrew (Ex. xxx, 18–22; xl, 30-33; Lev. viii, 6; Heb. x, 22; Eph. v, 26), all immersionists say are the divers baptisms of Hebrews ix, 10.

The only question now is, What was the mode of these

---

* Reflections on Wall's Hist. Inf. Bap., Letter IV, p. 94, vol. 2; Oxford Ed., 1862, in two volumes.

† Syriac, *amad, secho*; Arabic, *amada, gasala*; Latin, *lavo*; German, *waschen*, etc.

‡ Carrollton Debate, p. 186.

baptisms? As far as facts go we have given enough in the chapter on the laver baptisms. But we wish to take up the word wash in the Hebrew and Greek Scriptures and examine it on its own merits now, and see how the word stands as between us and Drs. Carson, Gale, A. Campbell, Conant, Bingham, J. R. Graves, and Elder Wilkes, etc., immersionists. Now—

1. No lexicon in existence ever defined the word [*rachats*] by immerse, dip, or plunge, or any equivalent word.

2. No immersionist we ever read or heard ventured to render it immerse, dip, or plunge.

3. Whenever it is rendered by a modal term, it is in every case either sprinkle, pour, or a word equivalent thereto. Proof—

(1) Fürst, the greatest of all Hebrew lexicographers, gives as its meaning, "to wash," and adds that its radical or primary meaning is "to flow, to pour out, to drip."

(2) It is rendered *cheo* ($\chi\acute{\epsilon}\omega$), to pour, in the Greek version [LXX] mainly used by the apostles.

(3) It is used where Joseph washed his face (Gen. xliii, 30). Was that immersion?

(4) It is translated in Jonathan's Targum by "washed his face with his tears."*

(5) It is of the same root of and akin to, *rachash*,† "to pour out."

(6) It is translated *nipto* in the Septuagint repeatedly, and several times where it is wash (*ek*) out of the laver, Hebrew *min*, out of. ‡

The washing effected by *rachats* in the Bible, was by only a little over one fifth of a pint of water, when not out

---

* *Shazzag min dimshon.*
† *Rachash effudit* (Castell).
‡ See the Laver Baptisms.

of the laver. Hence the washing, out of the jars, as given in John ii, 6, George Campbell, A. Campbell, render (Mark vii, 3), "Wash their hands often by pouring a little water on them." *Nipto* is the word there used. Hinton (Baptist) cites Jahn, Koenoel, etc. to sustain this rendering.

(7) In Arabic *rachats*, wash, and in Æthiopic, means primarily to sweat, perspire, sweat copiously. Then it means to wash, be washed, cleansed. Intensified, it is *rachash* in Æthiopic, and means "to bedew, make wet, same as the Hebrew *rachats*, to moisten, to water."*

WASH—רָחַץ—λούω—BAPTIZE IN THE NEW TESTAMENT.

(8) *Nipto* [νίπτω], wash is the translation of the Hebrew word *matar*, to rain, shed forth water. It always implies affusion. Its noun occurs in the Bible thirty-seven times, always implying affusion. The verb is rendered by the Greek (*brecho*†) rain, ten times. Yet this word is rendered *nipto*, wash. Nay—

(9) The place in our verson seized on as a favorite text by immersionists—Leviticus vii, 28, "rinsed in water"— is in the Greek washed or besprinkled with water.‡

(10) *Rachats* in Hebrew is often rendered in the Septuagint version by *louo*, wash, in Greek, which no lexicon ever issued ever defined by immerse, dip, or plunge, but by wash, cleanse. Whenever *louo* is rendered by a *modal* word it is either sprinkle, or pour, or both. See below.

(11) *Rachats* is rendered by *pluno* in the LXX also, which all lexicons render wash, and whenever *modal*, it is always sprinkle, or pour, or both. See below on it.

**Maduit, humidus fuit,* i. q. *Heb.* רָחַץ, *madefecit, rigavit.* Castell, Heptagl. 3721.

† *Matar;* Greek, βρέχω.

‡ Κλύσει ὕδατι, *klusei hudati.*

(12) This word *rachats*, thus translated and used in the Bible before apostolic times, is translated baptize (*tabhal*) frequently by the ancient Hebrew (Chaldee) Targums.

Is it not refreshingly cool, then, in Dr. Gale, indorsed by Drs. Graves, Carson, etc. etc., to say, "The word *rachats* always includes dipping and never signifies less"?

3. *Louo* [λούω] thus used, rendered also baptize in Syriac in Susanna, as shown in the chapter on Versions, is the word immersionists render as they do *rachats* in Hebrew, by "to bathe," instead of wash or cleanse, as if bathe were a religious or ceremonial use of water! Dr. Graves clings desperately to bathe.

Liddell & Scott's English edition: "*Louo*, to wash; properly, to wash the body; also to pour [water for washing];"* "*Loutris*, a woman employed to wash Minerva's Temple." Here her name is a "washer." Was the temple dipped?

What are the additional facts here? The native Greek lexicographer, Galen, born A. D. 130, defining this word *louo*, puts it thus: "*Louo*, to wash, to pour, or sprinkle." The *Etymologicon*, a native Greek lexicon, defines it thus: "To sprinkle, to besprinkle, and to wash."† Hesychius thus: To sprinkle, to besprinkle, etc.‡

Pickering, in his later new edition of his Greek lexicon, gives it: "*Loutron*, pl. [plural] *loutra*, libations for the dead." "*Loutrophoros*, one who brings water for bathing (Euripides, 358); a youth of either sex who brought water and *poured it on the tomb* of an unmarried person, (Demos., 1086, 15, etc.). Here the Greek word wash,

---

* Ingham (Baptist), Hand-Book on Bap., p. 445, thus also cites him.

† Αἰονάω [*aspergo*] καταχεέιν et λονέιν (Stephanus's Thesaurus).

‡ Αἰονάω, καταντλῆσαι, *perfundere, rigare, διάλελυμένον, igitur est pro* αἰονῆσαι. S.'s Thesaurus *sub* λούω.

"bathe," in verb and noun forms alike, refer to wash, bathe as effected generally by affusion, not by immersion. .

Under "*loutrocheo*" Pickering, so much relied on by Dr. Graves, gives, " to *pour out water for bathing.*"

Henry Stephanus's Thesaurus, the most elaborate lexicon of the Greeek ever published in the world, defines *louo* thus: "To wash. In Hippocrates [a Greek medical author] it is not merely to wash, but also *to sprinkle.* In like manner Galen uses it in his lexicon where—'for these are appointed, some to pour cold, the others to pour warm water upon those who are bathing.'" "*Loutrochoos,* pouring water for washing"—"sprinkled with cold water."* Let us now hear several of the latest and greatest Greek lexicons on wash.

Rost and Palm and Passow all define it alike, as well as the still later Pape, 1874, Liddell & Scott, thus: "*Louo*, to wash; properly to wash the body; also *to pour* [water for washing]." † Passow, Rost, and Palm, under *ballo*, which some think was the root of *bapto*, say, "In the middle voice, to sprinkle oneself, . . . to pour, to pour out, to sprinkle the water upon the body, i. e. *to bathe; . . . to besprinkle oneself with bath-water.*" ‡

Likewise Pape, under *ballo:* "That is, to besprinkle oneself with the bath-waters." § How does this "pan

---

* Ἐπιβαλλεῖν (δὲ θερμὸν) λελέουσι, . . . *aquam ad lavandam fundens, frigida perfundor.*

† This pet of immersionists still thus defines it, with the *bracketed words as above,* but Drisdel took it out of the American Edition, as in *baptidzo,* to appease Baptist fury.

‡ Im med. sich besprengen, χροα λουτροῖς (*louo*), wegiessen, ausgiessen, sprengen, . . . λουτρα ἐπὶ χροός (*louo*), i. e. baden, . . . wasser in ein gefass giessen, χρόα.

§ Λουτροῖς, SICH MIT BADE-WASSER BESPRENGEN. Here *louo* wash is *pour and sprinkle* for the BATH. Βάλλω . . . χρόα βάλλεσθαι λούτροις, sich mit bade-wasser besprengen.

out" for immerse as the bathe of the Greeks? But hear once more Liddell & Scott, Dr. Graves's favorite lexicon. Under *chutla,* plural noun from *cheo,* to pour "water for washing or bathing." "Hence *chuthō,* to wash, bathe, anoint." Thus from pour comes wash, bathe again.

Another word for sprinkle, *hudraino,* is defined by lexicons thus: "To wash, sprinkle, wet, moisten, bedew, pour out."* Does *rachats* or *louo,* wash, "always include dipping and never signify less"?† Liddell & Scott define *loutris,* noun from *louo,* wash: "A woman employed to *wash Minerva's temple.*" How did she dip or immerse this wonder of the world. It is in order for some good immersionist to rise and speak. *Rachats,* wash, is rendered often by the Greek word *pluno* in the Bible. Native Greeks define *bapto* and *baptidzo* by *pluno,* wash, also.

Stephanus defines *pluno* by wash, cleanse, and also by "to wash with tears, pour forth tears," and "to make wet," "watering by sprinkling with warm water." ‡

Passow, Rost, Palm, Pape define it in substance as the first *pluno,* "to wash, wash off, cleanse, purify," . . . fundamentally "to moisten, wet; Latin, to rain, flow." §

Thus we see that *pluno,* wash, comes from the word rain, sustaining all our views on philology and annihilating the bold assertions that wash necessarily implies dip or that it implies it at all. Pour comes to mean wash. Sprinkle means to wash. Rain comes to mean to wash. Yet they say wash, bathe, implies immersion.

* Graves gives it as above.

† Gale's Reflec. Wall's History Inf. Baptism; A. Campbell's Chris. Baptism, pp. 85-6; Chris. Baptist, 1101.

‡*Lachrymas effundere . . . madefacere et irrigans perfusio aqua fervida* (Thesaurus Greek Lin., Stephanus).

§ Passow: Πλύνω, waschen, spulen, auswaschen, abspulen, reinigen. . . . auschelten, strafen, wie unser einem den kopf waschen, . . . benetzen, befeuchten, we denn das Lat. *pluo* v. *fluo.*

WASHING, CLEANSING, BAPTISM. 345

In the Latin, as especially we have seen that all Latin-Greek lexicons translate βαπτιζω, *baptidzo*, by *lavo*, wash, when they come to the New Testament meaning of that word, we give all the best standards and latest.

1. Schiller & Luenemann, edited by F. P. Leverett (*Magnum Tot.*), etc.: "*Lavo* (*louo*, Greek), to be washed, to bathe. Figuratively, to wash or bathe; i. e. to moisten, besprinkle, bedew. Also to wash away, to remove."

2. Freund's great work *verbatim* as the above.

3. Ainsworth: "*Lavo*, to wash, to rinse, to bathe, to besprinkle."

4. White (1873): "*Lavo* (akin to λούω), to wash, bathe, lave; to bathe oneself, to bathe; to wash, of the sea, to flow over, wet; of tears—to wet, moisten, bathe, bedew, to sprinkle, wet."

As in all the cases, so here, wherever mode is expressed it is affusion. Yet they will tell you that wash was always to immerse in the Bible!

The laver baptism further confirms all the above. John ii, 6, shows it incontrovertibly as well. Compare 2 Kings iii, 11; Numbers xix, 21, 22; Leviticus x, 34; xv, 34-36; Lightfoot's Horæ Heb. 2, p. 416. "Elisha poured the water on the hands of Elijah" for his washing. This also Lightfoot's facts from the rabbins demonstrate: They allot one fourth part of a log for the washing of one person's hands; it may be of two; half a log for three or four; a whole log for five to ten, nay, to one hundred, with this provision, saith Rabbi Jose, that the last that washeth hath no less than a fourth part of a log for himself. A log is five sixths ($\frac{5}{6}$) of a pint. Now how could two persons be washed with the fourth of five sixths of a pint? One hundred washed with five sixths of a pint of water. Could they immerse their hands in it? Could one man immerse both hands in one ninth of a pint? Does not this show it was by sprinkling? In Lightfoot, from folio 21, 22, we read of Rabbi Abika, who being in prison, washed with half the water brought him to drink. Did he immerse his hands in the drinking vessel? No such thing was demanded or practiced. Yet in the face of all these undenied and undeniable records, with not one item to the contrary to be found any where, immersionists set up the claim that *rachats, louo, nipto, lavo*—wash—implies immerse every time in the Bible; that wash is derived from immerse—a thing so absolutely preposterous that not a word that properly and strictly means immerse in the whole world in any language ever means wash, or one that means properly to dip as its primary meaning. On the contrary, wash is constantly derived from words that primarily mean to sprinkle, to pour, to moisten or wet, to water, to flow, rain, shed forth. They all teach that *baptidzo* does mean to wash or apply to it; that *baptidzo* was implied always in the *rachats, louo.*

CHAPTER XXX.

MODERN COMMENTATORS AND CRITICS.

Immersionists cite commentators who admit, as all men do, that sometimes *baptidzo* means immerse and apply it as an admission that it never means sprinkle or pour or admits of baptism by such modes. Examples innumerable could be given from their earliest authorities to their latest. But we forbear to cite them so often.

1. Alford, on Mark vii, 4: "The *baptismoi*, as applied to *klinoi* (couches at meals), were certainly not immersions, but sprinklings or affusions of water." On Acts ii, 41, vol. 2, p. 25, he says, "Almost without doubt this first baptism must have been administered, as that of the first Gentile converts was (see chap. x, p. 47, and note), by affusion or sprinkling, *not by immersion*. Italics his.

2. Fairbairn: "The 'divers' [in Hebrews ix, 10—'divers baptisms'] evidently points to the several uses of water, such as we know to have actually existed under the law—sprinklings, washings, bathings."*

Baumgarten, another of the great modern scholars of Europe, German, "The Baptism of Saul" . . . he "is baptized . . . by means of the water poured upon him."† Again, "With a part of the same water" used in washing the apostles' stripes, "the keeper of the prison and all his

* Hermeneut. Manual, Art. *Baptidzo*.
† Com. on Acts ix, 1-36, p. 238-9.

were baptized . . . without the dipping of the whole body in the open, running water."*

4. Bengel, a universal favorite with all critics, "Gnomon," a commentary, like Alford's and Baumgarten's, only for the critical scholar: "Immersion in baptism, or at least the sprinkling of water upon the person, represented burial; burial is a confirmation of death." On Romans vi, 4, vol. 3.

5. Stier, one of the most careful, able, and voluminous of German commentators, says, "*Baptidzo* occurs often in the sense of mere washing." He supposes at times they may have been "dipped," "where otherwise baptism be administered by sprinkling, as probably with the thousands on the day of Pentecost." Reden Jesu, viii, 307, note.

6. Bloomfield, Greek text on Hebrews ix, 10: Baptisms—"*Bap.* denotes those ceremonial ablutions of various sorts, some respecting priests, others the people at large, detailed in Leviticus and Numbers." On Acts viii, 38: "Philip seems to have taken up water with his hands and poured it copiously on the eunuch's head." Mark vii, 4, he urges, "is not implied immersion."

7. Olshausen, one of the greatest and best commentators of any age, and the most impartial and profound, says on John iii, 25-27, "The dispute was on baptism—*katharismos*, equivalent to *baptisma* (baptism)." Mark vii, 4: "Ablutions of all sorts, among the rest those applicable to the priest (Ex. xxix, 18, *sq.* with Heb. ix, 10), were common among the Jews. *Baptismos* is here as in Hebrews ix, 10, ablution, washing generally; *klinai* here, couches on which the ancients were wont to recline at meals." Here he held that the legal sprinklings of John

Ibid., Acts xvi, 11-40, p. 134, vol. 2.

iii, 25-27; of the priests (Ex. xxix, 4, etc.), were the "diverse baptisms" of Paul (Heb. ix, 10). That the couches of dining were baptized as the Jews did—by affusion. Again, on Acts ii, he concludes the three thousand were baptized by sprinkling—"The difficulty can only be removed by supposing that they already employed mere sprinkling," etc. (vol. 4, 383).

8. Gerhard, of whom the late most scholarly Tholuck says,* "The most learned, and with the learned, the most beloved among the heroes of Lutheran orthodoxy," says, "Whether a man is baptized by immersion into water, or by sprinkling, or applying the water to him, it is the same" (Doc. Theol. ix, 137).

9. Reinhard: "Earthly or perceptible, pure, natural water in which a person is immersed, or with which he is partially sprinkled, is the baptism instituted by Christ." (Dogmat. pp. 570-572). Also—

10. Carpzov:† "Baptism is a Greek word, and in itself means a washing, in whatever way performed, whether by immersion in water, or by aspersion. . . It is not restricted to immersion or aspersion; hence it has been a matter of indifference from the beginning whether to administer baptism by immersion or by pouring of water" (Issagoge, p. 1085).

11. A. Clark: "Were the people dipped or sprinkled? for it is certain *bapto* and *baptidzo* mean both."‡ The same in substance he says on Mark vii, 4; Mark x, 16; Acts xvi, 32. He considers Romans vi, 4, refers to immersion among Jews in proselyte baptism, but that John

---

* In Herzog's Cyclop.

† Carpzov ranks among the most learned, along with the Buxtorfs, Lightfoots, Pococks, etc.

‡ On Matthew iii, 6.

baptized by sprinkling as well as those under the apostles most generally.

12. Lightfoot: "The word therefore, *baptismous* (washings), applied to all these [people, Pharisees, and all the Jews (verse 3), vessels, beds of Mark vii, 4], properly and strictly, is not to be taken of dipping or plunging, but, in respect of some things, of washing only, and in respect of others, of sprinkling only."*

13. Archbishop Kendrick (Catholic) has been misquoted so often, we cite him. On Hebrews ix, 10—"Baptism"—he says, "St. Paul calls the various ablutions of the old law, many of which were by aspersions, divers baptisms. . . Thus it appears manifest that the term was in his time used indiscriminately for all kinds of ablution" (On Baptism, p. 188). See him also page 322½ on Patristic Baptism—Augustine.

14. J. Wesley: "The Greek word [baptize] means indifferently either washing or sprinkling." Mark vii, 4. He argues that John did not immerse but sprinkled the multitudes he baptized; and the three thousand and five thousand in Acts, as well as the jailer, Saul, etc. were all baptized by affusion. He holds that Hebrews x, 22, alludes to the ancient manner of baptizing by sprinkling; while Romans vii, 4; Colossians ii, 12, allude to immersion as an ancient practice. See his note on Colossians ii, 12.

15. Beza, sixteenth century. The way Beza is habitually quoted may be seen in the various immersion works, as he is the favorite authority.* Now, while Beza says

---

* Horæ Hebraicæ et Tal. ii, 419, Eng. Ed. In edition of 1658, vol. 1, in Evang. Marci vii, 4. *Vox ergo βαπτισμοὺς ad hæc omnia applicata, propriè et strictè non accipienda est de tinctione aut immersione, sed quoad nonnulla de latione tàntùm, et quoad nonnulla de aspersione tantùm.*

† See Graves-Ditzler Debate, p. 520-1, as an example—same as in all standard authorities by immersionists.

a part of what they cite, yet they stop short and leave him testifying for their views and against affusion as baptism, just as they do Terretinus, Vossius, Witsius, Stephanus, Scapula, etc., etc. Here is what Beza says: "*Baptidzesthai* in this place (Mark vii, 4) is more than *cherniptein* [wash the hands], because that seems to be understood of the whole body, this merely of the hands. Neither indeed does *baptidzein* signify to wash except by consequence. For properly it expresses immersion for the purpose of dyeing." He then refers to Matthew iii, 11, where he defines it not only by "*mergere*," to sink, but by "*madefacere*," to make wet, and "*tingere*," to wet, to dye. That it answers to the Hebrew *tabhal* rather than to *rachats* and is used to express washing and cleansing.* Like Schleusner, Stokius, Witsius, Suicer, etc. he believes wash was a derived meaning from immerse as the classic meaning most in use. But, like them, he held that from wash, cleanse, it came to mean washing, cleansing, without regard to mode, and that affusion was practiced by the apostles for baptism, as the following words will show: Acts i, 5: "John indeed baptized with water." Beza says on this passage, "With the Holy Spirit. The prep. *en* is rightly omitted. . . . As if Christ had said, John indeed baptized you, but the Holy Spirit shall baptize you. But here is a double antithesis, if I mistake not, . . . when from the one [Father] emanated the Holy Spirit, the other is of the water poured by John and of the Holy Spirit falling upon the apostles, which mission

---

* Ut lavandi et abluendi, et lotionis vocabulo (Beza's Annot. on Matt. iii, 11, folio ed. 1598). What he says on *amad* is, in the above, that *amad* does not differ from it. But he there had .said *baptidzo* meant "*madefacere*," to moisten, make wet; to wash, then, was as above shown. It reads, "*madefacere et mergere*," and of that coming to mean *hamad* [*amad*], *quo utuntur Syri pro baptizare*.

of the Holy Spirit and POURING [of the water by John] is called by metaphor baptism." He thinks this "antithesis is better understood."* Here Beza shows that he held the old theory that, first, *baptidzo*, in classic usage generally meant immerse; second, as usual with them all, he finds that meaning to it in the later Greek writers, Plutarch being his first citation; third, that it came to mean wash, cleanse, by consequence; fourth, that from wash, cleanse, it came to mean wash, cleanse without regard to mode; fifth, that pouring became the settled practice of baptism even in John's day.

16. Terretinus, seventeenth century, a great authority, is cited for immersion constantly. Like Beza, he held that *baptidzo* properly meant to immerse in the classics of the age of Plutarch, etc. That it came to mean to wash, to cleanse, by consequence. We need not cite all he says, but admit it to the full. Yet he goes on to say, "There are not wanting various reasons for sprinkling also: (1) Because the word *baptismou* and the verb *baptidzesthai* are not spoken [or used] merely of immersion, but also of sprinkling (Mark vii, 4; Luke xi, 38)."† Then follow five arguments to sustain his position, urging that in the apostolic day, as on Pentecost, etc. the baptism was by sprinkling.

17. Witsius, A.D. 1685, held that "it is not to be supposed that immersion was so necessary to baptism as that the rite could not be performed by perfusion or sprinkling.

---

* *Johannes quidem vos baptizavit, sed spiritus sanctus vos baptizabit. Hic autem est antithesis duplex, ni fallor, una Johannis cum Christo vel Deo Patre, nam post βαπτιζησεθε, id est baptizabimini . . . altera est aquæ à Joanne* EFFUSÆ, *et spiritús sancti Apostolis mittendi; quæ spiritús sancti et effusio hic translatitie vocatur baptismus.*

†*Rationes etiam pro aspertione non desunt variæ;* (1) *Quia vox βαπτισμοῦ et verbum βαπτιζέσθαι, non tantum de immersione dicitur, sed et de aspersione* (Mark vii, 4; Luke xi, 38).

... It is more probable that the three thousand who were baptized in one day (Acts ii, 41), were perfused or sprinkled with water, than immersed." He then gives his reasons, and adds again, "Neither is it credible that Cornelius, and Lydia, and the jailer, baptized in private houses along with their families, had baptisteries in which they could be wholly immersed. Vossius brings examples of perfusion from antiquity, etc."* (2) "It is granted that *baptidzein* properly signifies to sink, yet also more generally it is used for any kind of cleansing, as Luke xi, 28." Here he cites authorities again, and goes on to cite Scripture for baptism, "for pouring," and "for sprinkling."

18. Vossius holds the same views as the above, and need not be further cited, since Witsius cites him for his views. Vossius gives as a leading New Testament meaning of *baptidzo*, "To sprinkle, or wash the body of any one sacramentally (Matt. iii, 11)."†

The list could be indefinitely extended, but to what good purpose? These are the masters, the others merely repeat. But these authors, by extensively applying their views of *baptidzo*, show how recklessly immersionists have

*Hermanni Witsi. ... "*De Œconomia Fœd. Dei*, 1685, p. 672, xiv, 6, *Non tamen existamandum est, adeo ad baptismum necessariam esse immersionem, ut perfusione vel aspersione rite peragi non possit. Nam et perfusio ac adspersio habent quo se tueantur. 1. Non si apostolos mersisse comperiamus, eo ritum hunc semper observasse consequitur. Probabilius est, eos ter mille, qui una die baptizabantur* (Acts ii, 1), *aquâ perfusos vel adspersos, quàm mersos esse*. ... *Neque credibile est, Cornelium et Lydiam, et commentariensem, in privatis œdibus una cum suis, baptizatos, baptisteria ad manum habuisse, quibus toti immergi potuerint. Perfusionis exempla ex antiquitate attulit Vossius Disput.* 1. *De Baptis. Th.*, ix, *quæ, eadem ordine, dissimulato tamen Vossii nomine, Lexico suo Antiquitatum Eccles.* p. 66, *inseruit Joshua Arndius.* 2. *Licet* βαπτίζειν *proprie significet mergere, tamen etiam generalius usupatur de quolicunque ablutione; ut Luc.* xi, 38, *etc.* ... *De Superfusione* ... *De Adspersione.*

†Vossius, "*Adspergere seu abluere corpus alicuijus sacrementaliter*" (Matt. iii, 11).

used their assertions, and how wildly and viciously they interpreted the old-school lexicographers.

19–21. Drs. Jameson, Fausset, and Brown, in their critical commentary, adopt Olshausen's words on Acts ii, 41, just quoted, and even on Philip and the eunuch adopt the view of Bloomfield, Baumgarten, and others, saying, "Probably laving the water upon him" (Acts viii, 38).

22. Wall, constantly misrepresented, says, "The word *baptidzo* in the Scriptures signifies *to wash* in general, without determining the sense to this or that sort of washing." He urges its use in Scripture is not that of secular authors. Then says of the Scripture use of *baptidzo* that it applies to such washing "as is by pouring or rubbing water on the thing or person washed, or some part of it" (vol. 1, 536-7, ed. 1862, by H. Cullon, London). He then quotes Mark vii, where they are to wash their hands. He cites 2 Kings iii, 11, to prove it was by water poured on them. He then says, "Now this washing of the hands is called by St. Luke the baptizing of a man" (Luke xi, 38). Again, "And the divers washings of the Jews are called *diaphoroi baptismoi—diverse baptisms* (Heb. ix, 10). Of which some were by bathing, others by sprinkling (Num. viii, 2)," etc. On patristic baptisms we cite only one out of many he cites (vol. 2, p. 520): "Origen here does plainly call pouring water on a thing *baptizing* it." He then cites the baptism of the altar, given far more fully in this work. Wall does complain bitterly of parties who merely touched the child with a few drops of water—opposes such sprinkling, but proves to his own satisfaction that sprinkling and pouring are baptism according to the Bible and the fathers.

23. Lange, held as an immersionist, says, on John i, 26, "'I baptize,' etc. . . . I baptize only with water; the baptism of the Spirit is reserved to the Messiah. . . . The

MODERN COMMENTATORS AND CRITICS. 355

Messiah is the proper Baptist of the Prophets, and his [the questioner] implied assertion—your interpretation of Ezekiel xxxvi, 25—is false. But because this true Baptist is here, I with my water baptism prepare him for baptizing with the Spirit."

Here Lange holds, with Rossenmüller, Hävernick, Bleek, etc., that the "sprinkle with clean water" of Ezekiel xxxvi, 26, was held by all Jews as baptism.

Again, on John iii, 5—"born of water"—Lange refers to Ezekiel xxxvi, 25 — "Then will I sprinkle clean water upon you"—as the baptism implied, as well as to Isaiah i, 16; Jeremiah xxxiii, 8, etc. [on John iii, 5].

24. M. Stuart is so often so garbled as to misrepresent him altogether, which necessitates a long quotation from him: "We have also seen, in Nos, 2, 5, 6, of examples from the Septuagint and Apocrypha, that the word *baptidzo* sometimes means *to wash*, and *bapto* to *moisten, to wet*, or *bedew*. There is, then, no absolute certainty, from usage, that the word *baptidzo*, when applied to designate the *rite of baptism*, means of course to *immerge* or *plunge*" (p. 76). Dr. Graves's ed. 1856, p. 73, he had proved that *baptidzo* was employed "to designate the idea of *copious affusion* or *effusion*, in a figurative manner." Page 84 he says of *baptidzo*, "Both the classic use and that of the Septuagint show that *washing and copious affusion* are sometimes signified by this word." Page 158—all in italics—"No injunction is any where given in the New Testament respecting the manner in which this rite shall be performed." "My belief is that we *do obey* the command to baptize when we do it by affusion or sprinkling" (p. 195).

On page 185 he urges that Baptists rely "on the exegesis of the fathers and the ancient churches. New Testament usage of the word in cases not relevant to this rite, clearly does not entitle you to such a conclusion with any confidence." Like Terretinus and others, he refers to the primitive and ancient church as distinct from the apostolic or New Testament church. He believes the three thousand (Acts ii, 41) and the five thousand, as well as Saul, the jailer, etc., were all baptized by affusion, and that Romans vi, 3, 4, does not refer to water baptism and was not immersion.

25. Dr. Barnes, being so often cited by immersionists, says of *baptidzo*, "Fourth. It can not be proved from an examination of the passages in the Old and New Testaments that the idea of a complete immersion ever was connected with the word or that it ever in any case occurred"* (Notes on Matthew iii, 6).

26. To these could be added Tholuck, Ebrard, Hävernick, Kühnoel, Bleek, Henstenburg, Rossenmüller, Schaaf, Watson, Geo. Hill, Doddridge, John Locke; but it is a waste of time and space to cite so many. But we close with the illustrious and renowned Lightfoot, the greatest luminary in these matters in that century of learning, the seventeenth. Luke iii, 16: "I baptize you," etc. "These seem to have been the words that he used in sprinkling or applying the water: 'I baptize thee,'" etc. "'With water,'" in the Greek it is indifferently with or in, answerable to the Hebrew preposition either local or instrumental." "So it is almost as little to be doubted that when they were there [into the river] he threw and sprinkled the water upon them." Works, vol. 4, p. 279, London, 1822. Of Christ's baptism he says, "He went into the water, had water sprinkled on him" (*Ibid.*, p. 305).

* But when he precedes this by saying that "baptize signifies originally *to tinge, to dye, to stain,*" he puts himself along with the careless class we have had to criticise so often; for all know that *baptidzo* has no such meaning, but *bapto* has.

CYCLOPEDIAS.

Dr. Graves and A. Campbell parade the testimony of cyclopedias. We could parade a number also, but as they merely copy each other, some abridging, the ten Dr. Graves (Debate, pp. 510, 511) adduces merely following Wall in the main. But the first one he quotes (Edinburgh Encyclopedia), and most elaborately, states what every scholar versed in the facts knows to be utterly untrue when it says, "In the Assembly of Divines, held at Westminster in 1643, it was keenly debated whether immersion or sprinkling should be adopted; twenty-five voted for sprinkling and twenty-four voted for immersion," etc. He then tells of Dr. Lightfoot, etc. This is utterly untrue as narrated. The facts are, the only debated question was, whether, in addition to sprinkling, ministers should be allowed to immerse where parties preferred or whether they should not be so allowed, and that was defeated. It was not debated whether they should allow of sprinkling or immersion. As Dr. G.'s first authority so falsifies these well-known historic facts, we pass all the rest.

CHAPTER XXXI.

CONCLUSION.

And now, dear reader, with the fruits of years of most painful study and research before you, in all fairness and kindness, with a serene trust and earnest hope that this controversy will speedily terminate, we do most solemnly and in the fear of God arraign before the bar of all these crushing facts our immersionist friends, and openly charge them with the awful responsibility of the divisions and rents in the body of Christ, the strifes and bad blood that have been too often engendered by their narrow proscriptions and intolerant aggressions. For years they have waged a dogmatic war all along the ecclesiastical lines. At times, when infidelity and crime were going hand in hand together through the land, smiting and threatening the very stability of society itself and sapping all the foundations of virtue, they have drawn off from the almost shattered and bleeding columns of the struggling army of truth and actually poured in a volley upon the worn flanks of the advancing yet reeling columns of the holy cause. In the fearful struggles of the great Reformation they turned against the heroic Luther and chilled the warm zeal of whole States. They split the Reformation. They filled the land with civil wars. They almost shattered the columns on which all Europe depended for deliverance from the thraldom and tyranny of besotted Rome. Even in the present age their historians boast of this crime against society and the world. Starting out with a cause so wretched, so destitute of fact, reason, or historic support, they have felt compelled from the start to garble authorities, misquote, interpolate, and blur and blot every record they have touched in history or literature. Hence it has been most common for their partisan writers to add to these offenses the crime of personal defamation and slander against all who boldly deny to them an entire infallibility on these questions. To break the force of exposure and opposition they often carry their opponent through all the distorting organs of detraction and abuse, while men who were besotted with prejudice and steeped in ignorance are held up as gods if they but support their cause.

To add to the evil, many of them have aimed with too much success to elevate a single command that had never before been hinted by Christ, never insisted on in the case of blessing any mortal while among the people over three years, into the old Pharisaical idea of "the great commandment," while they boldly proceed, like their predecessors in ecclesiastical narrowness, to unchurch all who fail to repeat their shibboleth. They have proceeded to blur and blot the simple, beautiful rite instituted by Christ, until the symbol of life is distorted into the supposed likeness of death. Baptism is a door. It is a death. It is a burial. It is a resurrection. It is a seal of pardon. It is a seal of the covenant. It is an initiatory rite. It is for remission. It is regeneration with others. Verily, is it not a god? They have so covered up the beautiful symbolism of this rite with the huge and indigestible mass of the *debris* of the old and wornout rubbish of antiquity and heathen superstition that it is a task from which a Hercules would have fled, to relieve it of the rotten mass, and would have regarded the Augean stable as a breakfast spell. Every fact is distorted that bears on the subject. To such a bold fanaticism have some of them come that they suppose the Eternal will mercifully forgive men who have spurned his offers, insulted his messengers, crucified his Son, trampled on his truth, yet will save them and pardon them of all crimes on confessing that they believe Christ is the Son of God—a fact that they never doubted—had believed all the time—and suffer themselves to be dipped in a pond of water! Yet he will not forgive you though you believe his whole Word, pray daily, live as spotless as a Paul, and fill the land with the praise of your good deeds if you fail of a dip of water!

It is the duty of all to obey God in all things. It is the duty of all to pray, to be baptized, to keep his commandments, pay their debts, be charitable. But it is rank idolatry to set up this rite to be honored and adored as above all his commandments. Our Gospel is not bound. Let the broad and noble principles of an enlightened and elevating Christianity expand our minds, enlarge the circle of our thoughts, and redeem us from evil.

INDEX.

	PAGE.
"Ænon near Salim,"	26, 66–67
Altar of Elijah baptized,	273
Amad, Baptist quotations on,	314
Lexicons on,	314–319
Literature of,	322–325
Syriac for baptize,	314
Versions on,	315–320
Apo, from, not out of,	31
Arabic versions on baptism,	328
Aristotle, *baptidzo* in,	260
Authors, blunders of,	1–3, 6
Baptidzo, lexicons on,	138–167
Ancient versions on,	311
Authorities on,	347
Classic usage of,	88, 217
How rendered by immersionists,	101
How translated (see Translations).	
In later Greek,	263
In the house of its friends,	203
N. T. use of,	88, 91, 94, 95
O. T. and N. T. sense of,	199
Patristic usage of,	271–289
Philology of,	168
Primary meaning of,	226, 301
Why not translate,	356
Baptism, administrator of,	11
Buried by, into death,	46–51
Design of,	11, 16–22
Eunuch's, the,	32
Five thousand and three thousand,	35

INDEX.

Baptism, mode of (see Laver, *Bapto, Baptidzo*, Translations, etc).
    Origin of, ... 15–21
    Symbolic import of, ... 72, 73
    With blood, ... 282
    With tears, ... 282
Baptists in harmony, ... 210
Bapto, classic occurrences of, ... 110–122
    Fathers and translations on, ... 122–125
    In Daniel, ... 122
    In N. T. and Septuagint, ... 22
    Lexicons on, ... 106, 107
    Philology of, ... 127
    Primary meaning of, ... 126–137
    Root of *baptidzo,* 126
Beza correctly reported, ... 213
Born of water, ... 52
Bury, meaning of, in Scriptures, ... 47
Ceremonial cleansing, ... 60
Changes in meaning, ... 88
Classic and N. T. Greek, ... 97
Classics, use of baptism in, ... 76, 217, 234
Codex Sinaiticus, ... 329
Commentators and critics, modern, ... 347
Conant on *baptidzo,* 263
Conclusion, ... 358
Convenience, ... 55
Criticisms, ancient—errors, ... 213
Cyclopedias, ... 357
Dale, errors of, ... 221
Decency in baptism, ... 55, 56
Dip not immerse, ... 243
Eis, to, into, at, etc., ... 26, 30, 31
En, with, and in, ... 27, 52–55
Epi, at, to, ... 29
Facts, summary of, ... 234–255
First occurrence of baptism, ... 308
Frequent baptisms (washings), ... 64, 65, 66
Gasala, Arabic for baptize, etc. (see Translations).
Graves, Dr. J. B., blunders and perversions of, 8, 10, 49, 90, 91, 98, 139–141, 143, 150–155.
Greek, classic and N. T., ... 88

INDEX. 363

Health,	55
History of baptism, facts on,	284
Immersion, arguments for,	11–14
Origin of,	285
To sink,	169
Jordan, swift,	39–43
Josephus on laver,	63
Kabas,	71
Laver, baptism at,	57–69
Laws of science ignored,	232
Learning in Dark Ages, revival of,	76–87
Lexicons,	76
Greek, on *bapto*,	105
Liddell & Scott's Lexicon, frequent changes,	155, 156, 157, note.
Louo, wash, pour,	342
Maimonides misquoted,	69–72
Matar,	183
Meanings, primary and derived,	88
Metaphorical uses,	37
Novatian, baptism of,	277
Origin and design of baptism,	15
Of immersion,	285
Patristic Greek, *baptidzo* in,	271–289
Baptism,	279
Pentateuch, "wash" in,	60
Peshito-Syriac,	315
Philology,	168
Principles of,	171
Science of language,	173, 176
Planted, what implied by,	47
Pouring,	38
Primary meaning,	91–93
Rachats, to "pour out,"	71
Roots and their meanings,	92
Saul, baptism of,	29
Shataph, Gesenius's definition of,	71
Solomon's temple, laver in,	61
Sprinkle or touch baptizes,	301–305
Stain, dye,	133
Standard folio lexicons,	292
Symbolic import of baptism,	72

INDEX.

Syriac, the, ... 311
    Versions, ... 320
Tabhal, Hebrew for *baptidzo*, ... 290, 306
    Primary meaning of, ... 71
Targum of Jonathan, ... 19, 63
Tingo, ... 246
    Drs. Graves and Toy on, ... 250
    Jerome on, ... 251
    Lexicons on, ... 252
Translations or Versions, ... 311, 328-337
    Æthiopic, ... 330
    Arabic, ... 328
    Basmuric, ... 332
    Coptic, ... 332
    Egyptian, ... 332
    German, ... 335
    Itala, ... 330, 334
    James's, made by immersionists, ... 86
    Persic, ... 333
    Sahidic, ... 333
    Syriac, ... 311
    Vulgate, Jerome's, ... 334
Tertullian first to name dipping for baptism, ... 281
Unscientific methods, ... 221
Versions (see Translations).
Wash, ... 199-202, 338
Washing familiar to all people, ... 22
Words change meaning, ... 88

Made in the USA
Monee, IL
31 January 2022